THE OPEN WOUND:

TRAUMA, IDENTITY, AND COMMUNITY

By

FRANK SEEBURGER

To Freya

Table of Contents

For if, when we love, our existence runs through Nature's fingers like golden coins that she cannot hold and lets fall so that they can thus purchase new birth, she now throws us, without hoping or expecting anything, in ample handfuls towards existence.

— *Walter Benjamin*
"Hashish in Marseilles"

Preface

Writing on trauma is hard. It is harder not to. Nor can one easily stop, once one has started. As an open wound that cannot close over without festering, trauma, if we do not write on it, begins to write on us. To heal, the wound must be kept open, and the writing on trauma never stops.

Accordingly, any given piece of writing on trauma is never more than a fragment. It is never complete. Insofar as it must be given a beginning and an end, to be held within the confines of a cover, where a book on trauma begins, and where it ends, remains a matter of chance—of the crossing of chains of innumerable factors, including simple whim. One must begin writing somewhere, but there is no one place to begin, so one just begins where one begins—then ends where one ends.

That applies to this book, which is a book on trauma. That means it is incomplete, no more than a fragment. What I have to say on trauma I began to say, it turns out, long before I knew myself that what I was saying had to do with trauma—long before I knew that what I kept finding myself talking about went by that name. I am still saying it—as I will, I am sure, continue to do in one fashion or another until I die. This book is just a series of reports of stages along the way of my own traumatic journey. I offer those reports in the pages that follow, solely in case they may prove to be of use to any others—whoever they may be, if any—to whom they might provide some guidance as they go along their own ways into and, eventually, back out of the traumas that come to them along those ways, as they will and do come to all who go upon any ways that really can be gone along at all.

Bibliographical information pertaining to the sources I cite explicitly in the following pages can be found at the end of the book under Works

Cited. Page references are given in the text, usually in parentheses, when pertinent. In a few cases, when the editions I accessed were electronic, page references are absent; but in those cases I have tried to give sufficient indications in the text itself to permit interested readers to find the relevant passages without too much trouble, in whatever edition may be available to them. Unless otherwise indicated in the text or in the list of works cited, all translations from German and French sources are my own.

I would like to acknowledge the University of Denver for providing me with two non-consecutive terms of relief from my regular classroom teaching responsibilities, during which I did some of the work that eventually became this book. I also want to acknowledge with gratitude the contributions to my thinking that students and readers of my work over the years since I began to focus on trauma almost a decade ago have made. Those contributors have been too numerous to name here, and the impact of their contributions upon my thought goes so deep that even I myself will never be able to plumb its full depths. My gratitude for them and for their gifts is as profound.

With the exception of the Introduction, earlier versions of the chapters that follow have already appeared in serial form as posts to my blog *Trauma and Philosophy*. Readers interested in my continuing thinking and writing about trauma since doing the work on the manuscript of the current book may also wish to consult that blog, for ongoing technical assistance with which I am grateful to my son-in-law, Nicolas Hadacek. It can be found online at traumaandphilosophy.wordpress.com. Although in at least one important sense, trauma itself may one day be gone, the work of trauma goes on. It always will.

This book is dedicated to my daughter, with love and gratitude to and for her, all boundless.

Introduction

OPEN WOUNDS AND THE SUBJECT

OF TRAUMA

I n agony, the wounded cry out for their pain to end. It never will.

For example, finding oneself suddenly and unexpectedly out of a job is traumatic. All too many people have found *that* out during the global "Great Recession" triggered by the collapse of the home mortgage market in 2008 and the lingering effects of which are still very much with us today as I write this, in the spring of 2012. In the United States, finding oneself still without work after many months of searching for new employment, when one runs out of unemployment benefits, even under the extensions granted since 2008, can be even more traumatic. That is assuming that one has not already been so thoroughly numbed into hopelessness already during the long months of unsuccessfully searching for a job—any job, even at massively reduced wages and/or only part-time, which is itself traumatic enough, surely—as to be beyond feeling any further shock. Shared traumas, even globally shared ones such as the current, ever-ongoing global economic crisis, affect humanity at the level of various sized human collectivities. In addition, they have devastating impact in the concrete lives of countless individual human beings, who can be cast without succor into physical-emotional and, in fact, all-encompassing misery by the exhaustion of all their resources.

Everyone must undergo such shared, historical traumas that strike the society or collectivity to which one belongs. In addition, every human being undergoes one's own personal losses throughout life: losses of loved ones, important personal property, physical strengths and abilities, or mental capacities and acquisitions such as memory, due to aging or illness, and so on, in all the innumerable variety of losses that can have traumatic impacts on those who suffer them. No human life is free of such personally traumatic losses, shared with none or few, any more than human life can be free of broad, collective traumas that affect one as a member of some collectivity. Both singly and together, up to and including humanity as a whole throughout the entirety of human history, past, present, and future, all human beings are struck by events that have traumatic impact.

Thus, trauma has always been part of the human experience. That is true at the level of humanity as a whole as well as that of human beings individually. With regard to the former, the history of humanity is largely the story of the innumerable collecive traumas, from primordial catastrophes remembered in such myths as the Flood or the Fall of Man, to the catastrophic 20th century with its World Wars, Holocaust, and mixed massacres and genocides, to September 11, 2001, down to the whiplashing rise and fall of the stock markets of the world in response to the daily ups and downs of the European debt crisis of 2011 and beyond. Trauma is timeless, in that there is no time, at least no human time, with no trauma.

Trauma is also timeless in another way. There is something *unpassing* about trauma, something about trauma that will never let those who are struck by it ever let go of it completely. Once traumatized, always traumatized. However complete one's "recovery" from a traumatic loss may be, the loss itself always remains just that, a *loss*. After the death of a spouse, for example, one may eventually be able to go on to other intimate relationships, perhaps even marry again and find happiness in life with a new spouse. Nevertheless, there will still always be the wound left by the loss of one's previous partner, the un-fill-able hole the dead spouse's absence hollows out in one's continuing life.

One of the strongest traditional images of how traumatic wounds remain open in a crucial way is that, from Christian scripture, of the resurrected Christ appearing to his disciples in the "upper room" where they have fearfully gathered after the Crucifixion. Christ tells his disciple Thomas, who comes to be known in subsequent Christian tradition as "doubting Thomas" because of his skepticism about the "Good News" of the Resurrection, to put his hands in the wound in Christ's side, from the Roman Centurion's blow with the lance while Jesus hung on the cross. Thus does he allow Thomas to become convinced that it is really Jesus who now stands before him. Even after the Resurrection, the redeemed body of the Christ still carries its wounds—and they remain *open*, even then.

Trauma is just such a never-to-be-closed wound, one that remains open even after the healing process has come to full fruition. The lesson of trauma, once learned, can never be forgotten.

The lesson of trauma, however, is never reducible to an easy—or at least easily formulable –"moral," as in such tales as Aesop's Fables. Rather, whatever general or universal truths trauma may convey, those truths can only be conveyed concretely, in the very details of one or another genuinely, deeply traumatic event. That is what, for example, graphic artist Art Spiegelman, author of *Maus*, the two-volume Pulitzer Prize winning graphic novel about the Nazi extermination of the Jews—which in effect meant, as I will discuss more thoroughly below, anyone whom the Nazis chose so to classify—in which the Jews are depicted as mice and their German persecutors as cats, found out, when he moved from his first three-page version of *Maus* to what became the eventual two-volume book version. In making that transition Spiegelman discovered that he could not just present general types or figures, leaving historical accuracy in any detail aside, and letting his creative imagination alone guide him, as might be done in a fictional work, as "fiction" is usually understood. Instead, he found he had to tell the all too real, singular, personal story of his own parents' suffering both in and after Auschwitz, and that story in turn intertwined with the story of his own experience growing up with those parents in New York in the post-war era.

In his very first, three-page version of *Maus*, first published in 1972 in *Funny Animals Comics*, Spiegelman had not concerned himself with historical verisimilitude, but had, indeed, contented himself instead with just free, wide-ranging imaginative, "fictional" constructions. However, when what had started as that three-page original eventually morphed into what became the full two-volume work, he found himself compelled to do careful, detailed research, and pay careful attention to the actual historical record, as well as to his father's recollections (his mother having committed suicide in 1968, before Spiegelman began *Maus*). As he writes in *MetaMaus*, his recent book exploring the creation, publication, public reception, and impact of *Maus* itself (page 120): "Only when I began working on the long book did I realize that, okay, I can use my cat and mouse heads but it would be fatuous to move in the direction of Aesop's Fables. The work would just turn fatuous and fake. Only through the specific could I imply the general."

Indeed, although Spiegelman does not say so himself, at least at that point in his text, to depict such a trauma as the Holocaust as just an instance of a type, an example of a general category, would be to dishonor the very victims of the Nazi's genocidal crimes. It would, although in an obviously less overtly violent way, reproduce the original, extermination-bound dehumanization process German Nazism inflicted on the Jews, that very dehumanization that emblematically expressed itself in stripping newcomers to Auschwitz of their very names, and branding their forearms with the numbers that would henceforth be their only official identification.

As Spiegelman's example can remind us, the timelessness of trauma is not the timelessness of generalities or formulas. It is the timelessness of the irreducibly singular traumatic event in all its concrete detail. Traumas are irreducible to type or species. Each trauma is unique, and demands to be respected in its uniqueness. Yet it is in respecting that very uniqueness that one singular trauma can show us what pertains to all traumas, because it pertains to trauma as such.

This is a book on the subject of trauma. It will deal at length with everything I have remarked upon so far, and much else besides. In doing so, it will often dwell on a single trauma, including, most especially, the same one with which Spiegelman's *Maus* is concerned, namely, the trauma often called the Holocaust—or just simply "Auschwitz," using the name of the largest, most notorious extermination camp as the symbol for the whole Nazi "camp-system" of imprisonment, dehumanization, and genocide. The reader should keep in mind, however, that in talking of Auschwitz, it only appears that we are talking about a now fortunately long-ago event that, as such, no longer concerns us. In truth, in talking of Auschwitz, or any other given trauma, we are talking about something still very much a matter of the present. We are talking about ourselves, and the timelessness of the suffering we still undergo right now, today, long after almost all of the survivors of Auschwitz, at least as we ordinarily understand that notion, have died.

So, as I just said, this is a book on the subject of trauma. However, that very phrase—"the subject of trauma"—is itself subject to more than one way of being heard, more than one interpretation of its sense. As it pertains to this book, in fact, there are three different but related senses in which what is at issue in the pages to follow is "on the subject of trauma." I will now turn to those three senses, one at a time. As is fitting, given what I have just cited from Art Spiegelman, I will begin to do that by first hearing from one survivor of that one already-mentioned trauma, the trauma that itself often serves as the very figure for all historical, collective traumas—the trauma of what is most often called the Holocaust, the trauma of "Auschwitz."

The First Sense of "the Subject of Trauma": Just Who Is Traumatized?

In 1943 in Belgium a young man named Hans Meier was arrested and forced, under torture, to acknowledge that five years before he had been forced to become, despite himself, a Jew. Five years after his arrest, the same man emerged from Auschwitz bearing the number that had replaced his birth-name for most of that time, and chose to become Jean Améry.* In *At the Mind's Limits: Contemplations by a Survivor on Auschwitz and Its Realities*, a book first published in 1966, he wrote the following

---

*   *Jean* being French for the German *Johann*, the shortened form of which is *Hans*, and *Améry* being an anagram of *Mayer*, an alternative spelling of his family name—his original German name being stripped from him, as he experienced it, when he was forced to become a Jew.

description of some of what had happened to him in 1943, after his arrest, (pages 32-33):

> In the bunker [to which he was being taken at the time] there hung from the vaulted ceiling a chain that above ran into a roll. At its bottom end it bore a heavy, broadly curved iron hook. I was led to the instrument. The hook gripped into the shackle that held my hands together behind my back. Then I was raised with the chain until I hung about a meter over the floor. In such a position, or rather, when hanging this way, with your hands behind your back, for a short time you can hold at a half-oblique through muscular force. During these few minutes, when you are already expending your utmost strength, when sweat has already appeared on your forehead and lips, and you are breathing in gasps, you will not answer any questions? Accomplices? Addresses? Meeting places? You hardly hear it. All your life is gathered in a single, limited area of the body, the shoulder joints, and it does not react; for it exhausts itself completely in the expenditure of energy. But his cannot last long, even with people who have a strong physical constitution. As for me, I had to give up rather quickly. And now there was a crackling and splintering in my shoulders that my body has not forgotten until this hour. The balls sprang from their sockets. My own body weight caused luxation; I fell into a void and now hung by my dislocated arms, which had been torn high from behind and were now twisted over my head. Torture, from Latin *torquere*, to twist. What visual instruction in etymology! At the same time, the blows from the horsewhip [one of his torturers carried] showered down on my body, and some of them sliced cleanly through the light summer trousers that I was wearing on this twenty-third of July 1943.

Even after the excruciating pain he experienced at that time was over, the torture went on, as Améry himself saw with complete clarity. Indeed, by his own account it went on long after all physical signs of his ordeal had vanished. In went on, in fact, up until Améry died by his own hand in 1978, thirty-five years later. '[T]orture,' he writes (page 34), 'has an indelible character. Whoever was tortured, stays tortured. Torture is ineradicably burned into him, even when no clinically objective traces can be detected.' Forever after, whoever has been twisted by torture remains twisted, with a twist that can never again be undone.

Throughout history all too many have been made to suffer the same sort of extreme physical torture Améry did — and all too often in all too many places still do today. Nevertheless, most of humanity can be grateful never to have had such excruciating pain inflicted willfully upon them at the hands of others.

Yet as Améry's own remarks about his own indelible torture make clear, it is not the pain itself, as undeniably excoriating as it was, that constitutes the core of what can never again be forgotten, no matter how one might wish it could be. Rather, the un-healable wound that torture inflicts upon the one being tortured already announces itself, Améry writes, at what he calls 'the first blow.' In his own case, that blow came when he was arrested, even before he was taken to the fortress where in the bunker he was literally left hanging on a hook by his dislocated shoulders. At that very first blow—and even though one struggles with all one's might to resist seeing it, just as someone being hoisted on a hook by one's arms joined behind one's back struggles with all one's might to keep one's shoulders from dislocating — everything is already visible. 'The first blow,' writes Améry (page 27), 'brings home to the prisoner that he is *helpless*, and thus it already contains in the bud everything that is to come" — everything, that is, that subsequent experience may finally force one to see, if one is unfortunate enough eventually to exhaust one's resources for avoiding the seeing, as it was Améry's misfortune to find them exhausted in the bunker to which he was led not long after receiving the first blow from one of those who arrested him.

'The first blow,' Améry continues, makes manifest to the one to whom it is delivered that those delivering it 'are free to punch me in the face, [as] the victim feels in numb surprise and [then] concludes in just as numb certainty: they will do with me what they want.' What is more, there will be no rescue, no possibility of help miraculously arriving to deliver the victim from the hands that are free to do to that victim as they will: 'Whoever would rush to the prisoner's aid — a wife, a mother, a brother, or friend — he won't get this far.'

In sum (page 28), for such a victim,

> with the very first blow that descends upon him he loses something we will perhaps temporarily call 'trust in the world.' Trust in the world includes all sorts of thing: the irrational and logically unjustifiable belief in absolute causality perhaps, or the likewise blind belief in the validity of the inductive inference. But more important as an element of trust in the world, and in our context what is solely relevant, is the certainty that by reason of written or unwritten social contracts the other person will spare me—more precisely stated, that he will respect my physical, and with it also my metaphysical, being. The boundaries of my body are also the boundaries of my self. My skin surface shields me against the external world. If I am to have trust, I must feel on it only what I *want* to feel.

Thus, understood as Améry understands it, 'loss of trust in the world' involves both a loss of any firm grip on one's self, and a loss of all 'expectation of help' from others (pages 28-29):

> The expectation of help, the certainty of help, is indeed one of the fundamental experiences of human beings, and probably also of animals. . . . The expectation of help is as much a constitutional psychic element as is the struggle for existence. Just a moment, the mother says to her child who is moaning from pain, a hot-water bottle, a cup of tea is coming right away, we won't let you suffer so! I'll prescribe you a medicine, the doctor assures, it will help you. Even on the battlefield, the Red Cross ambulances find their way to the

wounded man. In almost all situations in life where there is bodily injury there is also the expectation of help; the former is compensated by the latter. But with the first blow from a policeman's fist, against which there can be no defense and which no helping hand will ward off, a part of our life ends and it can never again be revived.

Once tortured, always tortured: the loss of trust in the world that torture shatters can never again be restored. Thus, at the end of his reflection on torture, Améry sums up as follows (page 40):

> Astonishment at the existence of the other, as he boundlessly asserts himself through torture, and astonishment at what one can become oneself: flesh and death. The tortured person never ceases to be amazed that all those things one may, according to inclination, call his soul, or his mind, or his consciousness, or his identity, are destroyed when there is that cracking and splintering in the shoulder joints. That life is fragile is a truism he has always known—and that it can be ended, as Shakespeare says, 'with a little pin.' But only through torture did he learn that a living person can be transformed so thoroughly into flesh and that, while still alive, be partly made into a prey of death.

> Whoever has succumbed to torture can no longer feel at home in the world. The shame of destruction cannot be erased. Trust in the world, which already collapsed in part at the first blow, but in the end, under torture, fully, will not be regained. That one's fellow man was experienced as the antiman remains in the tortured person as accumulated horror. It blocks the view into a world in which the principle of hope rules.

What remains of one's self, when all of one's identity has been stripped violently away from one? Just *who* is it, finally, who undergoes torture,

9

if the very process of undergoing torture irretrievably robs the one being tortured of all identity? Just who, then, is the very subject of torture, the one who undergoes it? Who is the subject of torture, if being subjected to torture robs one of one's own claim to sovereign subjectivity in the first place? Who am "I," the one who has been tortured, and goes on to speak of it?

And to just what community does that "I," whoever it may be, continue to belong, after once being twisted beyond recognition in the agony of torture? Since losing one's identity is losing all ties that make one into the member of some definite, distinct community constituted by sharing some trait or traits of a political, religious, vocational, or other sort, what community remains, to which one can still belong? Who are "we," if all we have in common is that we have all been stripped of any identify we can reference with the singular pronoun "I"?

Those are the intertwined, tangled questions that confront the one who has been tortured: fundamental—and henceforth, after being tortured, fundamentally unavoidable—questions of both individual and collective identity. In short, that tangle of questions boils down to one: Who is the subject of torture?

Because the figure of the torture victim also serves well as the emblematic figure of the *traumatized* person, that is also the fundamental, fundamentally unavoidable question with which trauma confronts the trauma victim: Who is the subject of trauma?

That is one of the major questions with which I will be concerned in this book. It is, accordingly, a book "on the subject of trauma" in that sense.

The Second Sense of "the Subject of Trauma": Identifying What Is Traumatic

As just discussed, torture in the sense relevant to Améry is more than, or at least different from, physical pain as such, no matter how excruciating. Similarly, trauma in the sense that the torture victim can stand as the emblematic figure of the traumatized human being is more than, or at least different from, a physical wound, no matter how grievous. The word *trauma* derives simply from the Greek for wound, and in the broad sense means no more than that. In the sense that is at issue in the recent, still burgeoning interdisciplinary field of contemporary 'trauma studies,' however, not every wound is traumatic, any more than every pain is torture in the sense that Améry was subjected to it. Indeed, in that narrower sense, not even every wound that permanently disfigures its recipient, permanently contorts or twists one's form to one extent or another, is a traumatic wound, properly speaking.

In the sense relevant to contemporary trauma studies — and to this book — only wounds that disfigure not only the body, but also the 'soul,' to use the same word Améry does to characterize how torture twists its victims, are genuinely traumatic. A wound that remains solely *somatic*, from the Greek word for body, is not yet a trauma in the modern sense of the term. Indeed, in the modern sense, a wound may be profoundly traumatic, even if it leaves the body as such completely untouched, as severe verbal or emotional abuse may do, for example. To be truly traumatic in the modern sense the wound must be more than, or at least different from, anything merely somatic. It must be a *psychic* wound, from the Greek for "mind"—or "soul," as the Greek word can and often should be translated.

Freud is the crucial figure in coining the modern sense of trauma. In his most famous discussion of the notion, which occurs in his relatively late *Beyond the Pleasure Principle*, he uses as the defining example a person who has been through a serious train wreck, and who has come through apparently unscathed, with no visible signs of damage at all. However, after a period of time, which Freud will label the period of "latency," the apparently unscathed train-wreck survivor begins to show such symptoms of an underlying, hitherto altogether invisible disturbance as recurrent nightmares or troubling returns of memory images from the accident, or "psycho-somatic" symptoms such as a nervous tic, or difficulty speaking, or loss of motor control. The Freudian term for this phenomenon, "the return of the repressed," long ago entered common speech, and is often used freely without even any awareness of its Freudian provenance.

Just as the recipient of the first blow from a police officer may be able to avoid, at least for a while, facing the reality that blow itself reveals, and may cling, for at least that same while, to the illusion that one can still trust the world, so does the trauma victim in general (and the first blow from the fist of a cop is just one case of a traumatizing blow, after all) manage to "repress" the trauma, at least for a while. Sometimes, that "while" may extend all the way to "the other side of the grave," to borrow an expression systems theorist Gregory Bateson used in an interesting discussion of alcoholism that dates back to the early 1970s. But however long a while it may be, after a while the trauma always "will out," just as murder will do, according to the old proverb.

At any rate, it is trauma in the modern, Freud-forged sense of it that is at issue in this book, which is in that sense, too, a book on the subject of trauma.

The Third Sense of "the Subject of Trauma": Becoming a Subject to Avoid Traumatic Reality

At the same time, this book is on the subject of trauma in yet a third sense, in which what is at issue is the relationship between "subjectivity" and the "subject," on the one hand, and trauma, on the other. The guiding question in that regard will be: Insofar as it is taken solely within the context of its relationship to trauma, just what *is* "subjectivity"? Since at least in a large class of cases (to borrow a phrase from Wittgenstein) the terms *subjectivity* and *consciousness* can be used interchangeably , the question might also be put as one that addresses just how, viewed in terms of its relationship with trauma, "consciousness" as such shows itself to function.

Various contemporary philosophers from Alain Badiou to Slavoj Žižek have even argued that there is an important sense in which the very emergence of "subjectivity" or "consciousness" as such occurs only in response to an antecedent trauma. The very event whereby in the first place the human being is struck into the mold of a conscious "subject" who posits before itself an "object" of which it is conscious—an event typically taken to have occurred in philosophy with Descartes—is seen as being inseparable from trauma.

In his treatment of trauma Freud defined the threshold of trauma as the point at which excitations overwhelm the "protective shield" or "crust" that an organism erects around itself precisely to guard itself *against* excitation. As he writes of the organism in section IV of *Beyond the Pleasure Principle* (page 30):

> This little fragment of living substance [that is, the living organism] is suspended in the middle of an external world charged with the most powerful energies; and it would be killed by the stimulation emanating from these if it were not provided with a protective shield against stimuli. It acquires the shield in this way: its outermost surface ceases to have the structure proper to living matter, becomes to some degree inorganic and thenceforward functions as a special envelope or membrane resistant to stimuli. In consequence, the energies of the external world are able to pass into the next underlying layers, which have remained living, with only a fragment of their original intensity; and these layers can devote themselves, behind the protective shield, to the reception of the amounts of stimulus which have been allowed through it. By its death, the outer layer has saved all the deeper ones from a similar fate—unless, that is to say, stimuli reach it which are so strong that they break through the protective shield.

When such breaching of the shield does occur, there is trauma, as Freud writes (page 35): "We may, I think, tentatively venture to regard the common traumatic neurosis as a consequence of an extensive breach being made in the protective shield against stimuli."

In *Beyond the Pleasure Principle* Freud places *consciousness*—"the system Cs.," in his notation—just *beneath*, as it were, the hard, protective shell that guards against external excitations. The job of consciousness is to receive the stimuli that are allowed to pass through the outer shell, now stripped of any excess intensity whereby they might threaten the equilibrium of the organism. This receptivity of consciousness, in turn, is itself in the service of assuring that the excitations that are allowed past the protective shield will indeed not be allowed to have any lasting effect—that is, that they be kept from registering any permanent effect on the psyche, any effect deserving of being rendered anything more than a moment's passing notice, which is just what consciousness renders them.

Thus, Freud suggests that (page 28) "becoming conscious and leaving behind a memory-trace are processes incompatible with each other within one and the same system," and lays down as an assertion deserving consideration "the proposition that *consciousness arises instead of a memory-trace.*" Accordingly, he goes on to write, "the system *Cs.* is characterized by the peculiarity that in it . . . excitatory processes do not leave behind any permanent change in its elements but expire, as it were, in the phenomenon of becoming conscious." The hard, dead protective shield of the outer layer of the psyche is, in effect, the first early warning system for securing the psyche against traumatic excitation. Then, if something does manage to fly in under the radar of that primary warning system, consciousness stands ready as the second line of defense, ready to shoot down into insignificance whatever has circumvented the primary protective shield.

In effect, then, his analyses lead Freud to view consciousness as belonging to the mechanism whereby the organism *avoids* anything breaching its defenses *against* significant excitation. To that extent, consciousness serves to *mask* reality, rather than to *reveal* it.

In *Unclaimed Experience: Trauma, Narrative, and History*, an important and influential work in contemporary trauma studies, literary theorist Cathy Caruth treats the relationship between consciousness, trauma, and dreams in Freud's work along similar lines. Reading Freud through Jacques Lacan's interpretation of his work, especially of *The Interpretations of Dreams*, which inaugurated Freud's psychoanalytic revolution when it was first published in 1900, Caruth argues (page 96) that "the wish fulfillment *of consciousness itself*" is not awakening, but sleep, or more precisely *to go on sleeping*. In *The Interpretation of Dreams* Freud, of course, argues that every dream is ultimately a hidden wish fulfillment. Yet Caruth goes further than that. In her reading, Freud's own analyses of dreams, most especially of the famous dream of the burning child recounted in *The Interpretation of Dreams*, suggest that "the wish behind any dream," not just that of the burning child, "is tied to a more basic desire, the desire of consciousness itself *not to wake up.*"

In the dream of a burning child, a father is sleeping in a room next to the corpse of his young son, recently dead of a childhood illness. "After the child had died," Freud writes (*Standard Edition,* vol. 5, page 509) the father

> went into the next room to lie down, but left the door open so that he could see from his bedroom into the room in which the child's body was laid out, with tall candles standing round it. An old man had been engaged to keep watch over it, and sat beside the body murmuring prayers. After a few hours' sleep, the father had a dream that *his child was standing beside his bed, caught him by the arm and whispered to him reproachfully: "Father, don't you see that I'm burning?"* He woke up, noticed a bright glare of light from the next room, hurried into it and found that the old watchman had dropped off to sleep and that the wrappings and one of the arms of his beloved child's dead body had been burned by a lighted candle that had fallen on them.

Freud sketches out his interpretation of this dream by remarking that it, "too, contained the fulfillment of a wish," as do, according to him, all dreams.

> The dead child behaved in the dream like a living one: He himself warned his father, came to his bed, and caught him by the arm . . . . The dream was preferred to a waking reflection because it was able to show the child as once more alive. If the father had woken up first and then made the inference that led him to go into the next room, he would, as it were, have shortened his child's life by that moment of time.

Thus, the dream preserves, at least for a moment, the illusion that the child is not dead. It perpetuates that illusion, letting the father avoid for that same moment the traumatic reality that his child is dead. To that extent, the dream of the burning child fits what Caruth (pages 96-97) cites, in a modified translation, from earlier in Freud's *The Interpretation of Dreams*:

> All dreams . . . serve the purpose of prolonging sleep instead of waking up. *The dream is the guardian of sleep and not its disturber. . .*
>
> *Thus the wish to sleep (which the conscious ego is concentrated upon. ..) must in every case be reckoned as one of the motives for the formation of dreams, and every successful dream is a fulfillment of that wish.*

However, by Caruth's analysis (page 97): "It is not the father alone who dreams to avoid his child's death but *consciousness itself* that, in its sleep, is tied to a death from [the reality of which] it turns away." Furthermore, as Caruth observes, folowing Lacan here, it is what eventually happens *in* the dream itself that finally wakens the father from his sleep:

> It is *the dream itself*, that is, *that wakes the sleeper*, and it is in this paradoxical awakening—an awakening not to, but against, the very wishes of consciousness—that the dreamer confronts the reality of a death from which he cannot turn away. If Freud, in other words, suggests that the dream keeps the father asleep, Lacan suggests that it is because the father dreams, paradoxically enough, that he precisely wakes up. The dream thus becomes, in Lacan's analysis, no longer a function of sleep, but rather a function of awakening.

A few lines later Caruth remarks that, "to the extent that the father is awakened by the dream itself, his awakening to death [which is here the figure for traumatic reality as such] is not a simple matter of knowledge and perception but rather, Lacan seems to suggest, a paradoxical attempt *to respond, in awakening, to a call that can only be heard within sleep.*" Indeed, where else but within sleep could one be reached by a call to wake up? Who is not asleep, has no need to be called to awake.

If we follow up a bit more on Caruth's Lacanian interpretation, we can also go on to say that awakening as such must be awakening not *of* or *to* consciousness—an emergence of consciousness itself—but, rather, awakening *from* consciousness—the liberation of the unconscious from its bondage to, and by, consciousness. In addition, such awakening can only occur *belatedly*, only "after the fact," namely, after the call to awaken has itself died away into silence insofar as it cannot be heard—cannot be heard precisely because there was no one awake to hear it, any possible hearer having fallen soundly asleep, and thus necessitating being called to awaken.

Freud saw and said clearly in *Beyond the Pleasure Principle*, with his example of the survivor of the railroad accident who emerges apparently unscathed and only later, after the accident has already completely receded, begins to manifest symptomatically any registration of that accident, that just such "belatedness" (*Nachträglichkeit*) characterizes traumatic events as such. Thus, awakening from sleep—which simultaneously means awakening from consciousness, as I have just said above—is itself, as such, *traumatic*. One falls into consciousness as into sleep, and can only be wakened after the fact by a call to awake that can never, in principle, be heard when it calls, but can only be heard in the recall, as it were, of its echoes.

That, in turn, is always and only an aleatory matter—a bit of luck, a stroke of good fortune. As is true of all such matters, the odds are against it happening in any given case. When it does happen, however, the possibility emerges that those to whom it happens can succeed in passing it on to others, thereby shortening the odds, perhaps even dramatically.

At any rate, when it does happen, those to whom it happens are freed to be . . . well, whatever one remains once one, in awakening, has been liberated from consciousness—or, to return to where this part of my discussion started, from "subjectivity." Who remains is whoever/whatever comes, then, "after the subject," to use a "postmodern" formula.

This book is on "the subject of trauma" in that third sense as well.

Nor are the three senses of that phrase unrelated to one another. I will explore some of the interconnections in the following section.

Trauma and Identity

In surviving Auschwitz, Jean Améry — whoever and whatever it was who went by that name after being liberated from the Nazi system of death — survived his identity. To survive something is, literally, to *live through it*, that is, to come out the other side of whatever it is one is said to have "survived." To survive something is to *outlive* it. In outliving Auschwitz, and all those who died there and in all the other camps, Améry outlived his own identity. He thus outlived *himself*, at least if being a "self" is a matter of having an "identity."

In one important sense at least, Améry surely desired and endeavored, directly and deliberately, to survive his imprisonment in the German death camps, which is what one would commonly mean by speaking of surviving 'Auschwitz,' in the synechdochal sense of that term, the sense that it has in Améry's own text, whereby that name of the largest of the Nazi extermination camps stands for the entirety of the Nazi death-camp system of death. However, he neither directly nor deliberately endeavored or desired to survive his identity, that is, to survive the complete loss of identity, the process of being robbed of all identity and left wholly bereft of himself, a process to which he was condemned in being condemned to Auschwitz. Only incidentally did he ever desire or endeavor to outlive himself. That is, it was only insofar as surviving Auschwitz also inseparably meant surviving the radical 'identity-theft' to which he was subjected in the death camps, that in willing to survive Auschwitz he also willed, inescapably, to survive his own identity by outliving it, living through its loss.

In "How Much Home Does a Person Need?"—the third essay in *At the Mind's Limits*—Améry recounts how he was robbed of one element of his erstwhile identity after another, until there was no identity at all left to him. The Nuremburg Laws of 1935 stripped all Jews within the Third

Reich of status as full German citizens, thereby depriving them of their very nationality, their very identity as Germans. In March of 1938, with the German march into Austria and the annexation (*Anschluss*) of Austria to Germany, those laws extended their sway over Hans Meier as well, and robbed him of his identity as an Austrian. Disowned by the country of his birth and entire life till then, he joined other newly de-nationalized Austrians and fled—in his case to Belgium, where his status was that of what today in the United States is often called an 'illegal alien.' As Améry writes (page 41), the Belgian 'customs officials and policemen would have refused us a legal crossing of the border, for we were coming into the country as refugees, without passport and visa, without any valid national identity. . . . [W]e knew they did not want us.'

"At that time," as he goes on to tell us (page 43), "I still did not bear the French-sounding pen name with which I sign my works today," when he is writing his account. He continues (pages 43-44):

> My identity was bound to a plain German name and to the dialect of my more immediate place of origin. But since the day when an official decree forbade me to wear the folk costume that I had worn almost exclusively from early childhood on, I no longer permitted myself the dialect. Then the name by which my friends had always called me, with a dialect coloring, no longer made much sense either. . . . And my friends, too, with whom I had spoken in my native dialect, were obliterated. Only they? Oh no; everything that had filled my consciousness—from the history of my country, which was no longer mine, to the landscape images, whose memory I suppressed—had become intolerable to me since that morning of the 12th of March 1938, on which the blood-red cloth with the black spider on a white field had waived from the windows of out-of-the-way farmsteads.

Then Améry comes to the very heart of the matter, in terms of my concerns in this book. So deprived of his very country, language, history, home, and other identity-forming affiliations, he became "a person who could no longer say 'we.'" So deprived, he is no longer permitted to count himself as a member of any of the groups, societies, fellowships, national or other communities, membership in which would make it possible for him to establish an identify for himself, even in his own mind. He is no longer part of any identifiable collective subject that could express itself through its members use of the first person plural pronoun 'we.' As no longer part of any definite 'we,' and thereby deprived of any referential ground for using that first person plural pronoun, he is also deprived of any such ground for using 'I,' the first person singular pronoun, thus becoming someone 'who therefore said 'I' merely out of habit, but not with the feeling of full possession of myself,' a self now stripped of all possibility of identifying itself. However, in truth: 'I was no longer an I and did not live within a We.'

Nor did he have anything "like a transportable home, or at least an ersatz for home," as religion can be for some more fortunate than he, or money can be for some others, or even fame or esteem for those who can cling to them. Having none of the four, religion, money, fame, or esteem— or any other ersatz for home to fall back upon when deprived of his home itself, the only possible "we" left for him to be a part of was the empty, purely formal community of "us anonymous ones," as he puts it in a telling expression (page 45).

Lest any of us who were not even alive in 1938 or, for that matter, were not even born, as I was not, until after Nazi Germany, along with Auschwitz and all the other German camps, had ceased to exist, be tempted to give thanks that we were never subjected to such total loss of home, and consequent infinite need for it, it is fitting to listen to what Améry says a bit later in the same essay. As already recounted, he first addresses his own plight as someone who is radically lacking in any home or possible ersatz. That is because all being at home and feeling at home in the world was stripped from him against his will by the Germany that forced him by law to be a Jew, which in that context just means to be a person deprived of all home or possibility of finding any ersatz for home. But then, having explained his own plight, he observes (page 55) that '[n]aturally, one can say: so what[?]' Not only have most of his actual or potential readers never had to suffer the horrors to which Améry was subjected, but we who never have may also think that the real loss is not all that great even for someone such as Améry, who has suffered those horrors. As he goes on to write (pages 55-57), in words which, if anything, are more telling today than they were forty- five years ago when they were first published:

> It is no great misfortune to lose his homeland and his fatherland. On the contrary, he grows with the area that he matter-of-factly regards as his own. Is not the emerging Little Europe [as western Europe after World War II was sometimes called], which in the traditional sense is neither fatherland nor homeland, already today for the Germans, French, Italians, Belgians, the Dutch, and the Luxem-burgers an accrued property? With the same assurance, so they say, they move about in Karlsruhe and Naples, Brest and Rotterdam. They imagine themselves in the situation of the man who is already rich and therefore also footloose and to whom the *world* belongs already. After all, jets take him faster from Paris to Tokyo, from New York to Toronto than a slow train took me scarcely four decades ago from Vienna to a village in Tyrol. Modern man exchanges his home for the world. What a brilliant transaction!

> La belle affaire! But one doesn't exactly have to be a dull obscurant, fixed to the spot, in order to doubt this too. For many a person who trades what yesterday meant home for a second-rate cosmopolitanism gives up the sparrow in hand for the kolibri in the bush. Just because someone travels in a subcompact from Fürth to the Côte d'Azur and there, on the terrace of the café, orders duex martinis, he immediately thinks he is a cosmopolite of the second half of the century and that he has already pocketed the profits from the world-for-home exchange. Only when he becomes sick and the

médicin prescribes him a local remedy does he get gloomy thoughts about French pharmacology and sigh for Bayer products and the Herr Doktor. Superficial knowledge of the world and language gained through tourism and business trips, is no compensation for home. The barter proves to be a dubious one.

But this is not to say that future generations will not be able to, will not have to, get along very well without a homeland. What the French sociologist Pierre Bertraux calls the mutation of the human being, the psychic assimilation of the technological-scientific revolution, is unavoidable. The new world will be much more thoroughly one than the dating dream of a Greater Europe pictures it today. The objects of daily use, which at present still imbue with emotion, will be fully fungible. Already, American city planners are thinking of turning the house into a consumable commodity in the future. One hears that at intervals of twenty to twenty-five years entire sections of the city will be demolished and rebuilt, since house repairs will be as little worthwhile as certain auto repairs already are. But in such a world, how would one still be able to form the concept of home at all? The cities, highways, service stations, the furniture, the electric household appliances, the plates, and the spoons will be the same everywhere. It is conceivable that the language of the future world will also be the purely functional means of communication [p. 57] that for the natural scientist it already is today. The physicists communicate in the language of mathematics; for the cocktail party in the evening, basic English suffices. The developing world of tomorrow will certainly expel the homeland and possibly the mother tongue and will let them exist peripherally as a subject of specialized historical research only.

The world that for Améry was still an imagined future has become all too much our daily reality today. In such a world, it is at best purely by accident that anyone at any given time can manage to preserve any illusion of still having any genuine home any longer. All one has to do is leave the United States, for example, and then return to pass through US customs, to be shown, if one just has the eyes to see, that an American citizen can be effectively stripped of all supposed rights of citizenship by no more than a whim of a custom's officer, a glitch in the airport surveillance equipment, or a shared last name with someone on some watch-list.

We are all homeless now. Homelessness is today everyone's standing virtual reality, activated randomly by mere chance and happenstance. None are immune from being suddenly and summarily turned out of whatever they call, as by a passing fancy, their "homes."

Today, the trauma of homelessness is universal.

Trauma, Identity, Nationality, and Community

Another way of saying that we are all homeless today is to say that today everyone is a Jew. That has been so ever since 1935 at least, the year the Nazi Nuremburg laws were enacted. If in 1935 someone such as Hans Meyer/Jean Améry, who had no cultural, linguistic, religious, or other affiliation with the Jewish community either locally or internationally, could suddenly be made to be a Jew by mere legislative whim, then anyone, anywhere can just as easily be made to be a Jew. In such circumstances, the circumstances that have prevailed at least since then, after all, to be a Jew just means to be virtually homeless, wherever and whoever one may turn out to be in terms of nationality or any other identity one may be entitled to claim — claim, at least, until one's virtual Jewishness happens to be activated, which may occur at any time.

Améry writes later in *At the Mind's Limits*, in the closing essay, significantly entitled "On the Necessity and Impossibility of Being a Jew," that insofar as someone such as himself, who had no "cultural ties or religious ties" to Judaism (page 83) and for whom, therefore, "being a Jew" never was or could be a "positive fact" (page 93) or identity, could be forced to be a Jew anyway, a Jew is simply and solely "a person who is regarded by others as a Jew" (page 94). Indeed, he goes on to observe (same page), "even if others do not decide that I am a Jew, . . . I am still a Jew by the mere fact that the world around me does not expressly designate me as a non-Jew.... As a Non-non-Jew, I am a Jew."

Because the world today is one in which by sheer happenstance one can be suddenly denied any status in terms of what, following Améry, we may call positive facts of identity, everyone today is virtually homeless — virtually a 'Jew' in the purely formal sense he explicates. Elie Wiesel, another Auschwitz survivor famous for having written about his experience, would say the same thing some years later.

Even later yet, Art Spiegelman, a very different author writing very different sorts of books in a very different time and place, will say the same thing yet again, and quote Wiesel in the process. Three years before his two-volume *Maus* was published, in "Looney Tunes, Zionism, and the Jewish Question," originally published in *The Village Voice* on June 6, 1989, and now available on the supplemental DVD to *MetaMouse*, Spiegelman, echoing Theodor Adorno among others, wrote that "western civilization ended at Auschwitz"—even though, for most of us in the western world today, "we still haven't noticed."

A little later in the same article, Spigelman writes:

> Elie Wiesel, in a television discussion that followed *The Day After*, the mini-series about nuclear destruction, noted that the word Holocaust echoes forward in time as well as back, that 'after Auschwitz we are all Jews.'. . . I agree totally. It is a profound statement. The Holocaust ought to have convinced the world that it must embrace the Diaspora Jew—that it must acknowledge, indeed, that it has become the Diaspora Jew. . . . After the Holocaust, we are all Jews . . . all of us. . . including George Bush, Dan Quayle, Yasser Arafat, and even Yitzhak Shamir. Now our job is to convince *them* of that.

Spiegelman is also no less aware than Améry that what is at issue in such convincing is no longer a matter of anything pertaining to 'nations' and 'nationality,' nothing, that is, to do with any 'we,' membership in which is vested in one by the fact of being born in a certain place (say the United States) or to certain parents (say U.S. citizens). Thus, just after noting that 'western civilization ended at Auschwitz,' even though most of us 'still haven't noticed,' and just before noting his agreement with Wiesel that 'after Auschwitz we are all Jews,' he asks if, before we all finally do notice what happened to us all in Auschwitz: 'Must every household — every room in every house — have to become a nation before we can evolve to some other social organization?'

Insofar as universally today everyone is a virtual Jew, even if that virtuality is not actualized at any given moment, everyone is virtually denationalized as well. Everyone is virtually an 'illegal alien,' to use the jargon of today in the United States, or a 'stateless person' to use a term more hallowed by time. The only 'we' to which everyone universally, without exception, absolutely belongs, in this day when all of 'us' are virtual Jews/illegal aliens/stateless persons is, to use a formulation Améry himself uses at one point in *At the Mind's Limits* (page 44), the "we" of "us anonymous ones."

The only "we" left for each and all of us virtual Jews today—which means, then, for all us "human beings" at all today—is and must be "anonymous," which literally means *without name*. We must all be nameless precisely because the universal 'we' that encompasses us all just as 'human beings,' all of us without exception and therefore with absolute universality, is beyond and apart from whoever we may be at the level of anything that can be named in us, in the ordinary sense — the level, that is, of whoever else we may be, besides virtual Jews: such things as Germans, Israelis, Christians, Muslims, Buddhists, fathers, mothers, daughters, sons, professors, students, and so forth, whoever we are at the level of any 'identity' the illusion of which the world still lets most of us continue to cling even today. The only universal 'community' to which all of us 'human beings' belong today, everyone everywhere with absolute universality, is, to use another expression from Améry, no 'positive community' such as all those just mentioned. Rather, it is a 'community of fate.' That is, it is the community of all of us who stand altogether *alone* before the inescapable *threat of catastrophe*, indeed, before the catastrophe of all catastrophes: the catastrophe of the actualization, which may strike at any moment whatever, with no ground or reason, descending upon us as our doom, of our universal "Jewery."

The only truly universal community is the community of all of us who are alone together before that trauma, the very "mother of all traumas," to paraphrase Sadam Hussein. To be forced to be members of that universal community of the damned is the curse under which all of us suffer today. As our curse and our doom, however, it is also the condition of the only hope left to us, all us anonymous ones, of constituting any genuine community at all today, this day "after Auschwitz." But that dawn itself can come only once we have at last "noticed," as Spiegelman puts it, what really happened at Ausschwitz—namely, that "western civilization ended." After Ausscwitz, after the end of "western civilization" (assuming that Auschwitz does not reveal that phrase to be an oxymoron) the only possibility of any of us coming together into any sort of genuine community lies solely in what, if anything, remains of "us" when we finally let that mother of all traumas, which reveals the very heart of trauma as such, traumatize us, rather than continuing to run from it into our willful ignorance.

This book is about that, too.

Chapter 1

THE TRUTH OF TRAUMA

By the *truth* of trauma I mean the *response that trauma itself elicits from those to whom it happens*—the response that lets trauma be the trauma that it is. The truth of trauma is the response to trauma that grants it a place to strike, to traumatize, rather than denying it any place to take place.

But just what response, then, does trauma elicit? What does trauma call upon us to do, if we are not to deny or avoid traumatization, but are, rather, to yield it space?

Let us begin with reflecting upon a powerful piece of fiction that in its own way addresses just that question.

In his fiction, contemporary American writer Cormac McCarthy depicts horrendous, traumatic events as they affect his diverse characters. That is certainly true of his novel *No Country for Old Men*, subsequently made into an award winning film. McCarthy ends the novel by depicting the retirement of Ed Tom Bell, a longtime border-town Texas sheriff and the moral anchor of the novel, in whose narrative voice McCarthy begins each of his chapters, before shifting to a neutral authorial voice. At the close of the novel, Bell is leaving his office on his last day as sheriff, to return home to his beloved and loving wife. Bell is retiring as sheriff because of his experiences, recounted in the preceding chapters, with Anton Chigurh, the new breed of soulless killer who is the engine driving all the considerable death and violence depicted in the novel.

Outside his office Bell gets in his truck, then sits there reflecting for a time, rather than leaving to go home right away. He tries to sort out his own emotions. McCarthy writes (p. 306): "He couldn't name the feeling. It was sadness but it was something else besides. And the something else besides was what had him sitting there instead of starting the truck." Then McCarthy alludes to an earlier episode in Bell's life, when Bell was a soldier in World War II, holed up with his unit in a French farmhouse, which is eventually shelled and destroyed around them: "He'd felt like this before but not in a long time and when he'd said that, then he knew what it was. It was defeat. It was being beaten. More bitter to him than death. You need to get over that, he said. Then he started the truck."

Grammatically, at least, McCarthy's text leaves the reference of the "that" which Bell needs to get over ambiguous. What Bell feels he needs to "get over" could be the "defeat," the "being beaten" he has experienced through Chigurh. But it could also be that what he needs to get over is whatever it is in him—in his own character—that makes such defeat so "bitter," "more bitter to him than death." That is, what Bell may feel he needs to get over may be, not defeat as such, but his making the avoidance of defeat so definitive for his sense of his own dignity. My own reading of the novel, especially its closing pages, leads me to that latter conclusion, as I will now try to explain.

McCarthy uses the passage just cited to end the next to last chapter of the novel. Then he casts the following, final chapter of only two pages entirely in Bell's own voice. In those closing thoughts, Bell recounts two things. The first is how earlier in his life, as a soldier in World War II, he had discovered, outside the French farmhouse soon to be destroyed around him and his unit at the end of the war, a water trough that had been patiently chiseled out of the rock there by some erstwhile inhabitant in an earlier age.

"I don't know how long it had been there," Bell reflects:

> A hundred years. Two hundred. You could see the chisel
> marks in the stone. It was hewed out of solid rock and it

was about six feet long and maybe a foot and a half wide and about that deep. Just chiseled out of the rock. And I got to thinking about the man that done that. That country had not had a time of peace much of any length at all that I knew of. I've read a little of the history of it since and I aint sure it ever had one. But this man had set down with a hammer and chisel and carved out a stone water trough to last ten thousand years. Why was that? What was it that he had faith in? It wasn't that nothing would change. Which is what you might think, I suppose. He had to know bettern that. I've thought about it a good deal. I thought about it after I left that house blown to pieces. I'm going to say that water trough is there yet. It would have took something to move it, I can tell you that. So I think about him setting there with his hammer and his chisel, maybe just an hour or two after supper, I don't know. And I have to say the only thing I can think is that there was some sort of promise in his heart. And I don't have no intention of carvin a stone water trough. But I would like to be able to make that kind of promise. I think that's what I would like most of all.

Doesn't the Psalmist singing of the transience of the rich and powerful and the triumph of the poor and lowly make just such a promise, too? And doesn't Bell's own father, of whom Bell speaks in the second and last thing he recounts to the reader in the closing paragraph of the book, to which I will now turn?

Earlier, the reader has learned that Bell's grandfather was a lawman, like Bell himself. Bell's father, however, was not. He seemed to lack whatever it was his own father, Bell's grandfather, and his son, Bell himself, had—whatever it was that let both of them become such figures of authority and prestige. Just after mentioning the water trough in the rock outside the long-ago bombed-out French farmhouse, Bell recalls his father (pp. 308-309):

The other thing is that I have not said much about my father and I know I have not done him justice. I've been older now than he ever was for almost twenty years so in a sense I'm looking back at a younger man. He went on the road tradin horses when he was not much more than a boy. . . He knew about horses and he was good with em. I've seen him break a few and he knew what he was doin. Very easy on the horse. Talked to em a lot. He never broke nothin in me and I owe him more than I would of thought. As the world might look at it I suppose I was the better man. Bad as that sounds to say. Bad as it is to say. That has got to have been hard to live with. Let alone his daddy. He would never have made a lawman. He went to college I think two years but he never did finish. I've thought about him a lot less than I should of and I know that aint right either. I had two dreams about him after he died. I don't remember the first one all that well but it was about meetin in town somewhere and he give me some money and I think I lost it. But the second one was like we were both back in older times and I was on horseback going through the mountains of a night. Goin through this pass in the mountains. It was cold and there was snow on the ground and he rode past me and kept on goin. Never said nothing. He just rode on past and he had this blanket wrapped around him and he had his head down and when he rode past I seen he was carrying fire in a horn the way people used to do and I could see the horn from the light inside of it. About the color of the moon. And in the dream I knew that he was goin on ahead and that he was fixin to make a fire somewhere out there in all that dark and all that cold and I knew that whenever I got there he would be there. And then I woke up.

What we owe the dead is everything, if we owe them anything at all. I will eventually return to the issue of our debt to the dead, but for now there is still much more to be said on the truth of trauma — the response trauma elicits from us. My argument will be that the truth of trauma lies in such responses to it as are embodied in Bell's long dead French farmer, or his more recently dead father, rather than in the sort of response Bell himself, outside his office after his last day as sheriff, initially has — the affective response of feeling defeated.

If we view philosophy itself as a response to trauma—for which there are some good reasons, including the fruitfulness of so viewing it, as I hope the following discussion will suggest—then philosophy, at least in its traditional, mainstream form, is a response of the same sort that Sheriff Bell's initial one represents in McCarthy's novel, rather than the sort represented by Bell's father and by the French farmer of Bell's memory, and expressed in Bell's own final hope.

In the great opening pages of his master-work *The Star of Redemption*, Franz Rosenzweig addresses the whole history of philosophy since Socrates, and contrasts it with the 'New Thinking' Rosenzweig himself endorses. He sees such New Thinking finally beginning to emerge only with Nietzsche, then coming eventually to be represented by Heidegger, for one, especially in the latter's famous disputation at Davos, Switzerland, in the 1920s with Ernst Cassirer about the interpretation of Kant. In those opening pages, Rosenzweig presents philosophy from Socrates down to Nietzsche as a sort of suicide. As Rosenzweig interprets it, the Socratic philosopher chooses to negate flesh-and-blood life itself in favor of a bloodless projected Ideal reality, making that choice in order never to have to face the fear of death, that always looming trauma, head on. By Rosenzweig's analysis, the 'otherworldliness' of philosophy until Nietzsche makes manifest an attempt to avoid the fear of death by avoiding ever fully living. It is a response to death—or, more precisely, to the fear of death—that tries to secure itself against death, but does so only at the paradoxical price of a permanent deadening, as it were. Philosophy stiffens itself against death by denying the very fear of it.

Just such stiffening in the face of what is perceived as threatening is also evident in another direction, one equally definitive of philosophy's own self-image. From its inception in the dialogues of Plato and embodied in those dialogues in the figure of Socrates, philosophy has conceived of itself not only in terms of its relationship to death, but also and inseparably in terms of its opposition to what counts for it as its "other"—what philosophy calls *sophistry*. Falling or degenerating into what philosophy traditionally calls by that name has functioned as a sort of "founding trauma," the compulsion to avoid which has always defined the philosophical endeavor itself. As contemporary French philosopher Jean-Luc Nancy puts it in his recent book *The Creation of the World, or Globalization* (page 77): "Philosophy begins as the self-productive technology of its own name, its discourse and its discipline. . . . In this operation, the best known and most prominent feature is the differentiation of itself from what is called 'sophistry' . . ."

Some two decades earlier, Philippe Lacoue-Labarthe, who for many years before his death was Nancy's colleague and frequent collaborator at the University of Strasbourg in France, had advanced a similar analysis, in the title essay to *Typography*. Lacoue-Labarthe sees philosophy throughout its history as an enterprise that must continually (re-)constitute itself as 'the *anti-mimetic* discourse"—recall how, for Plato, the "sophist," in the dialogue of that name, is defined as a kind of "image-maker," in contrast to the philosopher, that seeker of "truth" and "knowledge.

Thus, at least by such accounts as Nancy's or Lacoue-Labarthe's, from its inception philosophy has always defined itself by a movement of *exclusion*, the exclusion of that from which philosophy has always struggled to differentiate itself, precisely only in such differentiation becoming itself. Thus, in its founding movement philosophy gives priority to that *against* which it defines itself. It can come to itself only as the negation of its opposite, just as, for Nietzsche, the 'good' of the 'good/evil' distinction, in the first of the three essays that make up his *Genealogy of Morals*, can come to itself only as and in the exclusion of its opposite, which has a status independent of, and prior to, the 'good,' and to which the 'good' comes as a sort of afterthought.

Hence the obsessiveness of philosophy's incessant return to defining itself in its self-opposition to sophistry. Philosophy must perpetually and compulsively keep repeating its effort to set itself apart from sophistry, just because such a self-definition can never be accomplished for sure, once and for all. Only what needs no movement of distinguishing itself from what it extrudes and excludes in order to come to itself can ever fully 'accomplish' itself. Or, rather, only what never needs to accomplish itself at all, but what simply is, in its fullness, like the sun in Nietzsche's Prologue to *Thus Spoke Zarathustra*, can escape what we might call the excremental cycle—the cycle of excreting its own opposite and opposing itself to it in obsessive retention.

Influential contemporary Italian philosopher Giorgio Agamben's notion of the *ban* functions in just such a way. Thus, using Agamben's terminology, we could say that since its inception in Plato philosophy has bound itself to the ban of sophistry. No wonder then that philosophy always reeks of sophism, the very shit of philosophy.

What would a thinking that was *not* under such an excremental ban be like?

Wouldn't it have to be, in fact, a thinking that carries just the sort of *promise* McCarthy envisions at the end of *No Country for Old Men*? The defeat that leaves Sheriff Bell brooding in his truck outside his office just after his resignation has become effective—and just before the end of McCarthy's novel—is, we might say, a philosophical defeat. That is, it is a defeat of that which, since philosophy's beginning, has always been associated with philosophy: the defeat of the sort of manly stiffening before what threatens to overwhelm and dis-man man.

But that means it is a defeat of the dreaded 'feminine,' as the feminine has recurrently been conceived. Along just such a line of thought, Lacoue-Labarthe writes (*Typologies*, page 127):

> [T]here is, there will perhaps always have been, in the *theorization* of mimesis—from the *Republic* to [Jacques Lacan's] "The Mirror Stage," and whatever recognition might be given (despite everything and in different ways) to the ineluctability of the fact of mimesis—a kind of virile stiffening and anxious clenching as well as a resentment against the original

maternal domination and original feminine education, these being perhaps the sign, for the subject, of its constitutive incompleteness, of its belatedness (impossible to overcome) with respect to its "own birth" [Notice how, here, subjectivity itself emerges as and in *avoidance of trauma*, the ever renewed, ever failing/inadequate standing itself back up against and after the shock that has deflated it], and of its natural incapability of engendering itself (or at least assisting in or attending its own engenderment). *Anti-mimesis* is what will finally be revealed in the last, Hegelian dream of philosophy: absolute (in)sight, the subject theorizing its own conception and engendering itself in seeing itself do so — the speculative.

It is ironically fitting that a work of fiction—especially a late novel by such a masculine writer as Cormac McCarthy, whose fictions have for so long so well sung the praises of such admirably manly men as Sheriff Ed Tom Bell—should spell out the alternative to this dream of philosophy. It is fitting because the anti-mimetic, anti-sophistic—but never clearly emergent and enduringly sustained—self-erecting, self-stiffening structure of philosophy has not accidentally always also tied the critique and negation of mimesis to the equally virile rejection of all that deserves to go by the name of "fiction," as Lacoue-Labarthe joins in observing. After first remarking (page 129) that "what is threatening in mimesis is feminization, instability, *hysteria*," he soon concludes (page 131): "Hence the urgent need for a serious purification of language and a rectification of fiction. Moreover, it is clear that if it is absolutely necessary to redress discourse in order to install it [that is, set it up, erect it] within truth, it is not first of all because it is a lie—but more fundamentally because it is a fiction that 'writes' the 'subject,' that models it and assigns it an identity." What he calls (p. 130) "the entire (very) long critique [that Plato puts in the *Republic*] of traditional mythopoesis—of Homer and Hesiod, above all"—is, he goes on to say,

conducted in the name of that principle that demands—if the function of myths is to be, as Thomas Mann says, *re-cited* (or if life, as Novalis says, is a novel)—that we purify myth of all *bad examples*, which are of course always examples of *depropriation* (adultery, a lack of virility, or else a weakening of heroism, impiety, disrespect toward the just repartition of functions, ravaging laughter, furious madness, unworthy behavior, and so on).

Bell's father is just such a "bad example": someone who 'as the world might look at it," was a lesser man than Bell, one lacking in whatever it takes to make a 'lawman' like the father's son after him and the father's own father before him. He is an example of a man so feminized that he is more like a mother than a father, a womanly man who 'never broke nothin' in his son, no more than he did in the horses that he nevertheless, as the saying goes, 'broke' exceedingly well, apparently.

It is just such a "bad example" of a man, such a motherly misfit of a father, however, who carries the "promise" Bell addresses in his final reflections in McCarthy's novel. That is the same promise Bell also sees carried by the anonymous Frenchman who, in a land no less perpetually troubled than the borderlands that provide McCarthy the setting for this and so many other of his fictions (and of which his earlier novel *Blood Meridian* especially makes clear the all too grossly violent history), painstakingly and slowly chisels the water trough in the rock behind the farmhouse about to be destroyed in one of the endless rounds of wars that men like Bell the son struggle to erect around themselves.

Regardless of the author's intentions, there is something obviously suggestive of the feminine in the chiseled cleft in the rock behind the now long ago destroyed farmhouse in the French countryside of Sheriff Bell's remembering. What is more, if that which is always doomed in advance to go down to defeat in its bold and virile efforts to stand itself up again and again is to be, not even countered, but made irrelevant—made to vanish like mist in the morning sun or like the phantoms of the dreams one wakes from—by a promise issued even in the midst of all that irrelevancy, then it would seem that such a promise can only be feminine.

At any rate, it may be worth reflecting at this point on a certainly feminine voice that also speaks a promise, though no more uses that term than does Sheriff Bell's presumably male French farmer with a chisel, or his unmanly father with a horse-whisper, in McCarthy's novel. The voice I have in mind is that of Marguerite Duras, in *The War: A Memoir*, which Duras wrote in Paris during the Liberation as World War II was ending, but did not publish until 1985, both in the original French and, soon thereafter, in an English translation. At one point during her prolonged and anguished wait for news of her husband, Robert Antelme, arrested by the Nazis before the Liberation and sent off into the lostness of the Nazi camp system, Duras, along with the rest of France and the Allied world, begins to receive reports and photographs of the genocide that the Nazis had perpetrated in the camps. In response to that news, Duras writes (pages 46-47):

> We belong to Europe: it is here, in Europe [the same Europe where McCarthy sets Bell's story of the water trough], that we're shut up together confronting the rest of the world. Around us are the same oceans, the same invasions, the same wars. We are of the same race as those who were burned in the crematoriums, those who were gassed at Maidenek; and we're also of the same race as the Nazis. They're great levelers, the crematoriums at Buchenwald, hunger, the common graves at Bergen-Belsen. We have a share in those graves; those strangely identical skeletons belong to one European family.

A bit later comes an entry dated the next day, April 28, 1945 (pages 47-48):

> Those [around her in Paris] waiting for peace aren't waiting, not at all. There's less and less reason for not having any news. Peace is visible already. It's like a great darkness falling, it is the beginning of forgetting. You can see already: Paris is lit

up at night. . . . There's no room for me [who will not forget, but insists on remembering, as she continues to wait for her husband] here anywhere. I'm not here, I'm there with him in that region no one can reach, no one else can know, where there's burning and killing. . . . The lit-up city means only one thing to me: it's a sign of death, of a tomorrow without them [namely, without the dead themselves — or those who may as well be dead, given the public forgetting of them]. There's no present in the city now except for us who wait. For us it's a city *they* [the dead or may-as-well-be] won't see.

As for those dead (page 49): 'There are an awful lot of them. There really are huge numbers of dead. . . . This new face of death that has been discovered in Germany — organized, rationalized — produces bewilderment before it arouses indignation. You're amazed. How can anyone still be German?"

However, as though immediately realizing that to go the way opened up by that question is just once again to try to stand oneself up erect, repeating the very movement that inevitably involves exclusion, that very sort of exclusion that blossomed so hellishly in the Nazi genocide against the Jews — the very movement that *at best* leads to such resigned acceptance of defeat as Bell experiences at the end of *No Country for Old Men*—Duras lays out another possible response, a more promise-filled one (pages 49-50):

How can anyone still be a German? You look for parallels elsewhere and in other times, but there aren't any. Some people will always be overcome by it, inconsolable. One of the greatest civilized nations in the world, the age-long capital of music, has just systematically murdered eleven million human beings with the utter efficiency of a state industry. The whole world looks at the mountain, the mass of death dealt by God's creature to his fellows. Someone quotes the name of some German man of letters who's been very upset and become very depressed and to whom these things have given much food for thought. If Nazi crime is not seen in world terms, if it isn't understood collectively, then that man in the concentration camp at Belsen who died alone but with the same collective soul and class awareness that made him undo a bolt on the railroad one night somewhere in Europe, without a leader, without a uniform, without a witness, has been betrayed. If you give a German and not a collective interpretation to the Nazi horror, you reduce the man in Belsen to regional dimensions. The only possible answer to this crime is to turn it into a crime committed by everyone. To share it. Just like the idea of equality and fraternity. In order to bear it, to tolerate the idea of it, we must share the crime.

"We are all Americans now." That was the famous front-page headline in *Le Monde* the morning after the attacks on the World Trade Center and the Pentagon on September 11, 2001. What might have come to pass if, instead, following Marguerite Duras's line of thought, it had read: "We are all terrorists now"?

In *Traumatic Encounters: Holocaust Representation and the Hegelian Subject*, literary theorist Paul Eisenstein, specialist in German literature, suggests that what decent non-Jewish Germans should have done after the beginning of Nazi action against Jewish Germans on *Kristallnacht* in 1938 is what a few of them actually did when they put the Star of David in their own shop-windows, indentifying themselves with their vandalized Jewish neighbors. That is, Eisenstein argues, after *Kristallnacht* the only thing left for non-Jewish Germans of conscience to do was to proclaim that *they* were all Jews now. Those who did just that in one fashion or another chiseled their own water troughs of promise in the rock.

What Duras adds to the work of that promise is the insight that, once the Nazi extermination camps were opened, the only way all the prisoners of those camps could be set free and kept that way was for all those with a conscience, who so recently all needed to become Jews, needed to become, now that the Nazis were at last defeated, Nazis in their own turn. Paradoxical as it may seem, that was the only way, she saw, to turn aside from the Nazi road — or, better, from that long, long road of which only an all too long and too recent stretch bore the Nazi name, but which has borne many other names both before and since the Nazis. Only so could one wake from the dream, letting its phantoms dissolve in the morning sun while one went about one's daily business.

In *Traumatic Encounters* Eisenstein provides an excellent analysis of liberalism—in the classic sense of that term, not the modern, American one—as sharing with Fascism the endeavor to *avoid* trauma. But I am not sure that he fully appreciates what his own analysis shows, or at least what it showed me. I will use a line of Eisenstein's own, to point to what I think that is. He employs (page 42) the phrase 'the prevention of future catastrophes' to name the goal to the service of which he hopes his own analysis may contribute. (In the next sentence, he does go on to qualify that statement a bit, but not in a way that affects what I want to say here).

The argument he advances is that both liberalism and National Socialism end up "disavowing" the "traumatic kernel"—what French psychoanalyst Jacques Lacan calls the *point de capiton*, the 'quilting point'—that is 'internal' to any political order (like the point of 'decision' from which law and legal right themselves come, according to the right-wing German legal theorist Carl Schmitt, who used his thought to support the Nazi state, though Eisenstein does not draw that connection himself). They disavow that 'traumatic instability/inconsistency' that is internal to any and every social order, by turning it into a definite historical something—rather than keeping cognizant of what Eisenstein, using a Kantian terminology, calls its 'transcendence" by giving the traumatic kernel or quilting point (page 45) 'a context, a history, from the beginning.' Eisenstein uses 'the figure of the Jew' in National Socialism as his example. However, his analysis also applies just as well, so far as I can see, to the liberal construction of any such presumed actual historical starting point, whether that be 'the state of nature' of classical social contract theory, or even John Rawls's notion of 'the original position' in his contemporary reworking of such theory.

At any rate, what it seems to me Eisenstein himself may miss, or at least underemphasize, in his persuasive analysis is precisely what it brought most clearly to my own attention: that the very endeavor to 'prevent' such catastrophes as the Holocaust is itself a move of just the sort he so clearly exposes in liberalism and National Socialism. In short, it is precisely the endeavor to secure oneself *against* a future recurrence of catastrophe that counter-intentionally ends up generating just such recurrence—indeed, that requires such catastrophe to found itself and whatever order it imposes, found itself and its order in and as the very disavowal of the un-disavowable occurrence of trauma.

The discussion could also be cast in terms of the notion of *idolatry*. National Socialism, liberalism, and, if I am right, Eisenstein's own notion of 'preventing future catastrophes' are all 'idolatrous,' in that they all make the contextualizing, historizing move whereby a 'transcendence' is made into an 'object,' to use the Kantian language Eisenstein himself does. They all make God into an idol.

Eisenstein himself elsewhere in the same book all but sees and says the same thing, when he argues, contra contemporary American historian Dominick LaCapra, that what the latter calls "structural trauma" (which cannot be traced back to any datable event) is actually the very "precondition" for what he calls "historical trauma" (which can), that it is only by remembering or "repeating" the former that we can lessen the frequency of the latter. But what does that entail, if not that the very focus on "preventing" "historical" trauma engenders, against its own apparent intention, more and ever more of the very trauma it struggles to avoid? It is only, as Eisenstein argues, by remembering 'structural' trauma as such (as 'structural,' in a 'transcendental' sense) that we can stop keeping on doing deadly repetitions/recollections of it in the form of 'historical' trauma, acting the unacknowledged structural trauma out again and again and again. Just so, to use an example that is of concern to Eisenstein himself, the contemporary Israeli oppression of the Palestinians can be seen as a re-enactment of the Holocaust itself, with new victims and with the old victims now become victimizers.

Eisenstein's analysis in *Traumatic Encounters* can be profitably combined with that of Indian psychoanalyst Sudhir Kakar in his book *The Colors of Violence.*

Kakar draws a valuable distinction between 'community' and 'communalism,' to use his terms. Here is one way he formulates that distinction (pages 191-192): 'Communalism as a state of mind . . . is the individual's *assertion* of being part of a religious community, preceded by a full *awareness* of belonging to such a community. "The 'We-ness' of the community is here replaced by the 'We *are*' of communalism.' Thus, what Kakar calls 'community' is a state of *being*, the *assertion* of which becomes the focal interest of the state of *mind* he calls 'communalism.' It is important to keep in mind, here, that, all other things being equal, the felt need to *assert* something varies inversely with the felt assurance of being or having that same thing: The more secure — the more 'at home'—I feel about myself or whatever I have come to identify with myself—whether that be my looks, my intelligence, my sexuality, my community membership, or whatever, the less do I feel myself driven to assert myself or my having the identity at issue.

But what if the very "awareness" of *being* a member of a community—one's "cultural/communal identity"–does *not*, as Kakar says in the lines just quoted, 'precede' the 'assertion' thereof, except and unless it is a retrospectively cast myth or fiction of the origin of the community, membership in which is being 'asserted'? Just before the lines already quoted, Kakar borrows his psychoanalytic colleague Oscar Peterson's account of the stages through which one must go as "an individual who, as a consequence of a shared threat, is in process of self-consciously identifying with his or her ethnic group.' But isn't the very constitution of the ethnic group itself as a definite 'we' another retrospective projection of itself as already having been there all along? And isn't the very constituting of a threat as a 'shared' one a part of that very process–i.e., isn't the 'sharing' itself something that must be *communicated* in Heidegger's sense in *Being and Time*—whereby "*Mitteilung,*" the German for "communication," is taken seriously in its etymological meaning of *sharing-with*—in order to come into being at all?

Following Peterson, Kakar says the first stage of 'the change from community to communalism' is that 'I declare to all who share the crisis [whatever it may be, that has set off the whole process] with me that I am one of them a Hindu, a Muslim [or whatever].' With regard to that, it is striking to compare the post-9/11 *Le Monde* headline 'We are all Americans now,' and then go on to compare both (*Le Monde's* "all Americans," on one hand, and Kakar's example of all being Hindus or Muslims or the like, on the other) with Eisenstein's notion of all Germans of conscience identifying themselves as Jews after *Kristallnacht.*

Those three cases of self-identification with, or constitution of, a self-defining group are significantly different from one another, in ways that deserve to be studied. For example, there is something offensive to many about the *Le Monde* identification, especially insofar as it is an identification with the very community ('America') that itself marginalizes so many members of so many other communities, and silences, refuses to let be heard, and refuses even to hear, the voice of the marginalized that sounds in the 9/11 attacks themselves. In contrast, insofar as globalized capitalism marginalizes both Hindus and Muslims in the 'global market,' constitution of, and identification with, either of those two communities, 'Hindu' or 'Muslim,' has a liberatory potential completely lacking in the constitution of, and identification with, a global 'American' community, as in *Le Monde's* post-9/11 headline, which is not at all liberatory.

In contrast to both "we are all Americans" after 9/11, or "we are all Hindus" after some attack or other crisis for the Hindu community, "we are all Jews" in Nazi Germany after *Kristallnacht* is *wholly* liberatory, and *escapes* the very oppression of any "communalism" at all in favor of a constituting and identifying with a genuine, genuinely *open* community. Similarly and importantly, taken in their concrete historicity, Duras's willingness to affirm community even with the Nazis — her willingness literally to own up to their crimes: to take those crimes on as belonging

42

to us all, that is as being 'my own' crimes — is a movement of universal opening and inclusion, and is as such wholly liberatory and void of what Kakar calls communalism. Far from being a movement of assertion of identity via membership in some special group, Duras's affirmation that we are all Nazis is a turning aside from all such exclusion and exclusivity, such sticking to "one's own."

Duras's movement of universalization, made while she was still awaiting her husband Robert Antelme's return from the camps, or at least some clear news of him, one way or another, was, as it turned out, unknowingly but simultaneously reciprocated by Antelme himself, as he was later to recount in his own memoir, *The Human Race*, first written in 1946-47, but not published in France until ten years later, and eventually translated into English far later yet. The reference at issue comes near the end of the book, finally explaining the title thereof. Antelme begins by writing (page 219) that 'there are not several human races, there is only one human race. It's because we're men like them that the SS will finally stand powerless before us.' On the next page he elaborates:

> [I]f, facing nature, or facing death, we can perceive no substantial difference between the SS and ourselves, then we have to say that there is only one human race. And we have to say that everything in the world that masks this unity, everything that places beings in situations of exploitation and subjugation and thereby implies the existence of various species of mankind, is false and mad; and that we have proof of this here, the most irrefutable proof, since the worst of victims cannot do otherwise than establish that, in its worst exercise, the executioner's power cannot be other than one of the powers that men have, the power to murder. He can kill a man, but he cannot change him into something else.

Those lines are the culmination of his whole account of his experience in the camps in the preceding pages. Thus, much earlier (page 51) he writes: "For the most despised proletarians there is the reassurance of reason. He is less alone that the person who despises him, whose position will become narrower and narrower, and who will inevitably become more and more isolated and steadily weaker. The insults of these people are no more able to reach us than they are able to get their hands on the nightmare we have become in their brains: for all their denying of us we are still there."

Thus, Anthelme once again joins the Psalmist in affirming the impermanence and *irreality* of those who would exclude others to their own profit, of whatever sort, material or other, and, in contrast, the abiding reality of just what the excluders would exclude. Here, Anthelme gives that idea its most radical form, affirming the irreality of the Nazi camps, and the reality of the life those camps would deny and annihilate.

Anthelme returns to this theme a bit later (page 74), adding more detail. He begins with a reflection on the *spectator* to the calamity of the camps:

Th[e] passer-by who happens down the road and goes strolling past the barbed wire, a small dark silhouette against the snow — he is one of the world's forces. But if he sees us [that is, the camp inmates] behind the fence, if somehow the idea just enters his head that there are other possibilities in nature than being a man who walks freely along a road, if he launches out on some such train of thought, then it is very likely he will soon feel threatened by all those shaved heads, by all those figures not one of whom he has the slightest chance ever of getting to know, and who are for him of all things on earth the most unknown. And these men themselves will perhaps contaminate for him the trees that in the distance surround the fence, and this passer-by upon the road will then risk feeling himself smothering within the whole of nature, as though closed shut upon him.

The reign of man, of man who acts or invests things with meaning, does not cease. The SS cannot alter our species. They are themselves enclosed within the same humankind and the same history. *Thou shalt not be*: upon that ludicrous wish an enormous machine has been built. . . . [Yet:] They must take account of us so long as we are alive, and it still depends upon us, upon our tenacious hold upon being, whether at the moment they come to kill us they are made to feel utterly certain they have been cheated.

At the end of *Light in August* William Faulkner's "mixed-race" character Joe Christmas dies at the hands of proto-fascist, racist vigilantes. Yet while dying Christmas's lucid eyes displaying continuing vision escape and banish the attempt, by those who have just castrated him and left him to bleed to death, to erase the insufferable yet insuperable fact of his very existence. In just the same way, in Antelme's account the victims in the Nazi camps escape their captors' attempt to make it that they shall not be.

Equally, however, the perpetrators and their crime cannot be made not to have been. So Antelme continues: "But we cannot have it that the SS does not exist or has not existed. They shall have burned children, and they shall have done it willingly. We cannot have it that they did not wish to do it. They are a force, just as the man walking down the road is one. And as we are, too; for even now they cannot stop us from exerting our power."

An episode he then tells of an SS guard from the Rhineland effectively attests that power. One day, approaching Antelmne and another inmate in the basement of the camp factory, where the two prisoners are sorting parts, the Rhinelander holds out his hand to them. They shake his hand. Antelme writes (page 75):

> We had become accomplices. But he hadn't so much come to encourage us as to seek reassurance himself, to obtain a confirmation. He came to share in our power. Against that handshake there was nothing that could prevail, neither the barking of thousands of SS troops nor the whole apparatus of ovens, dogs, and barbed wire, nor famine, nor lice. . . . Nor did this covert and solitary gesture have a merely private character. . . . Any human relationship a German were to enter into with one of us was the sign itself of a deliberate

rebellion against the whole SS order. One could not do what the Rhinelander had done — could not, that is, behave as a man toward one of us — without thereby classifying oneself historically. . . as if they [that is, such human relationships as even a simple handshake] were themselves the paths, narrow and obscure, that history had there been forced to follow.

This example merits a moment's further reflection. For one thing, it contrasts with the self-serving — by self-exculpating — acts of the Nazi Auschwitz doctors who, as Robert Jay Lifton discusses in *The Nazi Doctors*, could continue to think of themselves as 'saving' lives in the very midst of taking so many. As Antelme presents it, the Rhinelander's gesture is a sort of sacramentally effective sign of humanity shared by the guard and the prisoners. *As* such a gesture, one that sacramentally *effects* the very solidarity it signifies, it is indeed, as Antelme has it, an act of genuine rebellion: an affirmation-demonstration of the very reality the camps sought to deny. It's value, however, lies solely in serving such a sacramentally effective lesson; it has no value at all for exculpating the guards, including especially the Rhinelander himself, insofar as he continues, by his very continuing SS membership if nothing else, to be an accomplice, as well, of the Nazis and their entire system.

Just such rebellion is already manifest in the assertion, already cited, *"I'm still here!'* made by the mere presence of the victim, just like Joe Christmas in Faulkner's novel. It is also still—and strongly — there even in the inmate dying or, what is more, already among the dead. Thus, Antelme writes (pages 93-94):

> There are moments when you could kill yourself just in order that the SS fetch up against this limit as it confronts the impassive object you'd have become, the dead body that has turned its back on them, that goesn't give a shit about their law. The dead man will at once be stronger than they are just as trees and clouds and cows, which we call things and incessantly envy. The SS undertaking is careful not to go to

the point of denying the daisies growing in the fields. And like the dead man, the daisy doesn't give a shit about their law. The dead man no longer offers them a handle. Let them savage his face, let them hack his body to bits, the dead man's very impassiveness, his complete inertness will counter all the blows they strike at him.

That is why we are not always absolutely afraid of dying. There are moments when, in a flash, death stands there as a simple way for getting away from here, for turning our back, for not caring anymore.

Here, death functions as does the retreat into fantasy whereby the prisoner being tortured by the representatives of the (only) apparently all-powerful and ubiquitous State at the end of Terry Gilliam's film *Brazil*. Thus does the victim escape even the executioner, whether by fantasizing or by dying — and displaying thereby the enduring *irreality* of "all that," of all the trappings with which the powerful seek to hide their own vacuity.

It is just such vacuity, such irreality of what passes itself off as to be taken seriously, that is, to put it paradoxically, unmasked by the masks of carnival, as Rebecca Solnit explores in her recent work *A Paradise Built in Hell: The Extraordinary Communities That Arise in Disaster*. The topic of her book is what she calls 'disaster communities,' those communities of 'mutual aid' that so often spring up after disasters such as the 1906 San Francisco earthquake, the munitions boat explosion in the harbor of Halifax, Nova Scotia, in 1916, the Mexico City earthquake of 1985, the attacks on the Twin Towers on Septmeber 11, 2001, or Hurricane Katrina in New Orleans in 2004, the five cases she studies in detail. Such disaster communities, she writes (page 17), are 'utopia itself for many people, though it is only a brief moment during terrible times, And at the same time they manage to hold both irreconcilable experiences, the joy and the grief [so often described by the survivors of such disasters, and of the communities that flower from them].' As she goes on to say a few pages later (page 21), such disaster communities are 'ubiquitous, fluctuating utopias that are neither coerced nor counter-cultural but universal, albeit overlooked" — overlooked, especially, by the mass media and, above all, the powers that be, the very powers behind those media. She adds: 'Elites and authorities often fear the changes of disaster or anticipate that the change means chaos and destruction.' Her analysis shows that to be just a sort of cover-fear for what such forces really fear, which is what she mentions next: 'or at least the undermining of the foundations of their power. . . . Too, the elite often believe [or at least wish they did] that if they themselves are not in control, the situation is out of control, and in their fear take repressive measures that become secondary disasters.'

This 'elite panic' sharply contrasts to the popular altruism and generosity with which 'disaster communities' themselves form and address the disaster in various sorts of mutual aid. Indeed, it is that very prospect of successful mutual aid that creates the panic among the elite, who fear not the disaster itself but that their own *irrelevancy* will be shown for all to see by the success of spontaneous, unregulated, mutual aid efforts that spring up to address the disaster's aftermath. As Solnit writes (pages 152-153, italics added), what takes place after most disasters is a sort of 'anarchy,' not the dreaded anarchy of rapacious selfishness and egotism depicted, for example, in William Golding's *Lord of the Flies*, but

another kind of anarchy, where the citizenry by and large organize and care for themselves. In the immediate aftermath of disaster, government fails as if it had been overthrown and civil society succeeds as though it has revolted: the task of government, usually described as 'reestablishing order,' is to take back the city and the power to govern it, as well as to perform practical functions — restoring power, cleaning up rubble. So the more long-term aftermath of disaster is often in some sense a counterrevolution, with varying degrees of success. The possibility that they have been overthrown *or, more accurately, rendered irrelevant* is a very good reason for elite panic if not for the sometimes vicious acts that ensue.

At least it is "a very good reason for elite panic" in the mind of the elite itself, whose very elite status is dependent on preserving the illusion of their own necessity—a dream from which the elite must hope that those over whom they set themselves to rule will never awake, since then such illusions would vanish like phantoms, just as the Psalmist sings.

It is just such irrelevancy, as Solnit goes on to argue, that is revealed in festivals of carnival, and such carnivalesque political movements as the Zapatista's in Mexico. She writes (pages 173-174):

> A disaster sometimes wipes the slate clean like a jubilee, and it is those disasters that beget joy, while the ones that increase injustice and isolation beget bitterness — the 'corrosive community' of which disaster scholars speak. Some, perhaps all, do both. That is to say, a disaster is an end, a climax of ruin and death, but it is also a beginning, an opening, a chance to start over. (It is also a way to start over for capitalism, creating markets for the replacement of what has been destroyed and more.) And in this light, we can regard the Puritan work ethic as a force of privatization, not only the spiritual privatization of Protestantism but also the privatization of what was hitherto public civic life. The moments of carnival, community, and political participation are in those terms nonproductive, wasted time, even — if you think of the seventeenth-century New England Puritans punishing those who celebrated Christmas — violations of belief. The widespread distrust of the life of unpoliced crowds, manifested in urban and particularly suburban design in the United States, in the bans by dictatorships on public gatherings, in the . . . plans for disaster are measures against carnival and popular power.

The utilitarian argument against fiestas, parades, carnivals, and general public merriment is that they produce nothing. But they do: they produce society. They renew the reasons why we might want to belong and the feeling that we do. The product is far less tangible than everyday goods and services but vital all the same — if absent from many contemporary societies. A festival is a sowing of wildness and a harvest of joy and belonging. An endless fiesta would be exhausting and demoralizing: the pleasure would go out of it, the masks would disguise only fatigue and apathy, and there would eventually be nothing to celebrate.* The ordinary and the extraordinary need each other, or rather everyday life needs to be interrupted from time to time — which is not to say that we need disaster, only that it sometimes supplies the interruption in which the other work of society is done. Carnival

---

* This remark and others like it, as well as the general force of Solnit's argument on the point, seem to have escaped Tom Vanderbilt in his review in the New York Times Book Review for Sunday, September 6, 2009, shortly after Solnit's book first appeared. Vanderbilt ends his review by asking: "As heady as it can be, would Carnival feel so energizing if it were the norm, and not the brief subversion of that norm?" By ending his review in that way, one suggesting that he is saying something Solnit has not considered, Vanderbilt reduces the issue to the level of the foolish child wishing Christmas could come everyday. As Solnit realizes—in the passage above and throughout her analysis—the issue is not to replace mundane time with a time of endless Carnival, but to change the time of everyday itself. Thus, on the very last page of her book (page 313) she writes that the sort of "paradise" that becomes visible in disaster communities "is the only paradise possible, and it will never exist whole, stable, and complete." Instead, she says that such a paradise "is always coming into being in response to trouble and suffering." In contrast to "[a]ll the versions of an achieved paradise [that] sound at best like an eternal vacation" (or, we might add, a sustained erection) she writes that "paradises built in hell are improvisational; we make them up as we go along, and in so doing they call on all our strength and creativity and leave us free to invent even as we find ourselves enmeshed in community." On the other hand, one might want to reflect a bit further on the extent to which the insistence on keeping such things as Carnival or Christmas within the banks of regularly recurrent annual celebrations may be little more than an effective ploy in the service of the preservation of elitist privilege, and against the threat that becomes patent in those very celebrations.

and revolution are likewise interruptions of everyday life, but their point is to provide something that allows you to return to that life with more power, more solidarity, more hope.

I would revise this overall compelling account on only one point, a point which Solnit herself touches upon a few pages later (page 178), when she cites a frequent remark from Subcomandante Insurgente Marcos, the most widely known of the masked zapatistas (which I will leave with an un-capitalized first letter, as they do) of the mountains of southeast Mexico. Marcos says that for the sort of revolution the zapatistas embody, "The means are the end." Insofar as that is so, then carnival and fiesta, or the mutual aid extended to another by those who encounter disaster, like the carnivalesque "political" acts of the zapatistas, do not so much "produce" society as they are that society itself. Solnit goes on to note something similar on the very next page, when she quotes Laura Carlsen, who went to Mexico after the 1985 Mexico City earthquake and remained there, re-porting on the aftermath of the quake as well as on such subsequent de-velopments as the zapatistas. As Solnit observes, Carlsen writes in her introduction to Marcos's *The Speed of Dreams:: Selected Writings 2001-2007* (page 20): "Unlike previous revolutionary movements, [the zapatistas] did not announce plans to take power and install a new state." Rather, says Carlsen, ever since they first appeared, "the zapatistas have deepened their commitment to building alternatives from the grassroots rather than controlling, competing for, or often even confronting the formal power of the state."

'The utopias achieved amid disaster,' Solnit writes in her own voice one page later (180), 'are perhaps the once and future ordinary arrangement of things.' If we remember that the expression 'the once and future' functions much the same as does 'once upon a time" — functions, that is, to dis-locate what is being said from the realm of history as journalistically understood, so to speak, history as some one time and not another, and to re-locate it instead in the always and everywhere of what is truly eventful — this amounts to saying that the utopias of 'disaster communities' are the reality into which we wake when we awaken from the dream that power would have us dream, and dismiss its phantoms as the illusions they are.

Significantly, on the preceding page (179), just before quoting Carlsen, Solnit writes this about Subcomandante Marcos:

> His 'real' identity became an obsession of journalists after the uprising [of 1994, triggered by the North American Free Trade Agreement (NAFTA) going into effect], and when one journalist took him at face value [when he said in an interview] that he had been a gay waiter in San Francisco, he wrote, 'Marcos is gay in San Francisco, black in South Africa, an Asian in Europe, a Chicano in San Ysidro, an anarchist in Spain, a Palestinian in Israel, a Mayan Indian on the streets of San Cristobal, a Jew in Germany, . . . a pacifist in Bosnia, a single woman on the metro at 10:00 p.m., a celebrant on the zócalo, a campesino without land, an unemployed worker . . . and of course a zapatista in the mountains of southern Mexico.' This gave rise to the carnivalesque slogan '*Todos somos* Marcos" ("We are all Marcos") . . .

That line, 'We are all Marcos,' used in that way, resonates with Alain Badiou's discussion of the early Stanley Kubrick film *Spartacus*, which ends with the leader of Rome's legions, who have 'defeated' the Sparticist uprising of gladiators and slaves in ancient Rome, offering the mass of the captured rebels a way out of crucifixion — namely, by 'identifying' Spartacus. In the film, when Spartacus (played by Kirk Douglas, to give Hollywood its due) steps forward from the ranks to save his comrades, first his young friend Antoninus (Tony Curtis), then one after another of the rebels steps forward too, each one claiming, 'I am Spartacus.' Obligingly, the Roman general (Lawrence Olivier) has them all crucified. However, as Badiou realizes and insists, by their refusal of the exclusionary 'identification' of Spartacus, by instead embracing a universally inclusive identification of everyone with one another, by and as the identification of all with and as 'Spartacus,' these rebels dispel the illusion of

Roman power and glory, emerging 'in truth' as the victors in their battle with Rome.

'We can go home.' That, according to Badiou, is the *truth* that takes place in the Spatacist rebellion. Importantly, Badiou also makes it clear that, so soon as that insight dawned on one gladiator or slave, then another and another, and those gladiators and slaves began to act in what Badiou calls 'fidelity' to the event of that truth, they were already at their desired destination, even as they struggled to escape Rome. And, having continued in their fidelity by their universalizing identification of themselves as being all Spartacus, even as they die on their crosses that is just where all the rebels remain at the end of Kubrick's film: home.

At the end of her next chapter, devoted to the disaster communities of mutual aid that formed in New York City after the attacks on the Twin Towers on September 11, 2001, Solnit quotes Astra Taylor, whom she describes (page 193) as 'a tall young woman from Georgia working at a left-wing publishing house in TriBeCa' on that day, who after the attacks 'went out into the street with hundreds of others to watch the extraordinary spectacle not so far away,' and ended up being caught up in the mass exodus of New Yorkers leaving the city on foot. Taylor, after remarking (quoted on page 194 in Solnit), 'The experience on television was so different than the experience on the street,' goes on (my emphasis added):

> 'I felt connected to the people on the street and I felt impressed by them. I also felt that *reality is not what I thought it was*, I still have a lot to learn. The reality that people would do this, commit this act of terrorism *but also the reality that people in the street would help you and that you would help*. Work — I really hate work — and it gets in the way so much: we're rushing to work and we're at work and rushing from work. We didn't go to work for a few days, and you had all this time to talk to people and talk to your family.' Taylor had a

lot of family on hand: two of her three younger siblings were with her in her warehouse in Brooklyn. Her wheelchair-bound younger sister wasn't threatened by the attacks either. She was terrified that her parents would make her come back home because of them, and she'd lose her newfound liberty. She didn't, and the usually reclusive Taylor put on an exhibition for the neighborhood in their home. Taylor summed up Brooklyn that week as an anarchist's paradise, a somber carnival: 'No one went to work and everyone talked to strangers.'

A bit later (on pages 221-222) Solnit expresses some chagrin about the subsequent history of the American response to 9/11:

It's possible to imagine a reality that diverged from September 11 onward, a reality in which the first thing affirmed was the unconquerable vitality of civil society, the strength of bonds of affection against violence, of open public life against the stealth and arrogance of the attack. (These were all affirmed informally, in practice, but not institutionally, and they constituted a victory of sorts, a refusal to be cowed, a coming together, and a demonstration of what is in many ways the opposite of terrorism.)

But isn't the very granting of 'reality' to the institutions of power that were so dissipated on 9/11 itself — those very institutions that Taylor sums up eloquently and accurately with the four-letter word *work*—exactly to accept the illusion on which such power feeds, and on which it must always feed to maintain itself?

"From that point on," continues Solnit in the passage at issue,

the people yearning to sacrifice might have been asked to actually make sweeping changes that would make a society more independent of Mideast oil and the snake pit of politics

54

that goes with it, reawakened to its own global role and its local desires for membership, purpose, dignity, and a deeper safety that came not from weapons but from a different role in the world and at home. That is to say, the resourcefulness and improvisation that mattered in those hours could have been extended indefinitely; we could have become a disaster society in the best sense.

That we *did* become just that, or, better, that we always *are* just that — just such a 'disaster society in the best sense" is, it seems to me, what the whole earlier discussion of Marcos and the zapatista's, as well as Solnit's own immediately preceding discussion of the testimony of Taylor and other New Yorkers on 9/11 itself, helps make clear. Furthermore, isn't her regret over supposedly lost opportunities a forgetting of Marcos's zapatista lesson that the 'the means are the end,' which is also, I would argue, the lesson of 'fiesta and carnival' in general?

Earlier in her discussion of 9/11 (page 189) Solnit quotes this from an email account of that day by a survivor who 'escaped with several coworkers from the eighty-seventh floor of the north tower': 'They [who made the attacks] failed in terrorizing us. We were calm. If you want to kill us, leave us alone because we will do it by ourselves. If you want to make us stronger, attack and we unite. This is the ultimate failure of terrorism against the United States. The very moment the first plane was hijacked, democracy won.' Solnit's own accounts of various other disasters in places other than the United States make it clear that if this survivor's insight holds, it holds not just for that one place, nor for any one political system. Rather, if the insight holds at all, it does so as one of universal applicability, pointing to the inevitable failure of all acts of what this survivor, following the general usage of that day and still this one, calls 'terrorism.' All such attacks are doomed to fail because they rest on an illusion, one dispelled immediately by the very response they first call up precisely from those being attacked.

However, cannot the same insight finally — indeed, above all — be applied to the very thing the attackers at issue on 9/11 thought they were attacking: that same United States the survivor just cited regards (falsely, I am saying) as especially immunized against such attacks, or at least against them succeeding? The so-called terrorists themselves could say the same thing to and about themselves that the survivor Solnit quotes does. Modified where indicated to fit, they also could say: '[The Great Satan (that is, the United States)] failed in terrorizing [or demoralizing, or annihilating, or destroying, or the like] us. We were calm. If you want to kill us, leave us alone because we will do it by ourselves. If you want to make us stronger, attack and we unite. This is the ultimate failure of . . . the United States. The very moment the first [Muslim] was degraded [(or the first Palestinian uprooted, the first African enslaved, or whatever), Islam (or Liberation, or 'the beloved community' of Martin Luther King, Jr., and the American Civil Rights movement, to which Solnit devotes a good discussion)] won.'

That is the important, deep truth of the 9/11 survivor's remark: Poor Satan (whatever or whomever that may functionally turn out to be for any given situation, whether it be 'the United States,' 'terrorists,' 'demon rum,' or some other thing or person)! No matter how hard the poor devil tries to do evil, good comes out of it! No sooner does the devil do his dirtiest, than everything is swept bright and clean again, even brighter and cleaner than before.

The survivor of 9/11 quoted above, as well as countless other survivors, not just of 9/11 but of countless other disasters, including those Solnit studies and as her own analyses make clear, did not just believe that to be so, or just hope that it might be. Rather, they *directly experienced* its *being* so, just as Marcos and the zapatistas did in the uprising of 1994 and their other 'actions,' when, as Marcos put it, they experienced that the means *were* the end.

Later in her book, not only after the remarks just discussed concerning 9/11 but also after her analysis of the zapatistas, Solnit remarks that she 'had long wondered whether there was a society so rich in a sense of belonging and purpose that disaster could bring nothing to it" bring nothing by way of an opportunity for the celebration of life and one another in disaster communities. That would have to be 'a society where there was no alienation and isolation to undo.' She makes that remark in one of her chapters devoted to New Orleans in the aftermath of Hurricane Katrina, and adds that she'd always thought she might find such a society 'in Mexico or a traditional community.' At any rate, she writes, 'I found a little of that in New Orleans.'

She returns to that theme in the concluding chapter of her book, in terms of the broad lessons her study of disasters and disaster communities has taught her:

> Who are you? Who are we? The history of disaster demonstrates that most of us are social animals, hungry for connection, as well as for purpose and meaning. It also suggest that if this is who we are, then everyday life in most places is a disaster that disruptions sometimes give us a chance to change. They are a crack in the walls that ordinarily hem us in, and what floods in can be enormously destructive — or creative.

As her preceding studies in the book have made clear, what above all determines which outcome a given disaster will have — the destructive one, or the creative one — is whether it is 'civil society' or 'elite panic' that wins the day. Thus, she continues the passage just cited as follows:

> Hierarchies and institutions are inadequate to these circumstances [of disaster]; they are often what fails in such crises. Civil society is what succeeds, not only in an emotional demonstration of altruism and mutual aid but also in a practical mustering of creativity and resources to meet the challenges. Only this dispersed force of countless people making countless decisions is adequate to a major crisis.

Yet isn't it really exactly this same thing, the 'dispersed force of count-less people making countless decisions,' that must be always at work be-neath surface appearances to let 'hierarchies and institutions" those very hierarchies and institutions whereby the elite maintain their status and power — function in the first place? Solnit's own discussions of the responses to disaster have surely made it clear that it is nothing other than the prospect that the people will suddenly come to realize that very point—when they find themselves in the carnival atmosphere of a mutual aid community that responsively forms after a disaster — that puts the elite into such a panic in the first place.

Thus, Solnit herself continues the passage cited above, after observing that it is only the 'dispersed force of countless people making countless decisions' that can address such major public disasters as she examines, by writing: 'One reason that disasters are threatening to elites is that power devolves to the people on the ground in many ways: it is the neighbors who are the first responders and who assemble the impromptu kitchens and networks to rebuild,' thereby making manifest the irrelevancy of the powers that be, with all their 'hierarchies and institutions,' and who do not even show up to help in such emergencies, phantoms that they are and are thereby shown to be, the illusion of their power dispelled in the process. Indeed, by her own analysis that is not just 'one' reason, but is, rather, *the* reason, at least in the sense of the most important and the sufficient reason, for 'elite panic' at the prospect of disaster or its aftermath. As Solnit herself goes on to write, such devolution of power upon the people after a disaster 'demonstrates the viability of a dispersed, decentralized system of decision making.' What is more, I would say, it demonstrates that exactly such a dispersed, decentralized system of decision making has been operative all along, giving the only substance they can have to the phantoms whereby the elite appear to themselves and the people as necessary, or even merely relevant.

'Citizens themselves,' notes Solnit as she continues, 'in these moments [of response to disaster] constitute the government — the acting decision making body — as democracy has always promised and rarely delivered.' However, that is so not only at moments of disaster or crisis, but also in moments of calm and 'business as usual.' *At all times* any actual government, as any hierarchy or institution at all, is sustained only insofar as all the anonymous individuals that constitute "the people" *continually re-enact them* — or, as Thomas Mann, or certainly as literary theorist and Jewish and German studies scholar Erich Santner, in his *Psychotheology of Everyday Life* would say, *re-cite* them, as though they did indeed have some sort of authority of their own. In that crucial sense, the 'democracy' Solnit mentions is far from *rarely* delivered, nor need its delivery even be promised, since it is always already given, whenever *any* government at all is.

So is the 'revolution' Solnit goes on to mention in her next sentence already there, for those who but wake from dreaming dreams of — and, even more, *for* — power: 'Thus disasters often unfold as though a revolution has already taken place.' It has.

We might say that community and revolution and all that goes with them—the "purposefulness, meaning, involvement" that Solnit lists on the next page (306), along with "the immersion in service and survival, and . . . an affection that is not private and personal but civic: the love of strangers for each other, of a citizen for his or her city, of belonging to a greater whole, of doing the work that matters"—are always there and active, even dominantly so, as *latent*, a word she uses in such a context herself toward the end of page 305. What disaster offers is the opportunity for that latency to become patent, as it does whenever one of Solnit's 'disaster communities' forms in disaster's aftermath.

At the beginning of these reflections on the truth of trauma, I said that what I meant by that phrase was the response that trauma itself elicits from those whom it strikes. Given that definition, what can be gleaned from the diverse sources I have considered above—from the fiction of Cormac McCarthy and William Faulkner, to the scholarly studies of Jean-Luc Nancy, Philippe Lacoue-Labarthe, Paul Eisenstein, and Sudhir Karak, to the survivors' memoirs of Marguerite Duras and Robert Antelme, to the investigative studies of Rebecca Solnit—might be put this way:

> *The truth of trauma is living in the irrelevancy of all relations of power.*

That way of articulating the idea is, perhaps, especially indebted to Solnit's work on what she calls "disaster communities," but it also fits the other sources I have considered. What Solnit's analyses claim to show is that such communities form on their own among those most directly affected by disasters. That applies whether the disaster be "natural"—as were, to stick with her own examples, the 1906 earthquake in San Francisco or the one decades later in Mexico—or brought about through human agency—as was the collapse of the Twin Towers in New York on September 11, 2001. By arising from the ground up among disaster survivors themselves as "mutual aid" societies, rather than being effected from above by official governmental agencies, independent charitable organizations, or the like, what such disaster communities effectively do, as Solnit herself puts it at one point (page 153), is to *render irrelevant* the official institutions of power.

Thus, the response that such disasters as Solnit examines elicit is to live in the situation of the irrelevancy of all such "official" channels and institutions, "governmental" or "non-governmental." Disaster calls upon those it strikes to live, instead, *in community* with one another, relying upon one another mutually, aiding and accepting aid as need and opportunity present themselves. Indeed, that is another way to formulate the truth of trauma—at least of such "public trauma" as Solnit discusses:

The truth of trauma is living in community.

The community trauma calls forth has nothing of the "communalism" against which Sudhir Kakar's *The Colors of Violence* warns us. There is nothing enclosed or enclosing about communities of trauma, Solnit's "disaster communities." Rather, they are communities in which aid is extended by all to all, and in which no challenging of anyone's claim to aid occurs, no demanding that aid claimants prove their need, certify their disabilities, or document their qualifications for receiving assistance.

The community called forth by trauma is in principle universal. It is the universal community of all those who have nothing in common save trauma, and who therefore cannot be sorted out, or sort themselves out, in terms of diverse identities and the exclusionary groups that go with such identities. In the community of trauma, everyone is a Jew, as Paul Eisenstein points out everyone should have been after *Kristallnacht*. But in the community of trauma everyone is also at the same time no less a Nazi, as Marguerite Duras knew she had to become as soon as the obscenity of being a Nazi became undeniable.

It is also the community of the broken, and of those who fall with no chance any longer of righting themselves, of standing themselves upright again, warding off trauma, as philosophy, according at least to Jean-Luc Nancy and Philippe Lacoue-Labarthe, has always struggled to ward off sophistry. The community of trauma is thus no longer a philosophical community.

But nor is it an *anti*-philosophical one, in the sense of still defining itself in terms of philosophy, as what it opposes. The community of trauma needs nothing against which to define itself, since it needs no "definition," no "identity," of its own in the first place.

In the same way, the community of trauma has no need to be "heroic." There is nothing rigid and "manly" about it. It is as soft and gentle as the voice of Sheriff Bell's father whispering to horses at the end of Cormac McCarthy's *No Country for Old Men*, the voice of that father who, by the world's lights was "less a man" than his son, but who "never broke nothin" in Bell, and to whom, therefore, Bell owes everything.

Such soft and gentle community nevertheless grows from, and embodies, the only genuinely effective *resistance* to the very structures of power the irrelevancy of which trauma demonstrates, as I will discuss in detail in the next chapter.

Chapter 2

RESISTANCE AND THE MEANING

OF TRAUMA

"The Secret of Joy"

In her 1992 novel *Possessing the Secret of Joy*, Alice Walker tells the story of Tashi, an African woman traumatized by female genital mutilation. In the novel Tashi eventually returns from the United States, where she has been undergoing recovery in therapy for the trauma that has come to define her, to Africa, where she kills the primary perpetrator of her traumatic mutilation. The novel ends with the soul of Tashi recounting how, handcuffed and on the way, back in Africa, to her execution for that homicide, Tashi finds clarity about 'the secret of Joy' on a poster some of her supporters unfurl for her to see as she moves on to her death. The poster proclaims that *resistance* is the secret of joy.

That conclusion drawn from Tashi's fictional story in Walker's novel is reminiscent of the conclusion Robert Antelme draws in his non-fiction memoir of internment in the Nazi camps, already mentioned in the preceding chapter. Tashi's very death from execution continues to be an exercise of resistance — and therefore something *joyful*, given the message Walker assigns Tashi's story to carry, as articulated above, from the very last page of the novel. Though the joyful element may not sound as clearly in Antelme's reflections, the pivotal point remains—that death itself, and the dead, can be a continuation of the very resistance that, according to Antelme, assures us that there is only one 'human race,' including even the Nazis, and thereby dispelling the phantom of the Nazi's own exclusionary dream

Echoed later by Walker's story of Africa, America, and Tashi's trauma, Antelme's experience that death itself, and the corpse it leaves behind, can constitute a resistance to everything the Nazi camp system stood for, also finds an important counterpoint in the reflections of another author who, like Antelme, survived the Nazi camps—"survived" them at least after a fashion, as I will soon explain.

Although Antelme did indeed undergo incarceration in the Nazi concentration camps, ending up at Dachau, the very first camp the Nazis opened, from which he was eventually rescued, he was never sent to one of the Nazi extermination camps as such, the 'death camps' properly speaking. In contrast, Jean Améry survived even Auschwitz, the paradigm of the death camps.

In *At the Mind's Limits*, in his preface to the reissue of 1977, after remarking that his reflections in the book 'stand in the service of an enlightenment," Améry warns the reader that what he is calling enlightenment 'is not the same as clarification" — or 'explanation,' to use another possible translation. He then explains:

> Clarification [Explanation] would also amount to disposal, settlement of the case, which can then be placed in the files of history. My book is meant to aid in preventing precisely this. For nothing is resolved, no conflict is settled, no remembering has become a mere memory. What happened, happened. But that it happened cannot be so easily accepted. I rebel: against my past, against history, and against a present that places the incomprehensible in the cold storage of history and thus falsifies it in a revolting way. Nothing has healed . . .

Later, in the body of his memoir, he writes (on page 14):

> What I felt [*sic*] to comprehend at that time [in Auschwitz] still appears to me a certainty: Whoever is, in the broadest sense, a

believing person, whether his belief be metaphysical or bound to concrete reality, transcends himself. He is not the captive of his individuality; rather is part of a spiritual continuity that is interrupted nowhere, not even in Auschwitz. . . . For the unbelieving person reality, under adverse circumstances, is a force to which he submits. . . . For the believer reality is clay that he molds, a problem that he solves.

This stands as a sort of confirmation in advance of what contemporary French philosopher Alain Badiou says about the 'eternity' of the 'subject,' as Badiou uses that term. For Badiou, the 'subject,' properly speaking, is always defined by a truth event and his 'confidence' in it. As truth—even that truth that can only occur as an *event*—is eternal, so is the 'subject' defined by its standing in that truth. Badiou thus opposes the eternity of the 'subject' to the mortality of the mere 'human animal,' the 'individual' as an indifferent unit of multiplicity.

Refusing Consolation

To this point it would seem to be Améry's 'believing person' who would constitute one of Badiou's "subjects," and not Améry himself or any other 'nonreligious and politically independent intellectuals' like him, as he goes on to put it. He insists that for such intellectuals Auschwitz deepened their *dis*belief not only in religious but also in secular notions that might have allowed them to make some sort of transcending sense out of all the horror and suffering. Thus, Améry writes (page 18), referring to Heidegger: 'Occasionally, perhaps,' for such intellectuals as himself in Auschwitz, 'that disquieting magus from Alemanic regions came to mind who said that beings appear to us only in the light of Being, but that man forgot Being by fixing on beings. Well now, Being. But in the camp it was more convincingly apparent than on the outside that beings and the light of Being get you nowhere.' On the next page he continues by referring back to an earlier citation of a stanza (the contents of which do not matter here) from the poetry of Heidegger's own beloved fellow Swabian, Friedrich Hölderlin. 'Like the lyric stanza' from Hölderlin, Améry writes, such 'philosophic declarations' as Heidegger's 'also lost their transcendency and then and there became in part objective observations, in part dull chatter. Where they still meant something they appeared trivial, and where they were not trivial they no longer meant anything.'

'We did not become wiser in Auschwitz,' he observes a few lines later. 'And yet,' he adds (page 20),

> the time in the camps was not entirely without value for us (and when I say us I mean the nonreligious and politically independent intellectuals). For we brought with us the certainty that remains ever unshakeable, that for the greatest part the intellect is a ludus [a fool playing at fool's games] and that we were nothing more — or, better said, before we entered the camp were nothing more — than *hominess ludentes*. With that we lost a good deal of arrogance, of metaphysical conceit, but also quite a bit of our native joy in the intellect and what we falsely imagined was the sense of life.

As he then sums up in the closing lines of the same page, the last lines of the first chapter of *At the Mind's Limits*, 'the word [whether of the poet such as Hölderlin or of the 'thinker' such as Heidegger, or even of the scriptures of religious believers] always dies where the claim of some reality is total. It died for us a long time ago. And we were not even left with the feeling that we must regret its departure.'

Picking up the same theme a few pages into his second chapter, 'Torture,' after noting (page 26) that most of the time, 'even in direct experience everyday,' what presents itself as reality is really "nothing but codified abstraction,' he writes that, in fact, '[o]nly in rare moments of life do we truly stand face to face with reality.' One such no doubt fortunately rare moment is the moment of torture itself. However, he observes, the moment of contact with reality 'does not have to be something as extreme as torture.' Rather, '[a]rrest is enough and, if need be, the first blow one receives,' a line I have already discussed in my Introduction, but which deserves further discussion here, in the context of reflecting on the notion of resistance.

Thus, it is a matter of *trauma*, where the datable occurrence is the occasion and/or emblem of the 'reality' that reveals itself through it. It is not the datable occurrence itself that is traumatic, but the revelation of reality that takes place *in* that occurrence. That reality can break in upon a person with the "first blow" that Améry has just mentioned, and with which he continues his reflections (page p. 27): 'The first blow brings home to the prisoner that he is *helpless*, and thus it already contains in the bud everything that is to come.' Thus, already at that first blow (p. 28), 'trust in the world breaks down.'

Life void of all such trust—*that* is what trauma gives us to understand, at least by Améry's analysis. Thus, the issue is to find out *what it is*, to "understand" that—to live continuously in the "knowledge that there is nowhere to go, no help to come, no room for such trust any longer."

As he notes a few pages later (page 35), under torture "[a] slight pressure by the tool-wielding hand is enough to turn the other — along with his head, in which are perhaps stored Kant and Hegel, and all nine [Beethoven] symphonies, and the World as Will and Representation — into a shrilly squealing piglet at slaughter.' Nor is there any possibility of return from that revelation the tortured are given, the revelation of the face of reality. Thus, concerning his own torture, Améry writes: 'It is still not over. Twenty-two years later I am still dangling over the ground by dislocated arms, panting, and accusing myself [in hopes of *that* stopping the torture — since he has no real information to divulge]. In such an instance, there is no 'repression.'"

'Whoever has succumbed to torture," he continues a few pages later (page 40), "can no longer feel at home in the world. The shame of destruction cannot be erased. Trust in the world . . . will not be regained. . . . It is *fear* that henceforth reigns over him. Fear — and also what is called resentments. They remain, and have scarcely a chance to concentrate into a seething, purifying thirst for revenge.'

The irremediable collapse of what Améry calls trust in the world is the issue of trauma. Especially when the trauma is experienced directly at the hands of others, as the tortured receive it from their torturers, what is lost is above all trust in others, replaced, in fact, by a now active *dis*trust. Nor need one have survived Auschwitz or torture in the narrow sense to experience such loss of trust. For example, as author Susan Cheever writes in *Desire* (page 135), her book about addictions, including her own, and how they can take root in trauma: 'The human balance that enables most people to live without mind-altering substances every day is fragile. It can be upset by trauma or by witnessing trauma. Once you see what people can do to each other, it's hard to go back to the level of trust in strangers and the human community that makes life bearable.'

Refusing even such recourse to addiction to mask what trauma reveals, Améry insists on facing the reality that trauma lays bare. He remains true to his own traumatic experience, stripped down by it to what alone remains after trust in the world has been lost beyond recall — his fear, and his resentment.

Concerning the latter, in *At the Mind's Limits* Améry writes (page 70) that his resentments themselves 'are there in order that the crime,' the crime that the Nazis inflicted upon him and so many other victims of torture and the camps, never be allowed to fade, never be forgotten, and above all never be forgiven. His resentments are there to make sure that, instead, the crime 'become a moral reality for the criminal, in order that he be swept into the truth of his atrocity.'

Like one of Badiou's 'subjects,' Améry remains faithful to a truth—the truth of his own trauma. As Badiou argues, such fidelity is all that remains of 'ethics' for one struck in the face by a truth. The only categorical obligation someone struck by trauma has any longer, is to stick to the truth of that trauma itself, refusing all consolation.

It is just that obligation that makes it necessary, in and after Auschwitz, for Améry, the thoroughly secularized and assimilated child of an equally secularized, assimilated Jewish family ('Jewish' at least through the Jewish ancestry of one of his parents, thought not of both), *to be a Jew*. Yet it is that very thing — being a Jew—that his secularization and assimilation have completely *voided* for him. By leaving him without any religious and cultural background in, or experiential connection to, Judaism, his own concrete, historical Jewishness as so secularized and assimilated have made it impossible for him ever fully to be, at least in any traditionally understood way, what the crimes of the Nazis have unconditionally obligated him henceforth to be, namely, a Jew.

Accordingly, in a chapter aptly entitled 'On the Necessity and Impossibility of Being a Jew,' Améry writes (page 94) that for a no longer possibly Jewish Jew like him, the impossible imperative placed upon him to *be* a Jew is also the imperative to live in a continual state of fear.

> [S]ince being a Jew not only means that I bear within me a catastrophe that occurred yesterday and cannot be ruled out for tomorrow, it is–beyond a duty–also *fear*. Every morning when I get up I can read the Auschwitz number on my forearm, something that touches the deepest and most closely intertwined roots of my existence; indeed I cannot even be sure if this is not my entire existence. Then I feel approximately as I did back then when I got a taste of my first blow from the policeman's fist. Every day anew I lose my trust in the world.

'Without trust in the world,' he continues on the next page, 'I face my surroundings as a Jew who is alien and alone, and all that I can manage is to get along with my foreignness.' Not only must he 'accept being foreign as an essential element of [his] personality.' Rather, he is even enjoined by the traumatic truth that has struck him (unbidden, one should note clearly) to 'insist upon' that foreignness, that being permanently out of place, wherever he may happen to be, 'as if upon an inalienable possession.' Struck by trauma into fidelity to what so strikes him, he then sums up his predicament neatly: 'Still and each day anew I find myself alone.'

Améry is utterly uncompromising in his refusal of all strategies of avoidance, and in his commitment to recounting as honestly as he can the truth, as he has been given to see it — or, more pointedly, been *struck* by it. It is a desolate, and desolating, truth. To *read* his faithful testimony to that truth is itself difficult and challenging, leaving the reader stripped of all possibility of justifying his or her own desperate efforts of avoidance.

Nor is it only in the face of torture and of the death camps that Améry maintains his defiance. It is also in the face of his own experience of aging, after surviving the camps, and even in the face of what he will eventually characterize, in his reflections on suicide, as the experience of radical 'failure,' the sense of the ultimate, devastating defeat of one's very life-endeavor.

In his preface to the first edition of his later work, *On Aging: Revolt and Resignation*, originally published in German in 1968, Améry writes that what he calls the "experiments" that make up the essays of the book—and this surely applies just as well to his earlier *At the Mind's Limits*—are "in quality more like searches" than like experimental research. He then goes on to say that such (re)searches "went from being an analysis to being an act of rebellion, whose contradictory premise was the total acceptance of inescapable and scandalous things."

The inescapable and scandalous things at issue in this later book are all the disturbing, degrading facts of the natural aging process, in the face of which Améry will no more permit himself any subterfuge or euphemistic evasion than he earlier permitted himself in the face of his experience of Auschwitz and the realities of torture. He writes (pages 76-77) that 'those who try to live the truth of their condition as aging persons,' as he insists on trying to do himself, must 'accept annihilation.' But such acceptance remains defiant, resistant, uncompromising, insofar as it is accompanied by a knowledge 'that in this acceptance they can only preserve themselves if they rise up against it." In so rebelling against their own aging, however, those who try to live such truth never lose sight of the fact "that their revolt—and here the acceptance is an affirmation of something irrevocable—is condemned to failure."'

Assured of such failure from the very start, those who practice such accepting rebellion or rebelling acceptance 'embark on an enterprise that cannot be accomplished.' However, it is only by choosing to embark on that very enterprise that the aging can find the possibility of preserving what is truly most their own—'the only possibility they have of truly aging with dignity.' All that is left to someone who makes such a choice is, as Améry writes in the final lines of the book (reminiscent of the final lines of Camus's *The Stranger*), the hope to have "done something to disturb the balance, expose the compromise, destroy the genre painting, contaminate the consolation," all consolation offered in the face of aging, decay, and death: "The days shrink and dry up. He has the desire to tell the truth.'

Writing about suicide a few years later, Améry demonstrates the same adamantine fidelity to the truth that he has already shown in his works on aging and, first of all, on his experience in Auschwitz. It is a fidelity above all to the truth of *resistance*—even and especially recalcitrant resistance toward that against which no resistance can ever hope to succeed, at least if success is measured by the standards of that very "reality" to which, in resisting it, one refuses to submit.

Thus, a few months before committing suicide himself, after being thwarted by the ministrations of others in an earlier attempt, Améry publishes *On Suicide: A Discourse on Voluntary Death*. He discusses a case he has recently read about in the news, one in which a housemaid smitten by a popular singer of the day kills herself rather than face the reality of not being the singer's lover. Améry compares the housemaid's case to the early twentieth century one of Otto Weininger. Weininger, misogynistic author of the widely read *Geschlecht und Charakter* (*Sex and Character*), was born a Jew, but became ardently anti-Semitic, and killed himself in 1903 at the age of 23. "Weininger," Améry writes (pages 25-26), "could not bear to be a Jew: he was one. My housemaid could not bear to be an anonymous woman upon whom the singer's attention was never bestowed: she was one."

By his analysis, both suicides attest to the same truth of hopeless resistance that he has earlier discussed in regard to Auschwitz and aging. By suicide, Weininger and the housemaid smitten with the singer did not become what they were not (a non-Jew or the singer's lover, respectively). Nevertheless, in a certain sense, according to Améry (page 27), 'at least in a foolish way in the moment before the leap,' each '*was*' (his emphasis) what he/she 'could not be because reality would not allow it to [him/her]: Weininger as a non-Jew, the girl with the broom as the sweetheart of the singer.' Each rose up against reality—and became, in that foolish instant, what reality would not let each be—*"by de-selfing their self themselves,"* as he puts it a few pages later (page 29, his emphasis).

Such suicide revolts neither against life as such nor against death. Rather, it revolts against the failure—Améry prefers and uses the French *échec* as more expressive, even just as a sound, of what he means—of one's life. Such failure is one of the two common conditions back of the decision to kill oneself, according to him, the other being 'disgust with life,' such as one experiences in (page 47) Sartrian *'naussée {nausea}*, one of the basic constituents of a human being,' wherein life, in the biological sense of the living as opposed to the "inorganic," is experienced as 'a malignant tumor,' as he puts it in parentheses a few pages earlier.

'What is suicide as natural death?" Améry asks (page 60). He answers: "A resounding no to the crushing, shattering *échec* of existence.' Such suicide is a refusal to live the life of 'a failure.'

The Affirmation of Resistance

At one point in *Heidegger and "the jews"* (page 27) Jean-Francois Lyotard suggests that we compare Robert Antelme and his book *The Human Race*, on the one hand, and Elie Wiesel and *Night*, on the other. "Two representations, certainly," he writes—that is, two representations of the horrors of the Nazi camp system. "But," he goes on, "Antelme resists, he is somebody who resists." Well, even granting that there is an important sense in which Antelme resists, whereas Wiesel does not, which is actually debatable in some ways, it is surely the case that in at least as important a sense Jean Améry, whom I have been considering, belongs, along with Antelme, among those who resist, despite whatever significant differences there may be between the two cases, Antelme's and Améry's in the sense of "resistance" at issue.

"It is certainly true that dignity can be bestowed only by society," Améry writes in *At the Mind's Limits* (page 89). "Still," he then adds, "the degraded person, threatened by death, is able to convince society of his dignity by taking his fate upon himself and at the same time rising in revolt against it.' On the next page he makes it clear that the "revolt" at issue is a matter of *actually striking back*: 'I finally relearned what I and my kind often had forgotten and what was more crucial than the moral power to resist: to hit back.' Yet another page further along he observes: 'I became a person not by subjectively appealing to my abstract humanity but by discovering myself within the given social reality [which is to say, within Auschwitz] as a rebelling Jew and by realizing myself as one.'

Returning to Lyotard, it is worth noting that he reads Antelme's resistance (still on page 27) as a "political resistance." As such, according to him, "[i]t is a compromise formation that involves learning to negotiate with the Nazi terror, to manipulate it, even if only for a little; trying to understand it, so as to outsmart it; putting one's life on the line for this; reaching the limits of the human species [that is, Antelme's *espèce humaine*], for that. It is war. Deportation is a part of the war. Antelme saves honor."

Such an idea of the limitations of resistance, of there being a "compromise," inherent to resistance, with what it resists, a sort of secret collusion with it, is not uncommon. Thus, another, younger, still-living French philosopher, Jean-Louis Chrétien, writes in his *The Ark of Speech* (page 146):

> Affirmation forms the sole place of struggle against evil. To say no to the no means to say no again, leading back one way or another to what one is opposing and making one dependent on it. To resist evil is to carry with one, permanently, the Trojan horse that contains it. To struggle against it can only mean attacking it, and only the diamond of the *yes* can really attack all negation, at its heart, without having to deny it.

Christianity — specifically, the Gospel insistence that one should not resist evil—is Chrétien's foundation here, as it is for countless recurrences in Western thought of this idea that resistance is somehow inherently coun-terproductive, defining itself by what it resists. Versions of the same idea can be found in non-Christian traditions, perhaps especially Buddhism. Yet it is above all to Christianity that we owe the injunction against resisting evil.

That Christian injunction is mutually reinforcing with another Christian motif, that of the redemptive value of *suffering*. So, to give a pow-erful example from recent Christian thought, French philosopher Michel Henry, who died in 2002 at the age of 80, goes so far as to equate suffering with joy itself, or at least to argue that, even in the worst affliction and the deepest suffering, the suffering self always also suffers, feels, *itself*, and in such auto-affectivity quite literally *enjoys* itself. Insofar as it is Christianity that teaches the truth of such absolute self-relation, as according to Henry it is, Christianity distinguishes itself from all other traditions precisely on that basis. Thus, as he puts it in his work *L'essence de la manifestation* (*The Essence of Manifestation*), originally published in 1963: 'In Christianity it is no longer a question of combating suffering, whether it be in trying to eliminate its exterior causes, as in the Western world of technology, or in abolishing all interior resistance against it, as in Buddhism, or yet in progressively blunting sensibility in the manner of winning through to a heroic sensibility, as in stoicism.' Instead, it is a matter of en-joying the suffering as such — turning suffering itself *into* joy.

However, the very example of Henry should give us reason to pause at this point, since not only was Henry himself active in the French Resistance during World War II, but he even experienced the clandestinity required by the Resistance as definitive of truth itself. He read clandestinity in and into the very heart of that "manifestation" the study of which defined his career as a philosopher.

Thus, while Henry would no doubt agree with Chrétien and the whole Christian tradition on non-resistance to evil, his own life give us reason to question any simplistic distinction between resistance and 'affirmation,' to follow Chrétien's usage. Indeed, the already considered case of Améry sug-gests that it is important to attend to the affirmation that is inherent to the very act of resistance as such.

Strong reinforcement of that suggestion comes from psychoanalyst Dori Laub's work on trauma, especially that of Holocaust survivors such as Améry. Cofounder of the Fourtunoff Video Archives for Holocaust Testimonies at Yale University, Laub is coauthor with literary scholar Shoshana Felman of *Testimony: Crises of Witnessing in Literature, Psychoanalysis, and History*, which has become a classic text in trauma studies. One interview he recounts having had with a woman who, like Améry, survived Auschwitz itself, is particularly relevant to the issue of the relationship between resistance and affirmation.

In her interview with Laub, the woman in question at one point talks about her experience, while at Auschwitz, of the rebellion of some of the other inmates near the end of World War II. As this survivor remembers and recounts it, all four crematoria chimneys were blown up, although "in reality" —at least in what the group of historians to whom Laub later recounts the woman's testimony take to be reality, in discounting the woman's testimony because of its "historical inaccuracy" —only one of the four was "actually" destroyed. What is more, the historians point out, the whole rebellion was a radical failure, with the Jewish rebels even being betrayed by the Polish underground, which had failed to live up to their promise of support.

Against such discounting, Laub defends the testimony of the Auschwitz witness, arguing that it is her testimony that reveals the very *historical truth* of the rebellion—and therewith, I would argue (and I think Laub would probably agree), the truth of 'Auschwitz' itself. As Laub discusses, the fact that *any* rebellion at all ever occurred at Auschwitz puts to the lie the purported "reality" of the entire system of the Nazi's "final solution to the Jewish question." Against the historians' dismissal of the whole rebellion as one that, "historically, made no difference" (*Testimony*, page 61), Laub writes (pages 62-63):

> On the contrary, it was her very talk to me, the very process of her bearing witness to the trauma she had lived through, that helped her now to come to know of the event. And it was through my listening to her that I in turn came to understand

not merely her subjective truth, but the very historicity of the event, in an entirely new dimension.

She was testifying not simply to historical facts, but to the very secret of survival and of resistance to extermination. . . . She saw four chimneys blowing up in Auschwitz: she saw, in other words, the unimaginable taking place right in front of her own eyes. And she came to testify to the unbelievability, precisely, of what she had eye-witnessed—this bursting open of the very frame of Auschwitz. The historians' testifying to the fact that only one chimney was blown up in Auschwitz, as well as to the fact of the betrayal of the Polish underground, does not break the frame. The woman's testimony, on the other hand, is breaking the frame of the concentration camp by and through her very testimony: she is breaking out of Auschwitz even by her very talking. She had come, indeed, to testify, not to the empirical number of the chimneys, but to resistance, to the affirmation of survival, to the breakage of the frame of death; in the same way, she had come to testify not to betrayal, nor to her actual removal of the belongings of the dead, but to her vital memory of helping people, to her effective rescuing of lives. This was her way of being, or surviving, of resisting. It is not merely her speech, but the very boundaries of silence which surround it, which attest, today as well as in the past, to this assertion of resistance.

There is thus a subtle dialectic between what the survivor did not know and what she knew; between what I as interviewer did not know and what I knew; between what the historians knew and what they did not know. Because the testifier did not know the number of the chimneys that blew up; because she did not know of the betrayal of the Polish underground and of the violent and desperate defeat of the rebellion of the Auschwitz inmates, the historians said that she knew nothing.

I thought that she knew more [than they did], since she knew about the breakage of the frame, [the same breakage] that her very testimony was now reenacting.

On the same page (63), Laub goes on to connect his experience of this Auschwitz survivor's testimony with his own ongoing experience in his clinical therapeutic practice.

It has happened to me many times that thinking back to a psychoanalytic session with a patient, I suddenly realize that I understand it. Everything falls into place and comes together. . . . Such sudden illuminations are not rare. They often do not last, however. I do forget them before my next appointment, and my patient and I sink back into the routine of everyday quabble. It is as though two simultaneous dialogues proceed and the ordinary one, the one that is commonplace, prevails.

Thus, Laub connects the issue of the 'historical truth' of an event such as the rebellion at Auschwitz, on the one hand, with the issue of what might be called 'the psychoanalytical truth' of neurosis. Insofar as, in the latter, *delusion* is in play to one extent or another, we might also call the truth at issue "delusional truth," in a sense of that phrase which would mean the truth that remains and calls out to be honored and preserved: to be borne witness to even after the delusion is over.

To bear such witness to the truth of trauma as Laub discusses—even and perhaps especially if it is a "delusional" truth—is itself as such to put up an effective *resistance*. Later in *Testimony*, Laub's coauthor, Shoshana Felman discusses Claude Lanzman's famous film *Shoah*. At one point (page 278), Felman quotes Philip Müller, one of the death-camp survivors interviewed in the film. Müller had belonged to one of the *Sonderkommando*, the 'special units' of camp prisoners who were allowed to live yet a while longer at the price of being forced to assist the Nazi's by performing such tasks as keeping fellow prisoners calm as they were being herded to the gas chambers, then cleaning out the mess afterward, so a new contingent of the doomed could be ushered to their deaths in turn. Müller, a Czech, recounts an episode in which he accompanied a group of fellow Czechs to the changing room, where prisoners were made to strip before entering the gas chamber, disguised as a shower-room:

> The violence climaxed when they tried to force the people to undress. A few obeyed, only a handful. Most of them refused to follow the order. Suddenly, like a chorus, they all began to sing. The whole "undressing room" rang with the Czech national anthem, and the *Hatikvah*. That moved me terribly. . .
>
> That was happening to my countrymen, and I realized that my life had become meaningless. Why go on living? For what? So I went into the gas chamber with them, resolved to die. With them. Suddenly, some who recognized me came up to me . . . A small group of women approached. They looked at me and said, right there in the gas chamber . . . : "So you want to die. But that's senseless. Your death won't give us back our lives. That's no way. You must get out of here alive, you must bear witness to . . . the injustice done to us."

Concerning this episode, Felman makes the following excellent observation:

> The singing . . . signifies a common recognition, by the singers, of the perversity of the deception to which they had been all along exposed, a recognition, therefore, and a facing, of the truth of their imminent death ... a repossession of their lost truth by the dying singers, an ultimate rejection of the Nazi-instigated self-deception and a deliberately chosen, conscious witnessing of their own death.

She then goes on to note on the very next page (279): "The singing challenges and dares the Nazis.' The act of singing, and of thereby bearing witness even in their very dying, embodies resistance among the Czech compatriots about to be gassed. But for Müller as a member of the *Sonderkommando*, someone who can survive, at least for the time being, resistance cannot mean giving up his life. Rather, for him it has to mean renouncing such very dying — which in this context also entails his continuing to act in apparent complicity with the Nazi killers themselves.

Later in a note to a passage on the same page (n. 52), Felman also quotes yet another Czech survivor, Rudolph Vrba, on his "decision to escape, after the suicide of [fellow inmate and Resistance figure] Freddy Hirsch that aborts the Resistance plan for the uprising of the Czech family camp: 'It was quite clear to me then that the Resistance in the camp is not generally for an uprising but for survival of the members of the Resistance.'"

For these two Czech survivors of Auschwitz, Müller and Vrba, continuing to live becomes as such the act of resistance. For the woman Laub interviews, the 'failed' *Sonderkommando* rebellion at Auschwitz near the end of the war—and even the joy with which she later (mis)remembers and (mis)recounts it—effects resistance. For Antelme, resistance is manifest even in the very act of dying, and even the corpses of the dead continue resistance to what the Nazi endeavored in vain to accomplish with all their killing.

So different on the surface — as different as life (in Müller and Vrba) and death (in Antelme)—all these cases are the same in at least two key ways.

First, in them all, the efficaciousness of the resistance they display has nothing to do with what would ordinarily be accounted the success or failure of the enterprise to which the resistance attaches. So, for example, Müller's choice to hear what the other Czech prisoners about to be gassed tell him, and therefore not to join them in the gas chamber, is as such already fully effective as resistance, and would have remained so, even if Müller had later been gassed or shot in turn, as was the standard Nazi practice for dealing with the members of a *Sonderkommando*, who only temporarily escaped such a fate. Similarly, as Laub's account makes so powerfully clear, that the rebellion at Auschwitz was a "failure" by historians' standards does not really touch its effectiveness as resistance. Finally, the corpses of which

Antelme speaks constitute a mutely effective resistance even though there is no sense in which they represent the success of any endeavor, including even the endeavor to resist as such. Rather, their resistance consists in their being at all, at a level that clearly has nothing to do with success or failure of anything.

The second way in which all these diverse cases of resistance are the same is really just the flip-side of what I have called the first way: They are all the same in that what they do is to "put the lie" to that which they resist, to use Antelme's way of speaking. Or, to use Laub's excellent way of wording it, they all, just as themselves and apart from all ordinary question of the "success" of the resistance they embody, "broke the frame" of that against which they resist. The *Sonderkommando* uprising breaks the frame of Auschwitz, even if it blew up "only" one smokestack and even if all the rebels were "betrayed" by the Polish underground and almost immediately killed after their rebellion had barely begun. For that matter, even the joy with which the woman who witnessed the rebellion recounts it, with however many "mistakes" in her recounting, also breaks that frame, just as effectively and completely as the uprising itself did. Finally, Antelme's corpses also break it no less.

Indeed, to do justice to what is in play in these examples, which could be supplemented with many others, we need to free ourselves from the notion that resistance is a reactive formation, dependent for its very meaning on the thing that it resists, which thing in that sense takes priority over all resistance to it. We need, instead, to recognize a peculiar *priority of resistance over what it resists*.

Interestingly, in their most recent book, *Commonwealth*, the final volume of their trilogy that begins with *Empire* and continues with *Multitude*, Michael Hardt and Antonio Negri argue for just such priority of resistance over the very power it resists. They base their position on a remark of Foucault's that power can only be exercised over "free subjects," since otherwise there would be nothing over which power would need to exert itself. They quote (on page 59) this remark by Foucault: "At the very heart of the power relationship, and constantly provoking it, are the recalcitrance of the will and the intransigence of freedom."

A little earlier (on page 56), Hardt and Negri have already noted that throughout his later works Foucault 'constantly theorizes an other to power (or even an other power), for which he seems unable to find an adequate name,' but for which '[r]esistance is the term he most often uses.' However, they observe, 'that term does not really capture what he has in mind, since resistance, as it is generally understood, is too dependent on and subordinate to the power it opposes,' just as Jean-Louis Chrétien seems to understand it in the remark from him I cited earlier. 'In our view,' Hardt and Negri conclude, 'the other to power that runs though [Foucault's works] is best defined as an alternative production of subjectivity, which not only resists power but also seeks autonomy from it.'

Returning to this same point later, they characterize (on page 176) "the conception of resistance" they have posed in the earlier chapters as one in which resistance "is prior to power since power is exercised only over free subjects, and thus, although situated 'within and against,' resistance is not condemned to reinforce or repeat the structures of power." Then, even later, they return to the point yet a third time, to write (pages 234-235): "Power can be exercised only over free subjects, and thus the resistance of those subjects is not really posterior to power but an expression of their freedom, which is prior. Revolt as an exercise of freedom not only precedes but also prefigures the forms that power will take in reaction."

By such a conception, then, what is crucial to an act of resistance is not what it resists. What is crucial about such an act is that to which it bears witness in and by resisting whatever it resists. Furthermore, that to which the act so bears witness is not only prior to, but also more enduring than, any exercise of power that—and this would be the internal structure of all such exercises of power, which one might well, following Hardt and Negri on this point as well, call "sovereign" power—seeks reactively and, therefore, parasitically and ultimately ineffectively, *impotently*, to suppress it.

It is just such a positive, active sense of the term 'resistance' that is necessary to capture what is at issue in the examples of resistance we have considered from the works of Antelme, Laub, and Felman—or, for that matter, in the examples from Améry, Duras, or even the fiction of Alice Walker. What is at issue is a sense of 'resistance' that finds, not the negation that Chrétien, for one, attributes to resistance, but, rather, the affirmation to which he eloquently appeals as the only possible way of ever successfully responding to evil, rather than succumbing to it.

As Hardt and Negri argue, only such active, affirmative resistance genuinely *subverts* sovereign power, rather than reinforcing it in the very endeavor to weaken it. Only such resistance escapes dialectical identity with the very power 'within and against' which it works, and the eternal recurrence of that same power under different guises, with a new "ruling power" just replacing an old one, but otherwise leaving everything the same, as always occurs unless such dialectical identity can be broken. Only such resistance 'establishes revolutionary decision making and the overthrow of the ruling power from within,' as Hardt and Negri require (page 351), and which explains their preference for 'subversion rather than oppositional responses' (page 372).

The active, affirmative, subversive resistance to which not only Hardt and Negri, but also the examples of Améry, Antelme, and the survivors whose testimony Laub and Felman let us hear, point, escapes the otherwise perpetual play and replay of sovereign power by *living in the irrelevancy and the impotence of such power.* Such resistance, in fact, laughs at the pretenses of "the ruling power," just as the crowd in Hans-Christian Anderson's story laughs at the emperor who has no clothes, once that laughter is released by no more than the simple honesty of a single child who says the truth, which is that the emperor has no clothes. And, as Hardt and Negri point out on the next to last page of *Commonwealth*, and therefore of the entire *Empire* trilogy, "the most adequate response" to "the arrogance of power"–indeed, on the basis of their own three-volume analysis, as well as that of the testimony of such survivors as those just mentioned, I would say the *only* adequate response—is, "rather than lamenting our poor lot and wallowing in melancholy," just such "laughter."

Resistance and the Refusal of Meaning

To recap to this point: If *resistance* is taken in the active, subversive sense conceptualized by Hardt and Negri in *Commonwealth*, then resistance, as they suggest, is also laughter in the face of trauma, at least in the face of that trauma that strikes by the hand of another, as an assertion of sovereignty and the power to rule. The laughter of resistance dispels the illusions with which ruling power surrounds itself in order to preserve its very claim to sovereignty and dominance.

However, what the examples of resistance I have been considering, above all the example of Jean Améry, suggest to be chief among the illusions whereby ruling power preserves itself is the illusion that the trauma to which the exercises of such power subjects those over whom it asserts sovereignty *has meaning*—that it somehow *"makes sense."* That is a point Susan J. Brison makes poignantly and powerfully, in my judgment, in *Aftermath: Violence and the Remaking of a Self*. Brison is a philosopher and a rape survivor. She was brutally raped and beaten, then left for dead in 1990, when she was living with her husband in the countryside around Grenoble, France. In *Aftermath* she effectively combines the account of her traumatic experience, and her recovery from it, with her reflections as a trained, professional philosopher.

In her preface to the book, Brison addresses (page x) "[t]he prevalent lack of empathy with trauma victims" that she had the misfortune to encounter firsthand after her rape. Through reflection on her own experience, she writes, she came to the realization that such lack of empathy "results . . . not merely from ignorance or indifference, but also from an active fear of identifying with those whose terrifying fate forces us to acknowledge that we are not in control of our own."

It is just such lack of control that trauma brings home to those it strikes. That is a lesson, however, no one wants to learn, and all want to avoid. Worth noting at the very outset is that it is not only others who want to avoid having to face the reality revealed to them by the stories of the victims of trauma—the reality of not being in control of their own fate. So, too, do trauma victims themselves want to avoid that reality. As Brison herself notes later in her book (on page 74), trauma victims will even go to the length of blaming their trauma upon themselves, if that is the only way they can preserve the illusion of having control. "Whereas rape victims' self blaming," she writes in that later passage (page 74), "has often been misunderstood as merely a self-destructive response to rape, arising out of low self-esteem, feelings of shame, or female masochism, and fueled by society's desire to blame the victim, it can also be seen as an adaptive survival strategy, if the victim has no other way of regaining a sense of control."

At any rate, to return to the prevalent lack of empathy by which others attempt to avoid what trauma victims have to tell them, in her preface Brison continues by observing that, '[n]evertheless, the trauma survivor must find empathic listeners in order to carry on.' She argues that the avoidance manifest in and as 'the prevalent lack of empathy for trauma victims' must be overcome, even and especially for the sake of those victims themselves. Victims themselves need such listeners, not so that they can continue to avoid what their trauma imposes upon them, but so that they can begin truly to face their trauma, and to recover from it. That is because, as Brison points out, '[p]iecing together a shattered self,' the very self shattered by the trauma in the first place, 'requires a process of remembering and working through in which speech and affect converge in a trauma narrative.'

Indeed, constructing such a narrative of one's trauma and recovery actually *accomplishes* recovery itself. Succeeding in constructing that narrative is succeeding, to use the way of putting it that Brison borrows from J. L. Austin and 'speech act theory,' in *performing* recovery as such. The narration "performs" the very healing the story of which it narrates, just as a minister or justice of the peace is not just advancing some claim about the relationship between two people, but is actually marrying them, when the minister or justice of the peace "pronounces" the marriage. Following Austin, such speech acts are said to be "performative speech acts," or simply "performatives."

Accordingly, Brison goes on, in characterizing her own goal in *Aftermath*: 'In this book I explore the performative aspect of speech in testimonies of trauma: How *saying* something about the memory *does* something to it. The communicative act of [survivors] bearing witness to traumatic events [that have befallen those survivors themselves] not only transforms traumatic memories into narratives that can then be integrated into the survivor's sense of self and view of the world, but it also reintegrates the survivor into a community, reestablishing bonds of trust and faith in others.'

A bit later, in the body of her book (page 20), Brison uses her own experience of her first attendance at a rape survivors' group she joined after eventually returning to the United States to make the same point concretely. Concerning the construction of a trauma narrative, she writes: "Our group facilitator [and herself a rape survivor], Ann Gaulin, told us that first meeting [in Philadelphia]: 'Although it's not exactly the sort of thing I can put on my resumé, it's the accomplishment of which I'm most proud.'" Brison then turns back to her own case (page 21):

> I am not the same person who set off, singing, on that sunny Fourth of July in the French countryside. I left her in a rocky creek at the bottom of a ravine. I had to in order to survive. I understand the appropriateness of what a friend described to me as a Jewish custom of giving those who have outlived a brush with death new names. The trauma has changed me forever, and if I insist too often that my friends and family acknowledge it, that's because I'm afraid they don't know who I am. . . .

> And I no longer cringe when I see a woman jogging alone on a country road where I live, although I may still have a slight urge to rush out and protect her, to tell her to come inside where she'll be safe. But I catch myself, like a mother learning to let go, and cheer her on, thinking, may she always be so carefree, so at home in her world. She has every right to be.

That the right at issue here needs to be so explicitly defended bears its own witness that trauma victims such as Brison herself have lost that 'right.' It is unfortunately all too alienable, as Brison herself goes on to discuss some pages later (pages 65-66), even referring directly to Améry in the process:

> . . . many trauma survivors who endured much worse than I did, and for much longer, found, often years later, that it was

impossible to go on. It is not a moral failing to leave a world that has become morally unacceptable. I wonder how some can ask, of battered women, "Why didn't they leave?" while saying, of those driven to suicide by brutal and inescapable aftermath of trauma, "Why didn't they stay?" Améry wrote, "Whoever was tortured, stays tortured" and this may explain why he, [Primo] Levi, and [Paul] Celan and other Holocaust survivors took their own lives decades after their (physical) torture ended, as if such an explanation were needed.

Only considerably later, near the end of the book, do we learn that the reference to suicide in the passage just quoted is not only thematically important for Brison's discussion of recovery from trauma. It is also biographically important for Brison herself, as she reveals by telling the reader that it was her own brother's death by suicide one day before Christmas in 1995 that (page 115) 'made [her] rethink the importance of regaining control in recovering from trauma.'

Up to that point, her experience of her rape and its aftermath had led her to think of recovery from trauma as entailing regaining a sense of control, especially by constructing a narrative in which the trauma becomes integrated into the ongoing life-story of the trauma survivor, in a process involving seeking out and being heard by empathic listeners. In succeeding in constructing and sharing such a narrative, the trauma survivor is able to "make sense" of the traumatic experience. However, her brother's suicide five years after she was raped—and it is well worth noting explicitly here that by experiencing her brother's suicide Brison herself survives yet another trauma, on top of the one she suffered five years earlier when she was raped and beaten—occasions her rethinking of the whole matter yet again.

"Maybe," she writes (still on page 115) concerning the results of her rethinking, "the point is to learn how to *relinquish* control" (emphasis added) rather than somehow to *regain* it. She then uses the Freudian distinction between 'acting out' an earlier trauma in one's ongoing behavior, as if one were trying at last to 'get it right,' in effect, and 'working through' the trauma. Learning to relinquish control, she comes to think after her brother's suicide, requires that we 'learn by going where we need to go, to replace the clenched, repetitive acting out with the generativity of working through.' Compulsive repetition, 'although [itself] uncontrollable,' as she notes, 'is, paradoxically, obsessed with control, with the soothing, numbing safety of the familiar,' and can go so far as to 'instill the dangerous, even deadly, illusion of invincibility.' In contrast, the process of working through 'is inventive, open to surprise, driven to improvisation,' and ' can provide the foundation of trust on which new life can be built, the steady bass continuo that liberates the other parts to improvise without fear.'

With these remarks toward the end of her book, Brison picks up and deepens a useful distinction she has earlier introduced between what she calls "living to tell," on the one hand, and "telling to live," on the other. Those who survive trauma directly inflicted by others, as Brison herself survived being raped and beaten, often report that what allowed them to survive their ordeal was their strong will to do so in order subsequently to bear witness to what they had gone through. For them, they had to live through the ordeal in order to tell about it later, eventually constructing a coherent trauma narrative and finding empathic listeners to hear that narrative, as has already been discussed.

However, Brison eventually discerns—no doubt as the result, given what she reveals to the reader only later, of the rethinking her brother's suicide occasioned for her—that there are definite limits to the healing potential of this process of living to tell, and that in order to continue to recover beyond those limits one must switch to the very different process of telling to live. Thus, she writes (pages 103-104):

> What I emphasized earlier in the book as the central task of the survivor—regaining a sense of control, coming up with a coherent trauma narrative and integrating it into one's life story—may be crucial to the task of bearing witness, of living to tell, but it may, if taken too far, hinder recovery, by tethering the survivor to one rigid version of the past. It may be at odds with telling to live, which I now see as a kind of letting go, playing with the past in order not to be

held back as one springs away from it. After gaining enough control over the story to be able to tell it, perhaps one has to give it up, in order to retell it, without having to 'get it right,' without fear of betraying it, to be able to rewrite the past in different ways, leading up to an infinite variety of unforeseeable futures.

My earlier discussions of the primary effects of trauma emphasized the loss of control and the disintegration of the (formerly coherent [as she *supposed*] self. My current view of trauma is that it introduces a 'surd'—a nonsensical entry—into the series of events in one's life, making it impossible to carry on with the series. . . .

I thought I had made a certain sense of things until the moment I was assaulted. At any rate I thought I knew how to carry on with my life—to project myself, through action, into an imagined future—the way one knows how to go on in a series such as 2, 4, 6, . . . Not that there was a unique pattern leading ineluctably into a predictable future. The series could have been continued in any number of different ways. . . . But the assumption was that I could find *some* way of carrying on the narrative of my life. Trauma shatters this assumption by introducing an event that fits no discernible pattern. The result is an uneasy paralysis. *I can't go on, I can't stay.* All that is left is the present, but one that has no meaning. . . .

Narrative, as I now think, facilitates the ability to go on opening up possibilities for the future through retelling the stories of the past. It does this not by reestablishing the illusions of coherence of the past, control over the present, and predictability of the future, but by making it possible to carry on without these illusions.

Trauma breaks the illusion of control. Even more fundamentally, it breaks the illusion of meaningful coherence on which that of control itself depends—the illusion that there is any *meaning* that can be made to encompass and "make *sense*" of everything. Trauma is what stands as an exception to the rule that everything has to make sense. It is the *ab-surd* of *non-sense*, we might say, building on Brison's remark that trauma "introduces a 'surd'—a non-sensical entry—into the series of events in one's life, making it impossible to carry on with the series." Trauma is the non-sense that breaks the frame of reference of sense itself.

Concerning the relationship between the endeavor of living to tell and that of telling to live, Brison suggests that it is only at the point of the ultimate collapse of the former that the latter can arise. The point of the breakdown of the endeavor of living to tell would thus also be the point of breakthrough for the opposed endeavor of telling to live. Indeed, Brison comes to see the final purpose or function of living to tell, as part of recovery from trauma, to be getting trauma survivors to that point of breakdown and, therefore, possible breakthrough. In effect, the whole point of living to tell would be to get to the point where living to tell no longer has any point, which is just the point where telling to live comes to have one. "It may be," Brison writes (pages 109-110),

> that the retroactive attempt to master the trauma through involuntary repetition is carried out, intrapsychically, until a listener emerges who is stable and reliable enough to bear witness to it. Perhaps there is a psychological imperative, analogous to the legal imperative, to keep telling one's story until it is heard. After the story has been heard and acknowledged, one can let it go, or unfreeze it. One can unclench.

What one can at last let go of, is not just the endeavor to make sense of what are supposed to be isolable cases of trauma, as if traumas were just isolated islands of meaninglessness within a vast, surrounding ocean of meaningful events. Rather, what makes trauma so traumatic in the fist place is that it reveals the nonsense of thinking that everything somehow ultimately makes sense, that there is some sort of ultimate meaning to everything that happens, some sufficient reason for its happening. Trauma is the revelation that "the principle of sufficient reason" is no principle at all but only, at best, a wish—and, I will add, though I will not discuss the point here, at worst, and all too often, a nightmare.

As Brison writes (page 116) a few pages after the passage above, the passage focusing on the notion of the self and referring to her rethinking, after her brother's suicide, of the nature of recovery from trauma: 'Recovery no longer seems to consist of picking up the pieces of a shattered self (or fractured narrative). It's facing the fact that there never was a coherent self (or story) to begin with.' Once one reaches the point where there is no longer any sense to be made, one can at last give up the compulsive struggle to make sense of things, including oneself.

At the point where the struggle to make sense out of trauma breaks down, the option of surrendering that struggle yet continuing to live in the non-sense, the absurdity, finally breaks through. From that point on, to live in such as way as no longer to avoid the trauma one has undergone, but, rather, to face it—to live, that is, in the truth that dawns in trauma itself—one must live in resistance to any claim that what one has suffered has some redeeming meaning.

The meaning of trauma is that there is no meaning to trauma. Accordingly, recovering from trauma is learning to reject any attempt to give it one. Recovering from a trauma requires, finally, refusing to grant the trauma any meaning, and insisting, instead, on its meaninglessness.

It is all "in vain."

That includes even the trauma of death itself. The same observation applies not just to some deaths, but to all of them: *Every* death is in vain. We owe it to the dead to remember that, as I will discuss next.

Chapter 3

OUR DEBT TO THE DEAD

*His soul swooned slowly as he heard the snow falling faintly through
the universe and faintly falling, like the descent of their last end,
upon all the living and the dead.*

James Joyce, "The Dead"

Robert Jay Lifton, Survivors, and Guilt

"One kind of anxiety is a sense of guilt," writes influential psychiatrist Robert Jay Lifton to begin an analysis of guilt in *Broken Connections: Death and Life Continuity* (page 132). What Lifton says about guilt is in the context of his decades-long research on survivors of such public, historically significant traumas as the atomic bomb attack on Hiroshima at the end of World War II or the American debacle in Viet Nam a few decades later. With regard to the latter, Lifton played a crucial role in the development of the concept of Post-Traumatic Stress Disorder (PTSD), and in eventually gaining official recognition of PTSD as a distinct diagnostic category, signaled by its inclusion in the third edition of the *Diagnostic and Statistical Manual* (*DSM-III*) of the American Psychiatric Association in 1980.

"Guilt feelings," he goes on to observe, "like other forms of anxiety, are associated with psychological pain and many kinds of psychopathology." Lifton's own concern with guilt, however, is not so much with pathological manifestations of it as it is with guilt's healthy forms. Thus, immediately after noting the connection between guilt and psychopathology, he writes that "guilt can also serve as a signal that the integrity of the organism, or moral integrity, is threatened." Thus, he concludes: "It follows that the capacity for guilt is necessary and useful on the one hand, and a potential source of severe psychological harm on the other."

Significantly, when Lifton turns to the topic of what has commonly come to be known as "survivor guilt," that is, the guilt that survivors of a trauma that strikes others as well as themselves often experience toward those who did not survive, he does *not* relegate such guilt, as one might expect, to the second camp, that of unhealthy manifestations of guilt. That is, he does not treat survivor guilt as a subset of pathological guilt, as tends to occur in contemporary popular psychological accounts of the phenomenon, where feeling guilt for surviving a traumatic event is typically treated as no more than a malady to be overcome, or at best a stage of the healing process—at any rate not as something that characterizes mature psychological health itself.

However, the contrary idea, that survivor guilt as such does indeed belong to mature psychological health, is just what Lifton's analysis ultimately suggests. Instead of relegating survivor guilt to the pathological side of phenomena of guilt, Lifton draws the distinction between the healthy and the pathological *within* survivor guilt itself. Thus, while not at all denying that survivor guilt can and often does indicate an underlying psychopathology, Lifton also insists that it can sometimes indicate psychological—and moral—vitality and health.

As he presents it in *The Broken Connection*, it is precisely his own earlier work with cases of guilt in survivors of the atom bomb explosion over Hiroshima at the end of World War II, as well as his work two to three decades later with American veterans of the war in Vietnam, which gives Lifton his guiding clues for characterizing not just survivor guilt, but even guilt in general. In effect, he de-pathologizes survivor guilt by placing it in the perspective of the larger view of guilt he derives from his earlier work with survivors.

The crucial step in Lifton's analysis is to focus upon survivor guilt in terms of the inexpugnable sense of a *debt to the dead* that survivors commonly experience. In turn, against the not uncommon tendency to treat the sense of debt toward the dead as itself mere evidence of immature or superstitious belief, he articulates the position that, as he puts it at the end of the chapter on guilt in *The Broken Connection* (page 146), "[i]ndividuation itself demands that the young organism…indeed develop the capacity for a debt to the dead…"

Two pages earlier (144), Lifton is careful to note: "The image of a debt to the dead conveys the idea of something one owes, a duty, an obligation, a matter in which there is some form of accountability." That last word, 'accountability,' provides the key for understanding Lifton's entire analysis, in my judgment. For him, the notion of debt is not to be read as a reduction of the idea of moral accountability or responsibility to some sort of economic exchange, as it is widely taken to be, especially in "deconstructive" accounts. Rather than arguing that the idea of a debt to the dead involves a sort of economicization of the idea of guilt, as occurs in such accounts, Lifton, as I read him, suggests that what is really in play is a *de*-economicization of the idea of debt, in which the very notion of economic debt gets read back into the broader moral context of accountability or responsibility.

What is more, I do not think it does injustice to Lifton's thought to remark that the tendency of his analysis is precisely to divorce the notion of debt, specifically of debt to the dead, from any attempt to treat such debt as something that could ever even potentially be "discharged." That is, debt to the dead in the sense at issue for him as I read him is nothing that could ever possibly be "paid off," leaving the living no longer indebted, and thereby freeing them to go on about their business, content in the good conscience of having repaid their debts to, and squared their accounts with, the dead.

Rather, the sense of debt to the dead to which Lifton's analysis points is a debt that is un-payable in principle. It is a debt that can never be discharged and which, more importantly, is misunderstood as soon as it is treated in terms of any possibility of paying it off. Indeed, I would argue that it is not pushing things too far to say that such "misunderstanding" is an all too motivated, self-serving one for those who entertain it: The attempt to reduce one's debt to the dead to something that might somehow someday be paid off, is actually the crucial attempt to shirk that very debt, to renege on it—in short, to cheat the dead of what one owes them.

However, the dead are remorseless, as it were. They never forgive the debt the living owe them. Nor do they ever "write off their losses." Instead, they stubbornly insist on asserting their claim on the living. The dead are inexorable creditors.

By Lifton's analysis the morally mature, healthy individual is, then, not someone who has somehow managed to pay her debt to the dead. Rather, even to think in terms that would allow one to make sense of the notion of ever writing "paid" to the living's debt to the dead would be a reliable sign of moral *immaturity*. In contrast, the morally mature and healthy individual would be someone who holds tightly to the knowledge that her debt to the dead can never be discharged, never be paid or made good. It is a debt, instead, that must be constantly borne.

Today, such a view seems completely counter-intuitive. It runs head on against some currently basic notions concerning debts, indebtedness, and the payment of debts. So deeply has the common contemporary understanding economicized the notion of debt that the very idea of the sort of debt Lifton's analysis suggests we owe the dead—a debt the sum of which cannot be calculated and for which no balancing of accounts would ever be possible—such a notion seems to be sheer non-sense, a violation of the very meaning of the term 'debt.' A debt that could never even conceivably be paid, with however large a sum of payments, seems void of all sense, given current dominant understandings.

It also runs counter to the still widespread idea of the foolishness, the childishness—the "primitive" nature—of all "ancestor worship" and "ancestor religion." Contrary to such derogation of ancestor worship, if Lifton is right in the general direction of his thinking about debts to the dead, then ancestor worship could well bear witness to the good and mature moral sense of those who practiced it, rather than to their moral immaturity.

But what sort of a bizarre debt would it be, that could never in principle be paid off, and that is owed to those no longer even living? Could it be anything more than a poor wordplay to talk of such a wholly non-indemnifiable debt?

In my judgment, Heidegger's famous analysis of guilt and debt in *Being and Time* can help to answer that question, as I will discuss in the next section of this chapter.

Heidegger's Guilt

In *Being and Time* Heidegger argues that "being guilty" (*Schuldigsein*) is a primordial existential determination of what he calls *Dasein*, his name for the human being, which is commonly left in the German even in English translations of his work. That is, far from guilt being a condition one acquires only on occasion, by acting contrary to how one "should" act, being guilty belongs, by his analysis, to the very being of a human being, the being of "being-there" or Dasein (*da*: there; and *sein*: to be). According to him, it is only because Dasein always already *is* guilty, that it is even possible for it to *become* "guilty" in the derivative sense of having committed some violation of some moral or social law or rule—become guilty, in short, through failure to do one's "duty," to do what one "should" or "ought to" do.

It is interesting to note that, like Lifton, Heidegger supports his analysis in part by referring to the etymology of the word *guilt* (*Schuld*, in German). The root of that term means "to owe," "to be owing to." In that sense, then, it means precisely to be in debt—namely, in debt to whatever or whomever one owes whatever it is that one owes.

In the everyday—but, for Heidegger, derivative—usage of the term 'guilt,' one acquires guilt by being the cause or agent of a violation of duty, broadly conceived. So understood, being guilty is not at all definitive for being human. Rather, it is an occasional state or condition acquired through specific acts (including failures to act) of a certain sort. The "debt" connected to such guilt is a debt accrued by such actions, and is, therefore, at least in principle something that could be "paid off" by some sort of payment, whether in pounds sterling or in pounds of flesh.

Such everyday usage clearly still accords well enough with the original, etymological meaning of the term 'debt.' In effect, contemporary usage just limits the notion of being in debt, of owing something, to cases in which the debt at issue is incurred by one's own specific choices and actions, or at least to debts capable of being paid off in one fashion or another. So, to give an example relevant to my concerns in this chapter, just such an understanding of debt would be in play in any account of so called "ancestor worship" that treated such worship as an attempt to keep the spirits of ancestors well disposed toward oneself or one's society by making them payments in the way of sacrifices of various sorts, from firstborn children to fumes of incense or ejaculatory prayers.

In contrast, both Heidegger's and Lifton's analyses of guilt suggest a very different account of the nature of debt as such—and, accordingly, a very different account of what is at issue in supposed ancestor worship. Certainly by Heidegger's analysis—and, if I am right, also by Lifton's—guilt, precisely as indebtedness, is not a condition acquired after the fact as a consequence of making certain choices or acting in certain ways. Rather, it is part and parcel of being human, as such: To be a human being *is* to be guilty, indebted, before and apart from any specific choices one might make or fail to make, or actions one might perform or fail to perform.

It follows, as well, that such guilt or indebtedness can never, in principle, be "paid off." Insofar as it defines the very being of the human being as such, even the payment of one's own life could never write "paid" over the debt at issue. No conceivable payment, no matter how large or difficult to make, could ever close one's account and put one in good standing, as it were.

It is perhaps worthwhile to take a few moments to contrast the notion of guilt and debt that emerges in Lifton and Heidegger with another analysis of guilt with which it might seem to be similar: the famous/infamous analysis of human guilt and indebtedness *to God* first fully articulated by St. Anselm in the 11th century, and still very much alive today within large parts both of Catholicism and of evangelical Protestantism—an idea that finds popular expression in billboards and bumper stickers that proclaim "Christ died for your sins." In line with such an idea, the supposed "fall" of humanity through Adam, the fall from grace by and into sin, is something by which human beings acquire an "infinite" debt to God. By the principle that full payment must be equivalent to what is owed, however, an infinite debt could only be paid off with an infinite payment, which is, in turn, a payment that only a being that was itself infinite could ever possibly pay. Accordingly, in order to pay the infinite debt incurred by sin, and thus liberate humanity from the burden of an otherwise un-relievable burden, it was necessary for the infinite God to become incarnate in Jesus and then to take on, as a sort of infinite scapegoat, all the infinite burden of sin, in order that, in His death on the cross, he could then pay Himself the infinite "ransom" demanded to liberate humanity from captivity in its own sin, and to reconcile it to Himself.

However, in contrast, Lifton's and Heidegger's analyses suggest, as I read them, that the debt the living owe the dead is one that even an infinite God could never pay. To capture what is at issue, we might say that the debt in question is infinite in the sense of *unending*, taken strictly. That is, it is *in-finite* in the sense of being literally *without end*—alternatively worded, it is *ever ongoing*. To put the point paradoxically, even if God were to pay himself an infinite payment (as "ransom") for the infinite debt of human sinfulness, humanity would still not be free of debt. It would still not re-ceive any "get out of jail" card in the game of divine monopoly. Humanity's debt to God would still be infinite, even after such an infinite payment. It would just keep going on. The debt would just keep "carrying over," and the "balance due" would remain infinite.

It may be helpful at this point to note that, more than twenty years after the publication of *Being and Time*, in what was eventually published under the title of "The Question Concerning Technology," Heidegger ex-plicitly connected the notion of "indebtedness" (*Schulden*) to the ancient philosophical doctrine of four-fold causation. Indeed, he uses the very term *Schuld* (debt/guilt) to capture what, according to him, is at stake in the ancient Greek notion of "*aitia*," normally translated as "cause." He says, in short, that what the Greeks meant by *aitia* was precisely that to which whatever was at issue was, in effect, *owing*.

In colloquial English, we often use 'owing to' in the way Heidegger has in mind. For example, in the fall of 2008, after a summer of record gas prices, many families across the United States might well have said that "owing to the price of gas" they had not taken any long summer vacation trips. Furthermore, though present usage of the term 'cause' is much more restricted than was the case for ancient Greek usage of the term *aitia*, it still does not sound especially strange to say that the cost of gas "caused" the families at issue to stay home. If asked why they took no trips, such families might well say that it was "because" of the cost of gas: *be-cause of* the price of gasoline—that is, by *cause of* it—they remained at home.

In that broad sense of the term, whereby a cause of an occurrence is anything that contributes to answering the question of "why" it happened, the causes of a given occurrence are the factors *owing to which* it occurred. The event *owes* its very occurrence to those factors, and is in that sense *indebted* to them.

An occurrence solely as such, however, is not itself "accountable" in its indebtedness—accountable "for" itself "to" the factors to which it is indebted. In contrast, it is not merely as *being* indebted—in the sense of "being owing to," as just addressed, in which "being indebted" is characteristic of anything whatever—but also as being *accountable for* their debts *to* their "debtors" that human beings are *guilty*.

Heidegger expresses this by saying that Dasein not only "is" a "null basis" of itself, but also itself "has to be" that null basis—that is, it "has" that null basis "to be," in accordance with Heidegger's general formulation to the effect that Dasein never simply "is" whatever it is, but always has being whatever it is "as an issue," or "at issue," for itself, and in that sense always "has its being [whatever it "is"] to be." That is what Heidegger in *Being and Time* labels the "existence" ("ek-sistence": literally, standing out from itself) of Dasein.

Consequently, when he eventually gets around to discussing guilt, Heidegger offers a definition whereby guilt is: *"having to be the null basis of a nullity."* For my purposes here—and based on Heidegger's own discussion of guilt or debt (*Schuld*), indebtedness (being-in-debt, or being-guilty: *Schuldig-sein*), and debts (*Schulden*)—being guilty can be taken to mean not merely being indebted or owing to something or someone, but in addition to be *accountable for* the debt at issue. In that sense, the debt at issue is a debt that lies at the very heart of the being of the person, prior to—and first making possible at all—the incurring of any debt or indebtedness in the more limited sense, where it is only through actions or failures to act that one can accrue guilt. Thus, even before and apart from any actions we might take or fail to take, we are not only always *in* debt but also always *accountable for* it. As such, we always must and always do—one way or another, like it or not—*take up* that debt, *assuming* it, as it were.

In our accountability *for* our always inescapable indebtedness, to *give an accounting* is always part of our standing debt: We always "owe an accounting" of our debt *to*—we are "accountable" to—whatever or whomever we are "owing" in the first place. Thus, first and above all one is accountable for any given debt to whomever or whatever one owes whatever it is that one owes—to whomever or whatever gave it to one in the first place: one's "debtor" or "creditor" for the debt in question. For example, in one line of one old version of the Christian prayer to "Our Father," one prays to God the Father explicitly as to just such a creditor, asking that God "forgive us our debts as we forgive our debtors." More mundanely, the bank that carries the mortgage on my home is my creditor for the sum of money involved (plus interest, of course); and I am a debtor in relation to them for that sum.

It is at least conceivable, however unlikely, that the bank holding the mortgage on my home might at some time forgive me that particular debt. If we are to believe many of the "believers" among us, then God does indeed forgive us the debts to Him we incur by "sin"—though there is disagreement among such believers about whether God must first be asked to forgive us the debt of our sins, as there is about the details required for the transaction. For example, there is disagreement among Christians about whether the Incarnation and Passion of Christ was the price that God had to pay Himself to "ransom" us from His own clutches, as Saint Anselm says.

To stay for a moment with that same Christian example, it remains a matter of debate among Christians whether the indebtedness at issue, namely, the indebtedness incurred by "sin," is so incurred by our specific, chosen actions and failures to act, or whether it is part and parcel of our being born in the first place. Whatever may be the resolution of that dispute among Christians, if there is any final resolution possible, the mere fact that there is such dispute points to an issue concerning guilt and debt that has more than Christian significance. That is the issue of how to address the indebtedness revealed by the preceding analysis, informed by Lifton's and Heidegger's works. How are we to address that indebtedness incurred by the very fact that we are born at all, an inescapable indebtedness which is implicated in our very being, before and apart from any indebtedness of a more limited sort that we might incur by our own decisions and actions, such as the decision to purchase a home on credit, or the act of stealing fruit from a neighbor's tree (as Augustine famously did)?

I will discuss that question in the next section of this chapter.

Our Debt to the Dead

If we are, as Heidegger argues, guilty or indebted with what we might, following his own terminology, call an *ontological* guilt or indebtedness, insofar as we are from birth accountable for a debt incurred without any choice on our part, then no payment at all, not even an infinite one, could ever possibly discharge our debt. No payment is equal to what we owe. Our debt is in principle un-dischargeable. It can never be cancelled, no matter what we do. The debt we owe for our very being is one that could not be discharged or cancelled even by our voluntarily ceasing to be — by taking our own life in suicide, for instance. There may be some circumstances in which, as Jean Améry argued, the choice to commit suicide has good and sufficient grounds and is, therefore, a thoroughly rational choice under those circumstances, to be respected as such. However, the idea that one could pay one's debt for one's very being by committing such suicide is not tenable. If anything, a suicide committed on the basis of the inescapability of one's ontological indebtedness would just incur further debt, adding more charges to one's account, in effect, in much the same way as leaving town and changing one's identity to avoid making payments on a bank loan only increases one's liability.

Whatever one's belief or lack of belief about such matters as God and sin, at least one debt that all of us do indeed incur by being born at all is *our debt to the dead*. For one thing, we are all first, last, and always in debt to the dead—as paradoxical as it may sound—*for their very dying*: To put the point bluntly, if the dead had not died, then there'd be no place for us among the living. By dying, the dead make room for us, as we in turn will make room for others in our own deaths.

Thus, we owe our very lives and any chance to live them to the dead, who, by their dying, make room for us to be born into life. Life itself is indebtedness to the dead for the gift of life opened to us by their dying. We are all born of the dying of the dead, and even giving birth is itself a matter of just such dying, that the newborn may be. It is the giving up of one's claim over one's own life, so that life may come forth in the other, the one being born. By dying, the dead give the gift of life to the living, bearing them to their births.

Such a link between bearing a child and dying oneself has often enough been noted. What has perhaps been noticed less often is that giving life to a child is also giving the same child over to death, to dying. As an old proverb says, as soon as we are born, we are old enough to die. That is true not just or even mainly in the trivial sense that at any moment after birth one may suddenly die, killed by such accidents as earthquakes, malevolent acts of others, or congenital defects of one's own. The truth in the proverb that as soon as we are born we are old enough to die is that we are all *born dying*: Living itself is "unto death" in a strong sense. Giving birth to a child is setting that child free to die, letting the child go, releasing it into dying. The dead, in dying, give us the gift of life, which is to say the gift that enables us to die ourselves: In dying, the dead give us not just "the gift of life," but also and inseparably "the gift of death," to use the title of one of Jacques Derrida's works. For that gift of death, a gift without which we could receive no other gifts at all (nor offer any, for that matter) we owe a debt to the dead.

Above all what we owe the dead for that gift—of life, of death, of life unto death—is no more and no less than *to accept the gift they have given us*. To accept the gift of death from the dead, however, is just to live unto death and into it ourselves, as the dead have done before us. In turn, to do that— to accept the gift of death from the dead by dying oneself—is to pass on the gift of death, by clearing space for others, "the next generation," to come forth, that they too may receive the same gift. By not clinging to life, but letting it go, we make room for others to be born and life to go on—go on, namely, in the living, which is always unto death.

The dead as such, however, are anonymous. Dying is entering into such anonymity. It is folly, therefore, to think that we pay our debt to the dead by remembering them by name. It is much more nearly the reverse: We pay our debt to the dead by letting them go forth into death, as into just such anonymity. It is in, and only in, anonymity that the dead are finally and truly let be *dead*. Anything short of that, however, and we are refusing the very gift we owe to the dead, the very gift of life itself; we are throwing that gift back in the face of the giver, which is the very definition of ingratitude.

"How can one escape what never sets?" asks Heraclitus rhetorically in one of his fragments. Millennia later, in *The Unforgettable and the Unhoped For* Jean-Louis Chrétien, whom I have mentioned before, teaches the paradox that only what can never be remembered is truly unforgettable. All its possible positive benefits for those who are still alive set aside, the endeavor to remember the dead by reading their names—as is done on the anniversary of the attacks of September 11, 2001, at the site where the World Trade Center once stood, for example—is not what the living must do, to give the dead their due. Insofar as such endeavors to cling to the memory of the individual dead actually drag the dead out of the anonymity within which death itself encloses them, those endeavors just make a fetish of the dead. To that degree, they refuse to honor the dead in their very being dead, and even begin to cross over into blasphemy against them.

Hope to be remembered individually and by name by future generations is hope in a sham-immortality. As the author of *Ecclesiates* knew, all that is vanity. Not only will all the survivors with all their memories of all their dead loved ones eventually vanish themselves in turn, but even while those survivors still live and still keep their memories of all their dead loved ones brightly burnished, the images so kept do not reveal but mask what they represent. A form of idolatry is involved, whereby the images of the dead come to replace the dead themselves in the recollections of the still living. The dead are thus denied their death, disrespected in their anonymous community in death.

In his classic literary biography of James Joyce, Richard Ellman at one point addresses the lines I used as the epigraph for this chapter, the last lines from "The Dead," Joyce's great closing story in *Dubliners*. Ellman argues that the Joycean snow "falling faintly through the universe and faintly falling, like the descent of their last end, upon all the living and the dead" must not be taken, as not a few have taken it, to be a symbol for death itself. Ellman maintains that such an understanding would involve Joyce in a very un-Joycean tautology, the tautology of death descending on the dead. Yet I would maintain, *pace* Ellman, that the snow of those lines is precisely death, and that it is just the fall of death upon *both* the living *and* the dead that brings both together into a single, universal community, the only community in which there is no "respecting of persons," because in that community all are equal—equal, namely and only, in their complete anonymity: All the living and all the dead are all alike alone together before death.

Only when the names of the dead are at last forgotten, are the dead themselves—all the anonymous dead alike—allowed at last fully to be themselves remembered, and no longer covered over by their very names and by our own needy memories of them. As only the monk who no longer knows he is praying is truly praying, according to the desert anchorites of the early centuries of Christianity, so are the dead truly worshipped only when the worshiper no longer knows just whom she is worshiping.

Some of the most pointed examples of experiencing the impossibility of repaying the debt that the living owe to the dead can be found among survivors of such horrible traumatic events as the detonation of the atomic bomb over Hiroshima, or the Nazi extermination of the Jews. Robert Jay Lifton, who worked with survivors of both cataclysms, makes a point of how both Hiroshima survivors and Auschwitz survivors commonly regard their survival as mandating them to bear witness to those who did not so survive. They experience themselves as guilty before those who died in the bombing or in the camps. Furthermore, no matter how often and for how long the survivors bear such witness, telling others about what happened to those who did not survive, the survivors never experience it as enough. They never experience themselves as acquitted of the duty to go on bearing witness. As they experience it themselves, the debt of survivors to those who did not survive can never be repaid.

Not just for survivors of Hiroshima or Auschwitz, however, but also for us all as "survivors"—those who are still alive in the face of all the dead—our debt to the dead is un-payable. For that very reason, any attempt to pay it accrues a sort of second order guilt, the guilt that comes from doing harm to another. We harm the dead in stripping them of their rest in the anonymity of death, insisting on calling them back from the grave by name, summoning them by our invocations, to serve as instruments for our own purposes. To honor them and acknowledge our debt is to refuse any longer so to abuse them. It is, instead, to let them be dead.

It is not by reciting the names of the dead at memorial occasions, or printing their pictures as "portraits of glory" in our newspapers, that we assume our debt to them and acknowledge our guilt before them. Rather, we can assume that debt and acknowledge that guilt only by what amounts to an opposite sort of movement, one in which we no longer try to detain the dead and keep them with us, but instead allow them to depart from us, and go forth into the holy anonymity of the grave.

Dying in Vain

"If I forget you, Jerusalem, let my right hand wither! Oh let my tongue cleave to my mouth, if I remember you not, if I prize not Jerusalem above all my joys!" sings the Psalmist (Psalm 136/137: 5-6, Grail translation). The question, however, is how to be sure it is Jerusalem one is remembering, and not some poor substitute—some mere image of the holy. So it is, too, with remembering the dead: To be sure it is the dead themselves we are remembering, and not some mere shade of our own imagining.

If we would remember the dead, and not substitute for them some idol of our own making, then we also need to remember, in effect, just why we should remember the dead in the first place. For just what do we owe the dead our constant remembrance? Just what have the dead given to us, the living, such that we have incurred such a debt toward them?

We owe the dead for their death. (So, at least, I have been arguing.) Their death, however, is a pure gift that the dead bestow upon the living. As a pure gift, the death of the dead is like the grits in an anecdote from psychiatrist and popular spiritual teacher M. Scott Peck, author of the multi-million-copy bestseller *The Road Less Traveled*. In *What Return Can I Make? The Dimensions of the Christian Experience*, Peck tells the story of how once when he was served grits on the side in a restaurant in the American South, he remarked to the woman waiting on him that he had not ordered grits. "You don't order grits,' she replied by Peck's account. "They just comes."

Peck uses that anecdote to say that God's grace is like grits: One doesn't ask for grace. It just comes.

St. Paul is the ultimate source for such a Christian understanding of grace. For Paul, grace is a pure gift freely bestowed by God upon those who receive it. The Greek word Paul uses for "gift" is *dōrean*. In *St. Paul: The Foundations of Universalism*, Alain Badiou—a very different writer than M. Scott Peck, whom Badiou nonetheless unintentionally echoes on this point—writes concerning that Greek term: *"Dōrean* is a powerful word; it means 'as a pure gift,' 'without cause,' and even 'in vain.'"

Any pure gift is always given "in vain" in that sense. That applies not only to God's grace as Paul conceived it, but also to the pure gift that the dead give to us, the living, in their very dying. Furthermore, as such a pure gift, the gift of their death is a gift that the dead give us altogether without any forethought or intention on their part, just by dying. In that sense, their bestowing of their gift upon us who are still living is *involuntary*, at least in one sense: It is not, as such, *intentional*.

Correlatively, the reception of such a gift is no less involuntary or unintentional. One receives it just by being born at all. It is for the very reason that both the giving and the receiving are involuntary or unintentional, however, that the debt incurred by the living toward the dead for the pure gift of their death is *in-finite* (literally un-ending) and *un-payable*. The debt is infinite and un-payable because the gift by the involuntary receiving of which we are placed in debt to the dead, is always without cause, always "in vain" in the sense Badiou explicates.

All death is in vain, and no one dies *except* in vain. There is no point or purpose served by death. It is non-purposive, a-telic—just like life itself, which, as Nietzsche observes, neither has nor lacks a meaning.

Accordingly, if it is *the dead* whom we are remembering and not some idol we are substituting for the dead themselves, we must keep in mind that their deaths were indeed *in vain.* Any attempt to give "meaning" to their deaths, to assure that they will *"not* have died in vain," in fact robs the dead of their very death. To pretend to give death a purpose, a point or justification, is one sure way precisely to fail to honor the dead, to *dishonor* and even to *blaspheme* against them.

In so doing, in fact, one accrues, with or without intention, the second-order ("moral") guilt of acting contrary to one's duty (which includes simply not doing it at all)—here, one's duty to the dead. One reduces the dying of the dead (e.g., the millions killed by the Nazis) to no more than a means to achieve some end (e.g., the founding of the state of Israel) external to, and imposed upon, them.

Dishonoring the Dead

What do we owe the dead? As I have noted before, in one way of taking that question—taking it, namely, to be a question concerning that *for* which we are indebted to the dead—the answer would be "everything." Furthermore, it is, as I have also noted before, in their very having died—that is, to put the same point a bit differently, precisely *as dead*—that the dead give us "everything."

However, another way of taking the question of what we owe the dead—a way of taking it that is different, yet nevertheless inseparable, from the first—would be to take it as an inquiry about what would constitute proper *response* on the part of us, the living, *to* the dead, for what they have given us, the "everything" we owe them in the first sense. Precisely given that what we owe the dead, in the first way of taking that notion, is "everything," then just what would constitute a proper "response" to the dead, for what they have given us? What response do the dead themselves, as dead, call upon us to make, given that we owe them everything?

What we owe the dead in that second sense of the question—that is, the response that would appropriately answer to the dead for what they have given us by and in their very dying—is to grant them in turn what I would like to call *indemnity*. We owe the dead "indemnity" in the original etymological sense of that term whereby it means to *keep from harm*, to *protect against loss*.

How can the dead be harmed, however? What more can they lose, given that they are already dead? The most common answer would seem to be that they might lose their place in the memory of the living, and thereby suffer the harm of being forgotten. Hence the common refrain of "Never forget!" For example, Israelis admonish one another and the entire world to "never forget" what was done to the Jews of Europe in the Nazi extermination camps. Or, to give a more recent example, bumper stickers and window decals carrying the same admonition never to forget those who lost their lives in the attacks of September 11, 2001, continue to show up on cars in the United States each fall.

Yet what we try in such ways never to forget will still eventually be forgotten, despite all our efforts at remembering. Sooner or later, but inevitably, memory will fail. The names of the dead, which we vowed never to forget, will be forgotten; and those who bore those names will sink into the great, anonymous mass of all the nameless dead of all the earlier ages.

Whatever can be remembered in the same sense that a name can be remembered, will inevitably be forgotten in time. And even while the name is still remembered, there will come a time when the one who bore the name will no longer be, and only the name will remain. As Chrétien sees clearly, whatever can be remembered will be forgotten, and only what can never be remembered is truly unforgettable.

Before Chrétien, Jean-François Lyotard wrote along the same lines, specifically with regard to the Jewish dead of the Holocaust. In *Heidegger and "the jews"*, in a passage to which I will return in a later chapter on trauma and "representation," Lyotard writes (page 27) that the Holocaust

> cannot be represented without being missed, being forgotten anew, since it defies images and words. Representing 'Auschwitz' in images and words is a way of making us forget this. I am not thinking here only of bad movies and widely distributed TV series, of bad novels or "eyewitness accounts." I am thinking of those very cases that, by their exactitude, their severity, are, or should be, best qualified not to let us forget. But even they represent what, in order not to be forgotten as that which is forgotten itself, must remain unrepresentable. Claude Lanzmann's film *Shoah* is an exception, maybe the only one. . . .

> Whenever one represents, one inscribes in memory, and this might seem a good defense against forgetting it. It is, I believe, just the opposite. Only that which has been inscribed can, in the current sense of the term, be forgotten, because it could be effaced. But what is not inscribed, through lack of inscribable surface, of duration and place for the inscription to be situated, ... cannot be forgotten, does not offer a hold to forgetting, and remains present "only" as an affection that one cannot even qualify, like a state of death in the life of the spirit. One *must*, certainly, inscribe in words, in images. One cannot escape the necessity of representing. It would be sin itself to believe oneself safe and sound. But it is one thing to do it in view of saving the memory and quite another to

try to preserve the remainder, the unforgettable forgotten, in writing.

It is to be feared that word representations (books, interviews) and thing representations (films, photographs) of the extermination of the Jews . . . by the Nazis bring back the very thing, . . . in the orbit of secondary repression. . . . It is to be feared that, through representation, it turns into an "ordinary" repression. One will say, It was a great massacre, how horrible! Of course, there have been others, "even" in contemporary Europe (the crimes of Stalin). Finally, one will appeal to human rights, one cries out "never again" and that's it! It is taken care of.

A few lines later Lyotard contrasts all such endeavors "never to forget" the Holocaust—endeavors which, despite what may well be their authors' own intentions, end up obfuscating and thereby perpetuating the very crime at issue—with what belongs "on the side of 'the jews'" themselves. He writes (pages 27-28):

One can represent the Nazi madness–make of it what it also is–an effect of 'secondary' repression, a symptom; a way of transcribing anxiety, the terror in regard to the undetermined (which Germany knew well, especially then), into will, into political hatred, organized, administered, turned against the unconscious affect. . . . But on the side of 'the jews,' absence of representability, absence of experience, absence of accumulation of experience (however multimillenial), interior innocence, smiling and hard, even arrogant, which neglects the world except with regard to its pain—these are the traits of a tradition where the forgotten remembers that it is forgotten; knows itself to be unforgettable, has no need of inscription, of looking after itself, a tradition where the soul's only concern is with the terror without origin, where it tries desperately, humorously to originate itself by narrating itself.

The SS does not wage war against the Jews. . . . The war merely creates the din that is necessary to cover the silent crime. . . . –a second terror, a horror rather, practiced on the involuntary witness of the 'first' terror, which is not even felt, not even lodged, but which is diffuse and remains in it like an interminably deferred debt. In representing the second terror one ineluctably perpetuates it. It is itself only representation. . . . One betrays misery, infamy by representing them.

Lyotard then sums up with a remark that can be generalized beyond efforts to remember the dead of the Holocaust, to apply to any efforts to remember any of the dead. "*All* memory, in the traditional sense of representation," he writes (my emphasis), "because it involves decision, includes and spreads the forgetting of the terror without origin that motivates it."

We owe it to the dead, then, *not* to remember them, at least if remembering is taken "in the traditional sense," wherein to remember the dead entails holding on to some "representation" of the dead, even if only their names. Paradoxically, all such endeavors to honor the dead by always remembering them end up *dis*-honoring them. It dishonors the dead by stripping them of the only thing left to them insofar as they *are* dead. Instead of keeping the dead from harm, it harms them in the only way left to do so, once they are dead. It harms the dead in that, far from protecting them against loss, it robs the dead of the one thing they still have: their very *death* itself. In an unusual but literal sense, it is a form of grave robbery.

Robbing the dead of their graves under the guise of remembering them is itself a way of attempting to gain control over death itself. It is a matter of laying claim to what Robert Jay Lifton in *Super Power Syndrome: America's Apocalyptic Confrontation with the World* — in which he drops, by the way and unfortunately to my mind, what I take to be his earlier fruitful suggestions, in *Broken Connections*, of a non-pathological concept of "survivor guilt" (which in this later work he calls "death guilt")—calls "ownership of death." The dreams and assertions of a power so fantastic that it can lay claim to ownership even over death itself are built upon "profound feelings of powerlessness and emptiness," as Lifton writes (page 178), to cover those feelings over and avoid facing them. What is behind such "a sense of megalomania and omnipotence" that extends even over death itself is, as Lifton observes a few lines later, "[f]ear of being out of control."

Our fear of not being in control is always, at bottom, the fear of death, which is precisely the point where we lose all control. To avoid facing that fear, we are willing even to dishonor the dead, robbing them of their very death under the pretense of remembering them.

However, before the alternative—that of facing the loss of all control—we can only *swoon*—as I will turn to next.

The Soul's Swoon, Jean-Luc Nancy, and the Prayer of Death

All efforts to hold death at bay by retaining the memory of the dead, even just their names, ultimately fail. Sooner or later, but inexorably, even the mere names of the dead vanish into the anonymous grave. To be forgotten is the final destiny common to all, the living and the dead alike. When at last all ways of avoidance are blocked, and one is finally forced, by the accidents of one's life, to face the abyss of death and the grave's oblivion and silence, all that the still living soul can do is swoon, as Gabriel's soul does at the end of Joyce's "The Dead."

Interestingly, toward the end of the same century near the beginning of which Joyce wrote his great story, John Updike painted a similar portrait of the soul's swoon. In *Memories of the Ford Administration*, which is at one level a novel about the distortions, limitations, and ultimate losses of memory itself, first published in 1992, the overall story Updike tells involves the interplay of two included lesser stories, one of which is that of James Buchanan, the fifteenth President of the United States (about whose dying Updike had earlier also written a play). Toward the end of the novel, in the final section devoted to Buchanan, Updike depicts him near the very end of his Presidency, when all his efforts to avoid the Union rupturing in two have finally collapsed in failure, and Buchanan himself knows that the nation is falling into the abyss of civil war. Buchanan, the United States' only bachelor President, is alone in his rooms. Updike writes (pages 316-318):

> He sleepily prayed, and the silence into which his brain poured its half-formed words, the sense melting like wax at the edge of the flaming wick, tonight seemed itself a message, tuned to his great weariness. He saw for a moment through not his own mismatched eyes but through God's clear colorless ones; he saw that *sub specie aeternitatis* nothing greatly matters: not his own life, his ambitions, his patient intricate craven search for power, nor, cruel as the thought might appear from a wakeful perspective, the lives of the nation, the millions as they strain toward him for rescue. The hordes of the Sennacherib invaded Israel, and the Temple was destroyed stone by stone, and yet within the beautiful dispassion of God these cataclysms had been cradled, and now slept unremembered but by a few. While Buchanan had been Ambassador to the Court of St. James, British educated opinion had been considerably agitated by the apparent discoveries, within geology, of tracts of time vaster than any the Bible disclosed: Buchanan now perceived a cause for serenity here, a vastness that dwindled all our agitations to a scarcely perceptible stir, and our mountains and chasms to a prairie smoothness, a luminous smoothness like that of Greenland, or of the unexpected southernmost continent first sighted by Captain Cook. Having been long troubled by the silence into which his prayers seemed to sink without an echo, Buchanan in his majestic figure appreciated that the silence *was* an answer, the only answer whose mercy was lasting, impartial, and omnipresent. . . . As if though the

gimlet eye of an eagle soaring in God's silent winds Buchanan saw the nation beneath him, a colorful small mountain meadow scurrying with frantic life; its life would perish but infallibly renew itself in the turning of seasons, in the great and impervious planetary motions. Thus reassured, the old man sank on a sustained note of praise into the void and woke with surprise into a still-stormy world where it seemed all but himself had tossed sleepless through the night.

To *swoon* in the face of death and the dead, in the sense that Joyce's Gabriel and Updike's Buchanan do, is to relinquish all claim to ownership over death and, therewith, over oneself. It is literally to "let oneself go"— both in the sense of "losing control of oneself" and in the sense of "allowing oneself to leave." Where one goes, once so let go, is into the same abyss before which one can only swoon: the very abyss of death, in all its silence and oblivion.

In swooning, we, still living, die ourselves in turn, thereby responding to the invitation—to follow them—that all the dead who have gone before have extended to us. To swoon as Joyce's Gabriel or Updike's Buchanan does is to accept that invitation, and enter into death ourselves.

Entering death in such a swoon has nothing necessarily to do with killing oneself, with taking one's own life, in the sense that we use those expressions to talk of suicide. Although under certain circumstances, such as those Jean Améry articulates, it may be that suicide is how a given soul's swoon takes shape, under other, probably far more common circumstances, suicide is a way of pressing one's claims to ownership, rather than abandoning them.

At any rate, there is nothing of self-assertion in the soul's swoon before death, letting itself go into the Joycean community in death of "all the living and the dead." Rather, as is implicit in Joyce and explicit in Updike, the swoon is *prayerful*. It is itself *prayer* in the most fundamental sense, in which to pray is to praise, just as Updike's Buchanan sinks "into the void" in "a sustained note of praise."

Independently of both Joyce and Updike, or at least independently of reference to either, French philosopher Jean-Luc Nancy has recently, in his book *Dis-Enclosure: The Deconstruction of Christianity*, articulated prayer in a way excellently suited to capture what is at stake here. At the end of an essay entitled "Prayer Demythified" he writes some final reflections that illuminate "fanaticism" as the most destructive form of the endeavor, in effect (though Nancy does not put it this way, at least at this point in his text), to *avoid* or *deny* the abyss of death, rather than prayerfully to swoon into it, as Buchanan does.

What Nancy says applies not only to contemporary religious fanaticism of whatever sort, whether Hindu, Muslim, Buddhist, Jewish, or Christian—the latter as exemplified recently by the murder in Kansas in the spring of 2009 of Dr. George Tiller, murdered in the name of the protection of the "rights of the as yet unborn," as it is sometimes put. It also applies to Nazi and fascist fanaticism, as Nancy's own remarks make clear, and to all other forms of political fanaticism, whether "religious" in professed motivation or not. Above all, Nancy's analysis casts light on the connections between distortions of language and the fanatical avoidance of death and its trauma.

Thus, at the end of his essay on prayer Nancy writes: "Fanaticism is nothing but the abolition of the intractable distance of the real [the traumatic structure of "reality" as such, in effect], and consequently also the extinction of prayer and all speech, in favor of effusive outpouring, eructation, and vociferation." In contrast to all such denial and distortion, prayer as such, as he has been arguing in the preceding pages of his essay, is nothing but the lifting up, the elevation, of the very speaking and saying that is prayer itself. Hence, he goes on, after his remark on fanaticism, to write:

> In the elevation of prayer, a supplication also, albeit "accessory," cannot fail to intervene, for in it [that is, in prayer] is revealed the "poverty" [of all human speech itself]. The fact is "poor humanity" may have nothing else to pray. Prayer thus conceived does not enrich, does not remunerate the

"poor humanity" that we today have just as many reasons to bemoan [as ever]. It carries poverty over to saying—and it isn't poverty but saying that is obliterated in this prayer. Does not the same apply (isn't it the same thing) to the saying of love, the saying of mourning, and the saying of speech itself?

However that may be—and clearly the questions function rhetorically here—Nancy concludes that to

concern ourselves with this empty remnant [Note that term!] of prayer, [to] remain faithful to this obligation [to pray the poor prayer of poor humanity]. . . , [f]or us . . . has the force of a categorical imperative, for nothing today is more important than this: to empty and let be emptied out all prayers that negotiate a sense, an issue, or a repatriation of the real within the narrow confines of our faded humanisms and clenched religiosities, in order that we may merely open speech once again to its most proper possibility of address, which also makes up all its sense and all its truth.

The gift that the dead give us in their very dying calls for just and only such prayer as response—a prayer that utterly exhausts itself in lifting up death and the dead themselves, and, in so *raising them up*, obliterates not death and the dead but the praying voice itself, which vanishes behind what it exhausts itself in lifting up. Such an empty remnant of prayer, which expropriates those who pray—dis-appropriating them of all their own property, in order that they may at last pray properly—is the *only* proper prayer—indeed, the only proper speech—of those remnant communities, as I would call them, and as I will discuss in more detail in time, that are the only real communities, in any world of shared death such as our own.

The prayer Updike's Buchanan offers up as he sinks into the void is praise of that same void, the void of silence and oblivion that is death itself.

In his soul's swoon Buchanan's prays the prayer of death, praising it and "raising up" the dead themselves, as I made a point of putting it above. In the prayer that exhausts itself in lifting up the dead themselves, there thus occurs what, following Nancy, who himself here follows a long Christian (at least) tradition, we can call a *resurrection* of the dead.

However, that could only be in the sense of "resurrection" that Nancy himself discerns in the writings of Maurice Blanchot. In "Blanchot's Ressurection," another essay in *Dis-Enclosure*, Nancy insists (page 89) that the "resurrection" in question is one which "does not escape death, nor recover from it," but which rather "constitutes the extremity and truth of the phenomenon of dying." The movement of such resurrection "goes into death not to pass through it but, sinking irreversibly into it," just as Buchanan sinks into the (same) void, "to resuscitate death itself."

Resuscitating death itself, Nancy goes on, 'is entirely different from resuscitating the dead,' at least insofar as that is taken to mean 'to bring them back to life, to bring life back where death had destroyed it.' That is, it is not a matter of what the Catholic theologian Hans Küng (persona non-grata to the Vatican since early in the papacy of John-Paul II) years before Nancy called, disparagingly, 'the reanimation of a corpse.' Not only Blanchot's resurrection, but also Küng's, involve no such reanimation of the dead themselves. "Resuscitating death is an entirely different operation," writes Nancy, the point of which is precisely "to let the dead *be* dead: thus, to resurrect or resuscitate death, and the dead *as* [still] dead."

To let the dead be dead is at the same time, Nancy also recognizes, to join them in dying, even while one still lives. As he writes earlier in *Dis-Enclosure*, in an essay on the book of James in Christian scripture, an essay he calls "The Judeo-Christian (on Faith)," "man" as he is emerging in ongoing changes "in the instituting configuration of the West" is (page 59)

> no longer the mortal who stands before the immortal. He is becoming the dying one in a dying that doubles or lives the whole time of his life. The divine withdraws from its dwelling

sites—whether these be the peaks of Mount Olympus or of Sinai—and from every type of temple. It becomes, in so withdrawing, the perpetual imminence of dying. Death, as the natural end of a mode of existence, is itself finite: dying becomes the theme of existence according to the always suspended imminence of *parousia* [literally, presence or arrival—used in Christianity to refer to the Second Coming of Christ].

In accordance with such an understanding of the inseparable inter-weaving—the "identity" in the Heideggerian sense of *"belonging*-togeth-er'—of death and life, Nancy goes on in his very next paragraph to dis-cuss the Christian sacrament of anointing the sick, especially the dying. Sometimes called the sacrament of 'extreme unction,' so marking the sick, writes Nancy, ' signs not what will later be called life eternal beyond death.' Rather, unction marks 'the entry into death as into a finite *parousia* that is infinitely differed or deferred. This is the entry into incommensurable in-adequation. In this sense, every dying one is a messiah, and every messiah is a dying one. The dying one is no longer a mortal as distinct from the immortal. The dying one is the living one in the act of a presence that is incommensurable.'

Nancy then considers the Christian doctrine according to which "[d]eath is tied to sin." Considerably later in *Dis-Enclosure*, in an essay called "The Deconstruction of Christianity," Nancy argues that *sin* is not a "misdeed," but a "condition." By his understanding, sin is the shared human condition of being in need of redemption (or salvation), insofar as in all human being there is a radical "indebtedness of existence itself" (just such indebtedness as I have tried to explicate earlier in this chapter in my discussion of Lifton and Heidegger on 'guilt'), which the human being is 'tempted' to deny or disavow, affirming instead the 'self' and the self's claim to independence, to ownership over itself, owing nothing to others before and apart from the self's own voluntary commitments. To 'sin' is to give in to the temptation toward such self-affirmation, in the literal sense of affirming a 'self' in the first place. Nancy writes (pages 155-156):

Temptation is essentially the *temptation of self*, it is the self as temptation, as tempter, as self-tempter. It is not in the least a question of the expiation of a misdeed, but of redemption or salvation, and salvation cannot come from the self itself, but from its opening . . . and as such it comes to it as the grace of its Creator. . . . Through salvation, God remits to man the debt he incurred in sinning, a debt that is none other than the debt of the self itself. What man appropriated, for which he is in debt to God, is the self that he has turned in upon itself. It must be returned to God and not to itself. *Sin is an indebtedness of existence as such.*

In other words, while Heidegger tends to detach existential *Schuldigkeit* [guiltiness] from the category of "transgression" or of "debt" (in the ontic sense of the term), I wonder, rather, whether that *Schuldigkeit* does not realize the essence of sin as the indebtedness of existence—"indebtedness of existence" meaning, at one and the same time, that existence itself is in debt, and that which it is in debt for is precisely for itself, for itself, for the ipseity of existence.

My own reading of Heidegger on guilt, as I presented it earlier in this chapter, is one that takes Heidegger to be in full agreement with Nancy's own interpretation of guilt, rather than at variance with it. At any rate, my own agreement with the sort of interpretation of guilt Nancy offers is almost without qualification, my only qualification being that I suspect his account may still leave the difference-in-interconnection of guilt as the existential "indebtedness" he emphasizes, and guilt in a negative sense of being to blame for some misdeed, less than sufficiently clarified. Yet his remarks themselves can be read in such a way as to point to the nexus of that interconnection-in-disconnection, insofar as they suggest that the basic "indebtedness of existence" grounds and manifests itself in the closure toward "self," which then and as such is the *refusal* of the debt the living owe for the very fact of being alive at all.

The refusal at issue is a hardening of the self into its own claims of ownership over itself, as opposed to the recognition of fundamental indebtedness to the generosity of others. It is stiffening of the self into selfishness, of the ego into egoism. As the influential phenomenologist Jean-Luc Marion, one of Nancy's French colleagues in philosophy, puts it in *Being Given: Toward a Phenomenology of Givenness*, by refusing not just some specific debt but all indebtedness whatsoever, the self or ego hardens into an attitude of total *ingratitude*, insisting that it does not owe anyone for anything. As Marion writes (pages 90-91):

> The ingrate is defined first not by a negative will or his impotence to repay good with good, but by incapacity, impatience, and exasperation simply in receiving it [that is, a gift]. He refuses the charge not only of acquitting himself of this debt (which would remain within exchange), but of ever having incurred—of ever having been offered a gift. He suffers from the very principle that a gift affects him by befalling him. He does not refuse this or that gift with or without this or that objective support: he refuses indebtedness pure and simple—or rather the admission of it. In a stubborn struggle against the evidence of the gift already given and without his consent, the ingrate has the presence to maintain that his consent alone decides the gifts given to him. He sticks strictly to the base principle that "I don't owe anything to anyone" . . .

In contrast, to face one's ineradicable indebtedness for even being at all is, as Marion writes a few pages later (page 101), to face "what phenomenologically and morally is the hardest ordeal" of all, the ordeal of "succeed[ing] in making an exception to the principle 'I don't owe anything to anybody.'"

At any rate, to return to the connection of death to sin, according to Nancy's interpretation in his essay in *Dis-Enclosure* on the Biblical letter of James—which stands in a relation of reciprocal reinforcement with what he writes in the essay, later in the book, on the deconstruction of

Christianity—to say that death is tied to sin is to say that it is "tied to the deficiency of a life that does not practice faith." However, as he then adds, in a remark especially significant for my present purposes, the faith at issue is not one that life just happens on occasion to fail to practice. Rather, life "*cannot* practice it' (my emphasis), at least 'without failing or fainting—at the incommensurable height of dying"—just as Joyce's Gabriel and Updike's Buchanan fail and faint.

"Yet despite this," Nancy concludes—and we might well change that to *because* of it — 'faith gives.' What it gives is 'dying precisely in its incommensurability (to give death, 'the gift of death,' he [that other "James," namely, Jacques—French for James — Derrida, in a book of that title] says): a gift that is not a matter of receiving in order to keep, any more than is love or poverty, or even veridicity (which are, ultimately, the same thing as dying).'

So, too, is prayer "the same thing as dying," especially that prayer in which the living raise up the dead, dying after them in turn. In that dying, we indemnify the dead, keeping them safe from harm and loss, allowing them their rest in the silent, silencing keep of death.

That is our debt to the dead.

Chapter 4

TRAUMA AND REPRESENTATION I:

THE SOVEREIGNTY OF THE IMAGE

Obscene Images

Men and women, sometimes even holding hands, jumping from the upper floors of the Twin Towers, preferring that way of dying to being burned alive by the fires raging behind them: For many horrified spectators around the world watching on television during the events that took place in New York on September 11, 2001, there was something obscene about what seemed to be the compulsive broadcasting and rebroadcasting of those images. Hundreds of millions worldwide saw them in the endless loop of replays that continued for a time after the Towers collapsed, before the mass media began to hold them back, in real or pretended sensitivity to how offensive they might be to large segments of their audience.

However, just wherein did the obscenity of the broadcasting and rebroadcasting of those images consist, for those who did perceive them as obscene? Were the broadcasting and rebroadcasting obscene insofar as some sort of blatant exploitation of those horrible images for private gain might be suspected—for example, that some television network or other outlet might have been using them to build ratings? Yet even many viewers who imputed no such motives to the broadcasters still experienced something obscene about what came across to them as the compulsive broadcasting of the images at issue. What seemed obscene to such viewers was that those images were broadcast at all, regardless of the broadcasters' motives. To them, or at least some of them, there is something obscene about the very endeavor to represent such trauma in images at all.

There is a sense in which any representation whatever of such public traumas as "9/11" or, to introduce another example (or reservoir for countless examples), "Auschwitz" (that is, the Holocaust) can be taken to entail a sort of exploitation of the suffering of others, regardless of conscious intention. For such an understanding, the very representation of traumatic events, or at least of such public, historic ones as the attacks of September 11, 2001, or the Holocaust, is in a way a moral violation of the victims of such trauma—a perpetuation and repetition of their traumatization or wounding, a compounding of the harm and suffering already inflicted upon them. By that way of perceiving things, the mere endeavor to represent trauma constitutes a sort of obscenity and blasphemy against those who have been most traumatized. As Jean-Francois Lyotard writes (page 28) in *Heidegger and "the jews,"* already cited in the preceding chapter: "One betrays misery, infancy [he is speaking here especially of children in the camps] by representing them."

As the title of his book suggests, Lyotard makes that remark in the context of discussing the Holocaust. Lyotard sees something morally problematic about any effort to represent the Nazi "extermination" of the Jews in pictures or even in words. "If one represents the extermination," Lyotard writes (page 27), "it is also necessary to represent the exterminated." Accordingly, one ends up representing "men, women, children [being] treated like 'dogs,' 'pigs,' 'rats,' 'vermin,' subjected to humiliation, constrained to abjection, driven to despair, thrown like filth into the ovens." However, in so representing those who were exterminated, "this representation forgets something," something essential to remember. "For it is not as men, women, and children that they are exterminated but as the name of what is evil—'jews'—that the Occident has given to [its own] unconscious anxiety."

Thus, under the very pretense of protecting the memory of the exterminated, representing them as men, women, and children—and how else is one supposed to represent them?—one inadvertently ends up perpetuating the very movement of extermination, of erasure of the truth about what was done to those exterminated. Once again they are themselves thereby reduced to just another representation, as they had already been reduced by their executioners, their "exterminators," to mere representatives of incarnate evil—"the jews," as Lyotard puts it—to be exterminated in the first place.

Avoiding such unintentional exploitation of the victims of trauma is no easy matter, however. Even critics who explicitly discern such exploitation in others' representations, in works of cinema, books, or other forms, tend to fall prey to the same fault in their own accounts. So, for example, in *The New York Times* for Sunday, January 9, 2009, in a piece called "Telling the Holocaust Like It Wasn't," Jacob Heilbrunn comments critically on a rash of recently released films all of which concerned the Holocaust in one way or another. Heilbrunn sets the tone for his whole critique by citing a scene from one of those films: "Toward the end of the new film about postwar Germany 'The Reader,' a Holocaust survivor in New York curtly instructs a visiting German lawyer named Michael Berg that he would do well to remember that the camps were neither a form of therapy nor a university. 'Nothing,' she says, 'came out of the camps. Nothing.'" Heilbrun insists that the films at issue, including *The Reader*, end up forgetting that point, by making the Holocaust serve some sort of "narrative of redemption."

Later, however, at the beginning of his own two-paragraph closing, Heilbrunn effectively takes back what he has earlier given the reader in that opening passage. "Perhaps," he writes at the end of his article, "nothing came out of the Holocaust other than the determination to prevent a repetition of the crimes." Yet with such an ending Heilbrunn, despite himself one may assume, undercuts the very critique he has just given. Having written that "the further the Holocaust recedes into the past, the more it's being exploited to create a narrative of redemption," he turns right around and offers nothing short of a redemption story of his own. Thus, he too ends up exploiting what, by his own lights, is never to be exploited.

Images of Avoidance

"Nothing like commemorating an event to make you forget it."

Graphic-artist Art Spiegelman makes that remark in Plate 10 of *In the Shadow of No Towers*, his graphic-novel on September 11, 2001. Spiegelman, the son of Holocaust survivors, earlier won the Pulitzer Prise for *Maus*, his two-volume graphic novel of the Holocaust and its aftermath in the lives not only of survivors themselves but also of their offspring. A native of New York who has lived there all his life, he and his wife and children were in the city when the attacks on the Twin Towers occurred.

In a two page essay that begins *In the Shadow of No Towers* Spiegelman tells the reader that in the first few days after 9/11 he 'got lost constructing conspiracy theories about [the American] government's complicity in what had happened.' Then he writes: "Only when I heard paranoid Arabs and Americans blaming it all on the Jews did I reel myself back in, deciding it wasn't essential to know precisely how much my 'leaders' knew about the hijackings in advance—it was sufficient that they immediately instrumentalized the attack for their own agenda."

What is at issue in cases such as the second one Spiegelman mentions, involving something such as a governmental co-optation of trauma for its own purposes, fits generally within the category of what, for one, Dominick LaCapra, a contemporary American historian with special expertise in trauma studies, especially as it pertains to the Holocaust, calls "founding traumas." That is, what is at issue is the use of a trauma for the purposes of justifying and then repeatedly reinforcing some institution or institutionalized behavior, as the Holocaust itself is used to justify the foundation of the state of Israel after World War II, and then extended to justify Israel's ongoing policies toward the Palestinians and toward neighboring Arab states into the present. Similarly, the Bush administration used "9/11" as a "founding trauma" to justify the wars in Afghanistan and Iraq, passage and implementation of the Patriot Act, holding "enemy combatants" indefinitely without trial in Guantanamo, "rendition" of prisoners to countries practicing torture, and so forth.

The other case Spiegelman mentions, that of his "paranoid Arabs and Americans blaming it [9/11] all on the Jews," fits a different category that LaCapra also addresses. As an example of this second category LaCapra also uses the figure of "the Jew," only in his case is it the use of that figure by the Nazis to justify the "final solution" of "extermination" of millions in the Holocaust. Concerning this category of what, following Spiegelman, we can appropriately call the instrumentalization of trauma, LaCapra writes in *History and Memory after Auschwitz* (p. 187): "Particularly when one avoids recognizing the sources of anxiety in oneself (including elusive sources that are not purely empirical or historical in nature), one may be prone to project all anxiety-producing forces onto a discreet other who becomes a scapegoat or even an object of quasi-sacrificial behavior in specific historical circumstances."

At any rate, although Spiegelman himself in the lines cited above—about "paranoid Arabs and Americans blaming it all on the Jews," on the one hand, and the official American governmental response of using the attack to further its "own agenda," on the other—may conflate the two kinds of cases, there are important distinctions that need to be drawn between the two categories of such instrumentalization involved. In the next chapter ("Representation and Trauma II: The Image of Sovereignty") I will discuss the crucial differences between the two in greater detail. For my purposes in this present chapter, however, what interests me is not how the two cases differ from one another. Rather, it is the *similarity* between the two, such that they can come to be coupled as Spiegelman couples them. What is it about the two, such that reflecting on one can yield insight into the other?

Apparently, what connects them for Spiegelman is simply that both do indeed involve an "instrumentalization" of the attacks on 9/11. Both involve treating the attacks as mere means for achieving prior, independent ends—that is, ends prior to and independent of the response that the attacks themselves demand of us. Both deflect the impulse to respond to the attacks themselves, directing it into preset channels, and *distorting* it in the process.

What is at issue in both cases, then, would be literally a *making-use* of the attacks, a *giving usage* to them. Thereby, the attacks are forced to make sense, rather than allowed to stand there in their full awfulness as the horrifyingly senseless catastrophe that they truly are.

Such shanghaiing of trauma to do service for some outside agenda has about it the same air of offense, even of obscenity, that for so many observers accompanied the incessant media loop of images of the attacks on Manhattan's Twin Towers, especially the images of men and women, sometimes hand in hand, jumping to their deaths rather than suffering immolation. Spiegelman himself is not unaware of the connection, as he demonstrates by writing, on the second page of the same opening essay on the first page of which he remarks on the two cases of "instrumentalizing" 9/11, that he "wanted to sort out the fragments of what I'd experienced from the media images that threatened to engulf what I actually saw." Indeed, the instrumentalization of the 9/11 attacks and the flood of images of them in the mass media worked together, each feeding and reinforcing the other, to increase the threat of such inundation, in which the events themselves would be buried beneath the waves, at risk of sinking so deep into the sea of images as eventually to be beyond all possibility of salvage and recall.

The same inseparability of the proliferation of images of trauma and the instrumentalization of it is already manifest in the simple attempt to "get over" trauma, even aside from any commitments to special causes, such as both of Spiegelman's examples involve—as does LaCapra's, of the Nazi use of the image of "the Jew." The mere endeavor to "put it behind us" in order to "go on with our lives" already contains, in effect, a betrayal of the traumatized, including ourselves when we are among the wounded. Thus, for example, Thomas Zengotita wrote of Americans in a piece called "The Numbing of American Mind: Culture as Anaesthetic" a few months after 9/11 in the April 2002 edition of *Harpers* magazine that—at least "if we were spared a gaping wound in the flesh and blood of personal life" as the result of losing someone close to us personally—"we inevitably moved on after September 11." He then expresses clearly the connection between "moving on" and the reduction of 9/11 to images: "We were carried off by endlessly proliferating representations of the event. . . . Conditioned thus relentlessly to move from representation to representation, we got past the thing itself as well; or rather, the thing itself was transformed into a sea of signs."

In fact, even for someone who does suffer significant personal loses, leaving "a gaping wounds in the flesh and blood of personal life," as Zengotita says, the same process of "moving on" still typically occurs eventually, though it may take prolonged therapy for that to happen. Indeed, the very production of any representation of trauma, any encapsulating of trauma in an image—which production or encapsulation does indeed, to borrow Zengotita's fitting word, "inevitably" occur after trauma—serves that same process at least to some degree. Inevitably, then, even apart from all betrayal by others, traumatized persons, in all their flesh and blood concretion and with all their gaping wounds, will betray themselves, substituting images or representations for "the thing itself," which here means the still surviving, deeply wounded traumatized person herself or himself. As Orly Lubin, Chair of the Department of Poetics and Comparative Literature of Tel Aviv, writes in "Masked Power: An Encounter with the Social Body in the Flesh," her contribution to the post-9/11 collection *Trauma at Home*, after citing Zengotita's remarks:

> Representation, then, is in the service of creating an imagined community that will provide an easily digested set of morals applicable to representations rather than to flesh and blood. The ethics of representation (should Jules Naudet photograph the two people on fire to show the world the results of the wickedness of the terrorists, or would that be invading their privacy?) replaces the ethics of policymaking, since the results of the latter are prevented from [reaching] the community as they do not become representations due to the ruling ethics of representation. The community provides the representation as a gateway away from the horrors of responsibility [for oneself as an individual] and then accountability [as belonging to a group].

I will return to Lubin's essay later in this chapter, when the time comes to address what alternative there may be to betraying trauma by burying it beneath a sea or signs, representations, or images. For now, however, what I want to emphasize is how accounts such as hers or Zengotita's allow us to begin to trace the betrayal of trauma and the traumatized back into the internal structure of trauma itself. What such accounts point to is, in fact, a characteristic that has been attributed to trauma at least since Freud, with his insistence on the peculiar temporality of trauma, which always involves what he calls "belatedness" (*Nachträlichkeit*). Freud's classic example, mentioned before, is of someone who lives through a serious train wreck with no immediately apparent ill effects from the accident, but who later—after a period of "latency," as Freud calls it—develops such symptoms as nightmares, problems sleeping, phobias, or other mental-behavioral difficulties. Thus, as has already been discussed in preceding chapters more than once before, the *manifestation* of any "wound," which is to say of any trauma itself, does not occur until some time *after* the presumably traumatic event itself first happened. It is as if the trauma, the wounding, does not occur when it first occurs, but only belatedly, as a sort of after-effect, an aftershock of an original shock.

In contemporary trauma studies a distinction is sometimes drawn between trauma resulting from a single significant event or episode, such as the railroad accident of Freud's definitive example, and trauma resulting from a series of repeated events or episodes, such as a child who has been traumatized by a long history of abuse. Trauma of the latter sort is sometimes called "recurrent" trauma.

However, given the 'belatedness' characteristic of trauma, at least in Freud's account of it, one might well argue that at bottom *all* trauma is "recurrent," so to speak. Insofar as trauma is defined by Freudian *Nachträglichkeit*, the very "occurrence" of trauma must be characterized in terms of a *re*-occurrence, as it were—the coming back around again of what was denied a place to take place in the first place, one might say.

To put the same point a bit differently, phenomenologically trauma always has the structure that Jean-Francois Lyotard in *Heidegger and "the jews,"* to which I have already referred more than once, calls a "double blow." He couples that notion with the distinction Freud draws—and which plays an even more important role in Jacques Lacan's rereading of Freud—between "originary" or "primary" repression and "secondary" repression.

"The *double blow*," according to Lyotard's description in *Heidegger and "the jews"* (on pages 15-16), "includes a first blow, the first excitation, which upsets [what Freud likes to call] the [psychic] apparatus with such 'force' that it is not registered.' Hence, in such 'originary repression,' in one sense nothing at all is 'repressed,' strictly speaking, since nothing has 'registered' in the first place, such that it would need to be or even could be 'repressed.' Accordingly, Lyotard writes: 'The discovery of [such] an originary repression leads Freud to assume that it cannot be represented. And it is not representable because, in dynamic terms, the quantity of energy transmitted by this 'shock' is not transformed into 'objects,' not even inferior ones, objects lodged in the substratum, in the hell of the soul, but it remains potential, unexploitable, and thus ignored by the apparatus"—though 'ignored' may be a misleading word here, since one can only ignore what is at least first given, whereas the 'first blow' is precisely one that is not at first given at all, exceeding as it does the very capacities of reception of the psychic 'apparatus.'

"The first blow, then," as Lyotard goes on to say, "strikes the apparatus without observable internal effect, without affecting it"—that is, without being felt in the first place, not even as a blow. Thus, what he calls the first blow "is a shock without affect."

The first blow, however, is not the only one. The first blow is eventually followed by a second one. Whereas the first blow is a shock without affect: 'With the second blow there takes place an affect without shock.' Lyotard's example shows that what he means is the 'belated' manifestation, in symptoms that appear only after a period of 'latency,' that there has been an earlier traumatic occurrence:

> I buy something in a store, anxiety crushes me, I flee, but nothing had really happened. . . . And it is this flight, that feeling that accompanies it, which informs consciousness *that* there is something, without being able to tell *what* it is. . . . The essence of the [traumatic] event: that *there is* comes before *what* there is.

This 'before' of the *quod* [the "that"] is also an 'after' of the *quid* [the "what"]. For whatever is now happening in the store (i.e., the terror and the flight) does not *come forth*; it *comes back* from the first blow, from the shock, from the 'initial' excess that remained outside the scene, even unconscious, deposited outside representation.

To this way of thinking, then, all trauma as such would have the paradoxical structure of a "return of the repressed" in which there is a re-turn of what was denied any turn in the first place, as we might say. In that sense, *all* trauma would be "recurrent" trauma.

What is more, the "recurrence" of the trauma in the appearance of symptoms after a period of latency is itself a matter of *representation*, in the sense of a substitution of *images* or *signs* for "the thing itself," Lyotard's "first blow"—that "'initial' excess" that does not itself really initiate anything, at least not anything "representable," since it has always "remained outside the scene, even unconscious, deposited outside [all] representation." Thus, this manifestation in belated symptoms, substituting representations, images, or signs for that which is always already *beyond* all representation, imagination, or signification, is necessarily a *distortion* and *falsification* of what it manifests. Such "secondary repression" thus becomes repression in the genuine sense of a pushing down and away, a burying, of what it pretends, in effect, to represent or signify. It becomes the *"willful* ignorance"—to borrow an expression that 20th century avant-garde American novelist John Hawkes uses, in *Adventures in the Alaskan Skin Trade*, to define "stupidity"—whereby the very victims of trauma themselves practice the denial and avoidance of the fact of their ever having been traumatized in the first place.

Thus, the belated symptoms that represent earlier trauma themselves turn out to be images of avoidance. The representing itself, as such, constitutes the "repression" of what, prior to its being *mis*-represented in the representing image, was not yet ever available, such that it might have been *pushed back down* (repressed) before then. The letting-come-forth and the pushing-back-down are *simultaneous*: The representation *re*-presents, in and as an image, what theretofore had never been given as *present* at all. The *re*-presentation is the manifesting *presentation* itself—the only one possible at all. Here, the *re*- has the sense of making that which it prefaces *emphatic*, rather than that of indicating an "again," at least in the ordinary sense of the duplication of a preceding original.

The Fiction of Trauma

Coincidentally, in the same January 9, 2009, Sunday *New York Times* that contained Jacob Heilbrunn's criticism of recent films depicting the Holocaust, discussed earlier in this chapter, there also appeared a book review by Richard Lourie of H. G. Adler's novel *The Journey*, first written shortly after World War II, but the English translation of which appeared only in 2008, the year before Lourie's review. As one learns from that review, as well as from translator Peter Filkins's introduction to the English version of the book itself, Adler was born in Prague in 1910 into a secularized Jewish family, and was himself a survivor of both Theresienstadt and Auschwitz. Adler survived eighteen other members of his family who died in the Nazi camps, including his wife, her mother, and his own parents. After liberation, Adler eventually settled in London, where he wrote, among other things, *The Journey*, detailing in fictionalized form his own journey during the Nazi era.

Both Lourie's review and Filkins's introduction, as well as Adler's son Jeremy Adler's afterword to *The Journey* also acquaint the reader with the journey of its own that Adler's book—written in German during 1950-1951, we are told in the son's afterword—itself had to take before it was finally published in Germany in 1962. In all three places—Richard Lourie's review, Peter Filkins's introduction, and Jeremy Adler's afterword — we are told that the influential German publisher Peter Suhrkamp vowed that the book would never be published in Germany, so long as he lived. And it wasn't. Even after publication, the book languished, little known and little read, until only recently, as is indicated by an English language translation not appearing until 2008.

Both Lourie and Filkins connect Suhrkamp's insistent stance against publishing the book at all, with the dominance at the time of the aesthetics of Theodor Adorno, who famously declared that literature was no longer possible after Auschwitz. Adorno argued that the very idea of transforming the horror of the Holocaust into fiction or poetry was morally unacceptable. It was blasphemous and obscene, to use the same terms I already used myself, in an earlier part of this chapter, to characterize any "exploitation," as Heilbrunn appropriately names it in his review of recent films focused on the Holocaust, of "Auschwitz" — any exploitation, that is, of all that that name has come to stand for—even and especially for the sake of telling any tale of redemption that would give the Holocaust meaning after the fact.

Interestingly, H. G. Adler himself refuses to tell any such redemption tale in *The Journey*. Nevertheless, the background story about his novel's own journey helps to focus the issue with which Adorno and many since him, including Heilbrunn and historian Dominick LaCapra, whom I also have already mentioned earlier in this chapter, are concerned. As we might put it, given the background of the history of Adler's novel, what is at issue is the morality of fictionalized representations of such shared, historically significant, intentionally perpetrated traumas as the Holocaust or, to give a later example, 9/11. Especially in such cases, does fictional representation of trauma and its victims cross over into perpetuation of the traumatic abuse involved?

The broader, framing question to which that of the morality of creating and disseminating fictional images of trauma belongs is the question of just where representation in images as such begins to cross over into morally treacherous territory. At just what point does such representation begin to risk falling into blasphemy and obscenity?

With regard to that general question, I want to maintain the following thesis: All other things being equal (note that important qualification), the *less* "fictional," which is to say the *more* "realistic," the representation or image, the greater the risk of such blasphemy and obscenity. To put the point hyperbolically, I might say that, with regard to such traumatic events as 'Auschwitz,' the more *photo*-graphic, the more *porno*-graphic. That is, the more closely the representing of such traumas comes to what Walter Benjamin called "mechanical reproduction," in his often-cited article "The Work of Art in the Age of Mechanical Reproduction,' as it does in photographic images, the more morally questionable it becomes: The closer representation comes to reproduction in and as such an image, the greater the risk of blasphemy and obscenity.

There is something *voyeuristic* about the fascination with which those who occupy a position of spectator with regard to the traumas of others look upon photographs of the suffering involved. Susan Sontag reflects on that voyeurism in *Regarding the Pain of Others*, her return after a quarter-century to the concerns she first addressed in *On Photography*, originally published in 1977. It is worth noting that in *Regarding the Pain of Others* she raises the issue of voyeurism in relation to photographs of trauma by first contrasting such photographic images to other visual images that, no matter how graphic and "realistic," involve imaginary, and in that sense fictional or "invented," events. Thus, she writes (page 42):

> An invented horror can be quite overwhelming. (I, for one, find it difficult to look at Titian's great painting of the flaying of Marsyas, or indeed at any picture of this subject.) But there is shame as well as shock in looking at the close-up of a real horror. Perhaps the only people with the right to look at images of suffering of this extreme order are those who could do something to alleviate it—say, the surgeons at the military hospital where the photograph was taken [as in an example she has earlier discussed]—or those who could learn from it. The rest of us are voyeurs, whether or not we mean to be.

Near the end of her book, Sontag returns to the same issue of the moral inappropriateness and illegitimacy of trafficking in photographic images of trauma, adding another dimension to her critique. In addition to opening the door to voyeuristic abuses, the proliferation of such images serves, even aside from the intentions of those involved in its production, the powers at work in the perpetration and perpetuation of trauma inflicted by some upon others. Thus, against the not uncommon idea that the dissemination of such images on television and in other mass media brings spectators to greater understanding and sympathy for the victims of traumatic abuse, Sontag writes (pages 102-103):

> The imaginary priority to the suffering inflicted on others that is granted by images suggests a link between the far-away sufferers—seen close up on the television screen—and the privileged viewer that is simply untrue, that is yet one more mystification of our real relations to power. So far as we feel sympathy, we feel that we are not accomplices to what caused the suffering. Our sympathy proclaims our innocence as well as our impotence. To that extent, it can be (for all our good intentions) an impertinent—if not an inappropriate response. To set aside the sympathy we extend to others beset by war and murderous politics for a reflection on how our privileges are located on the same map as their suffering, and may—in ways we might prefer not to imagine—be linked to their suffering, as the wealth of some may imply the destitution of others, is a task for which the painful, stirring images supply only an initial spark.

However, Sontag is not some sort of Luddite, calling for dismantling the engines that proliferate the images of others' sufferings. Her view in *Regarding the Pain of Others* is a carefully crafted, nuanced one in which she even takes issue with her only earlier views, as expressed in *On Photography*. It is not simply a matter of replacing the idea that the proliferation of such images creates sympathy with the idea that it deadens sympathy, as she had thought at the time she wrote that earlier book. Rather, it is a matter of reframing the entire discussion. Thus, just two pages after the passage cited immediately above, she writes in *Regarding the Pain of Others* (pages 105-106): "As much as they create sympathy, I wrote [in *On Photography*], photographs shrivel sympathy. Is this true? I thought it was when I wrote it. I'm not so sure now." Then she reframes the whole issue as follows:

> The question turns on a view of the principal medium of the news, television. An image is drained of its force by the way it is used, where and how often it is seen. Images shown on television are by definition images of which, sooner or later, one tires. What looks like callousness has its origins in the instability of attention that television is organized to arouse and to satiate by its surfeit of images. Image-glut keeps attention light, mobile, relatively indifferent to content. Image-flow precludes a privileged image. The whole point of television is that one can switch channels, that it is normal to switch channels, to become restless, bored. Consumers droop. They need to be stimulated, jump-started, again and again. Content is no more than one of these stimulants. A more reflective engagement with content would require a certain intensity of awareness—just what is weakened by the expectations brought to images disseminated by the media, whose leaching out of content contributes most to the deadening of feeling.

Two pages later, on page 108, she adds:

> Since *On Photography*, many critics have suggested that the excruciations of war—thanks to television—have devolved into a nightly banality. Flooded with images of the sort that once used to shock and arouse indignation, we are losing the capacity to react. Compassion, stretched to its limits, is going numb. So runs the familiar diagnosis. But what is really being asked for here? That images of carnage be cut back to, say, once a week? More generally, that we work toward what I called for in *On Photography*: an "ecology of images"? There isn't going to be an ecology of images. No Committee

of Guardians is going to ration horror, to keep fresh its ability to shock. And the horrors themselves are not going to abate.

"Images," Sontag later (on page 117) recapitulates the view that even she had once espoused, "have been reproached for being a way of watching suffering at a distance, as if," she importantly and ironically concludes, "there were some other way of watching." Then on the next page she continues:

> It is felt that there is something morally wrong with the abstract of reality offered by photography; that one has no right to experience the suffering of others at a distance, denuded of its raw power; that we pay too high a human (or moral) price for those hitherto admired qualities of vision [those that once caused the ancient Greeks to heap praise upon vision above all the other senses]—the standing back from the aggressiveness of the world which frees up for observation and for elective attention.

"But," Sontag replies against such contemporary disparagement of vision, in contrast to the original praise of it by Plato and the other ancient Greeks, "this is only to describe the function of the mind itself." Thus, she continues: "There is nothing wrong with standing back and thinking. To paraphrase several sages: 'Nobody can think and hurt someone at the same time.'"

Sontag knows, of course, that there is a perfectly ordinary sense of "thinking" in accordance with which it is all too easy to do just that, "think and hurt someone at the same time." In that sense, torture is always a very thoughtful activity: the torturer must plan ahead and be attentive to what he is doing, to cause the torture victim the maximum of pain, at maximal duration. In making her remark, however, Sontag is, as it were, thinking of "thinking" in the most highly morally responsive, contemplative sense—the very sense, I might add, that is supposedly at issue in philosophy.

In that high sense, a truly thoughtful response to "the pain of others" requires precisely the sort of distance that a photograph introduces between the viewer and what is in view in the photographic image. It is because of the power of photographs to create such necessary distance that, as Judith Butler has recently put it in *Frames of War: When Is Life Grievable?* (page 96): "In the last chapter of *Regarding the Pain of Others* [on page 115], Sontag seeks to counter her earlier critique of photography. In an emotional, almost exasperated outcry, one that seems quite different from her usual measured rationalism, Sontag remarks: 'Let the atrocious images haunt us.' "

On the next page, Butler again quotes the same line, calling it "Sontag's imperative." And, in fact, both Sontag's original discussion and Butler's later reflections on it serve to show that there is indeed a sort of moral obligation upon those who occupy the position of spectators in relation to the trauma of others—an obligation not to turn away from others' pain but, instead, precisely to look and see what they have suffered. Those who, voluntarily or involuntarily, find themselves in such a spectator's position are ordered, as it were, by the very spectacle they are given to see in such photographs of the pain of others, to continue to "regard" that very pain in those images. They are obligated, that is, to hold the pain of others so im-aged "in a firm, fixed gaze," a steady gaze in which, in the etymologically original sense of *regard*, they "keep guard" over that pain, *letting themselves be "haunted" by it*, as Sontag insists they should do.

However, Sontag's own remark, cited above, on page 42 of *Regarding the Pain of Others,* about her own difficulty in viewing such images as Titian's painting of the flaying of Marsyas, suggests that, paradoxically, it may well often be in just such "invented" images—such *fictions* or imaginative con-structions—that the imperative to continue to look and see others' pain speaks most clearly, most imperatively. That is not only because, as Sontag herself observes in the same passage, beholding the fictional or invented representation can engender in the spectator a pure horror, unadulterated by the shame at one's potential or actual voyeurism with which "real" or photographic representations tend to mix the horror. It is also because, as fictions—literally, things made or created—"invented" images carry the message of their own *having been made or created* as part of their very representational content. As I argued years ago in *The Stream of Thought*, following Heidegger's remarks along the same lines in "On the Origin of the Work of Art," that is one of the crucial ways in which "invented" images, to use Sontag's term, differ from photographs, especially those that count as what we call "snap-shots."

Significantly, to use Butler's own prime example for her discussion in "Torture and the Ethics of Photography: Thinking with Sontag," the second chapter in *Frames of War,* the notorious photographs of American torture of Muslim prisoners during the war in Iraq in the prison at Abu Ghraib were just such "snap-shots." As Butler's discussion makes clear, it is only insofar as those photographs have been taken up by others than their original producers and consumers (the American guards at Abu Ghraid themselves) and disemminated "outside the scene of [their] production," as Butler writes at the end of her chapter on Sontag (page 100), that their "circulation . . . has broken up the mechanism of disavowal, scattering grief and outrage in its wake." That is, she argues that it was only when such "outside" circulation occurred that the photographs of torture came to have the power to let us see the very "frame" that otherwise "blinds us to what we see." According to Butler, "if there is a critical role for visual culture during times of war it is precisely to thematize the forcible frame, the one that conducts the dehumanizing norm, that restricts what is perceivable and, indeed, what can be."

That means, however, that considered *in* the scene of their production and in terms of their representational content—what is actually photographically visible *within* that same scene—the photographs from Abu Ghraib just do *not* problematize that "forcible frame" itself. They presuppose it, rather than calling attention to it, and thereby leave it "out of the picture" altogether. Only when the photographs are, as it were, forced *out* of that "forcible frame," does the fact, manner, and significance of their own production, their own having been made, come "into the picture."

In contrast, it is in the "invented" visual image—or in the "fiction" in general—of torture and abuse that *what* is so brought into the image is itself revealed in its own having been made, its own having been invented. In the fiction, the fictive nature—which is to say the non-"natural"-ness, the artificiality, the "forc-ed"-ness—of what is represented, in the scene of its own production, its own making or invention, is brought to attention.

In sum: In the face of the fictional representation of trauma inflicted upon others, the spectator is brought face to face with the fic-tion, the pro-duction, of such trauma itself. The fictional trauma lets us see the fully fictional status of what purports to be an "act of God" in the sense that insurance companies use that expression to get themselves off the hook of liability for a disaster: The fiction of trauma in the "objective" sense (that is, the fiction "of" trauma in the sense of the fictive, as opposed to photographic, imaging of trauma) lets us see the fiction of trauma in the "subjective" sense (the sense in which trauma itself creates fictions, makes up stories, about itself).

That holds, at least, for trauma perpetrated by some upon others, as the American guards perpetrated trauma upon the prisoners they tortured at Abu Ghraib, or the Nazis perpetrated it upon the Jews. However, I will begin the next section of this chapter with some reflections suggesting that it holds for all trauma, not just for that in which we can distinguish per-petrators from victims. I will argue that the internal structure of trauma is such that trauma makes a fiction of itself.

Screen Memory

"Ruth" is a Jewish Berliner who survived Auschwitz. She is one of three such survivors the accounts of which make up the first part of French soci-ologist Michael Pollack's book *L'experience concentritionaire*. According to her own testimony, Ruth was an inmate in the camp at Auschwitz for a full *six months* before the reality of everything happening around her finally broke through into her own consciousness. Here is her own description of that moment:

> The selections in the camp (as opposed to the [camp] "infirmary" [where Ruth was assigned regular duties]) were perfectly unforeseeable and arbitrary, like the lottery. I lived

through six. One day, everyone standing and lined up [for a roll call] had to count off, from 1 to 514. And then they [the camp guards] said: from 501 to 514, one step forward. I was among the 14. Up to 500, all were led to the gas. Another time, we were made to count off, one-two. And the women numbered one disappeared. I began to comprehend. The next time, the same game: there, I was a one. But that time, it was the number twos who disappeared. I felt anguish, the fear of death. I broke out in a sweat, I went in my pants. But that time, it was the number twos who disappeared. . . . [ellipsis in original] One more time I escaped. Six times in all. But the third time, I was already completely apathetic. One day, I was working in the commando sorting clothes. It was a cellblock where we gathered all the clothes of the newly arrived, and we had to sort them according to their nature and their quality: shirts, pants, coats. . . And another commando had to unstitch the hems of the coats and the pants to search for currency the deportees might have hidden there. Actually, one found many things there. And it was the things of people being led straight to the gas! One day, I was sitting there and, among all the items, I came across a little baby bib on which "her mama's darling" was embroidered. At that, suddenly, my eyes were opened: but these are the things of those being killed! And look at you, in the middle of all that, and even you sometimes accept it. . . For me that was the grand revelation and a great shudder of horror. Do you understand? All at once, I said to myself that I could just as easily come across the blouse of my mother, being killed at the same moment. There, suddenly I understood what game was being played in the camp. It was a rational system the purpose of which was to exploit people and kill them. It was, so to speak, just simply an enterprise, a factory for killing people after having exploited their resources for work and after having used different parts of their body: hair, bones, etc. And those clothes, those mountains of glasses, of gold denture crowns, of little valises, all those goods were sent to Berlin. During at least six months, I stayed under my glass jar [namely, of her denial, her incomprehension]. I heard everything, I saw everything, but nothing came through to me. It was too incomprehensible, too unimaginable. The dead, the people beaten, the hung in front of whom one passed by. All that, I saw and heard it all fine, but I didn't realize. At the end of six months, I admitted to myself where I was: in a factory the sole function of which was murder.

Such an incredible ability to blind oneself to what one is seeing all too clearly—to stay asleep, as it were, in the face of such horror—was not only a strange gift given to such Holocaust survivors as Ruth. The same capacity for not knowing what one knows, not seeing what all one's senses clearly record, was also displayed by some of the perpetrators of the Holocaust. So, for example, even such a figure among the survivors as Primo Levi can come to write, in *The Drowned and the Saved*, his last work before his own death by apparent suicide, with a certain sympathy for Albert Speer.

Once Speer was finally released from Spandau and his memoirs had been published, Hety S., one of Levi's German correspondents—"among all my German readers," writes Levi (page 197), "she was the only one 'with clean credentials' and therefore not entangled in guilt"—visited him. Levi cites (page 196) Hety's remark, in one of her letters to him, that she believes Speer when that latter says that for him, too, 'the Auschwitz slaughter is a trauma.' Hety goes on to observe that in the postwar years Speer became 'obsessed by the question of how he could 'not want to see or know,' in short, [how he could] block everything out.' Hety adds that she does not think Speer is just 'trying to find justification,' that is, some rationalization of his own criminal behavior. Rather, she thinks Speer is genuinely at a loss to account for his own strange blindness to what was so obvious: 'he would like to understand what, for him, too, it is impossible to understand.'

In his introduction to *The Shell and the Kernel*, an influential collection of writings by the psychoanalysts Nicolas Abraham and Maria Torok,

Nicolas T. Rand writes that Abraham's and Torok's "most radical contribution to psychoanalytic theory" is "the claim that the patient may be the bearer of *someone else's* trauma." Yet the examples of both Ruth, the Holocaust survivor, and Speer, one of the main architects of the very camp system, suggest that for them, too, the trauma is experienced, as it were, as "someone else's." They lived in the midst of the trauma of the Holocaust itself as though nothing unusual was happening at all. As Ruth puts it, none of what was really occurring succeeded in "getting through" to them at the time. No more, for that matter, does the railroad accident in Freud's original example of trauma in *Beyond the Pleasure Principle* get through "at the time" of the imagined accident to Freud's imagined victim. Indeed, the very "belatedness" that Freud uses that example to capture—a belatedness definitive of trauma as such, according to him—assures that trauma will always belong to "someone else," at least until the period of "latency" comes to completion.

Trauma distorts and displaces, both spatially and temporally, and in the process it disconnects, disorients, dissociates, and, in general, *dis-appropriates*. Yet it is solely such radical *dis*-appropriation that makes anything either *appropriable* or even *appropriate*—in all senses of that term—possible in the first place. We might try to approach the point—or, more properly speaking, to respect the point in its always unbridgeable distance, its never more than asymptotic (un)approachability —by saying that all *temperance* as well as all *tempering*, whether of our metals or our emotions, as well, for that matter, as all taking of any *temperature*, depends upon an originary, though never itself original, *distemper*.

In just that sense, indeed, *time* and *space* themselves are *traumatic*.

So, for example, in *After God* American "postmodern" theologian Mark Taylor writes of the dislocation that defines time. At issue is not only the dislocation between past, present, and future, the self-division of time into its three dimensions. Rather, the dislocation at issue is also, and even more crucially, *within* each of those three temporal dimensions. It is an inescapable dislocation or dis-juncture or Heideggerian ex-stasis within each of time's three so called dimensions, which dislocation is what alone first of all makes possible the division into three temporal dimensions in their mutual interrelation, that interrelation constitutive of time itself as such. Of these three never crossing yet always interrelating dimensions themselves, Taylor writes (page 118): "This past that was never present eternally recurs as the future that never arrives to disrupt the present that never is. In this way, the originary absence of the past is the condition of the inescapable openness of the future. Since the past is never accessible, the present is never present, and the future is never closed."

Then, on the very next page (119) Taylor goes on to address the absence that defines *presence* itself not only in the temporal sense of being *now*, but also in the spatial sense of being *here*: "*The present, understood both temporally and spatially, is always gift or present* [that is, always a "present" in the sense of a gift] *pre-sent* [that is, literally sent in advance] *by (the) nothing that is (not) present.*" Thus, the very condition of the present's possibility lies in what itself is *always* "absent," always somewhere else some other time, never here and now—what itself can never be present at all and is, for that very reason, really no "something," no "what," at all, but, rather, a "nothing" in relation to whatever is or ever could be given or presented.

In "Carrots, Noses, Snow, Rose, Roses," a delightful essay in his collection *The World Within the Word* (page 288), philosopher and avant-garde novelist William H. Gass imagines a "discornered dunce" who comes across a snowman only "persistently to wonder what a carrot [is] doing in this mound of snow: pointing at it, laughing, and then growing suspicious when we told him he was looking at a nose (not a snownose, naturally, yet the nose of a snowman)." Gass remarks that, were we to come across such a discornered dunce, "we should have to conclude that he hadn't grasped the set of crossed contexts which establishes the figure, and therefore that he couldn't understand the carrot's ontological transformation."

What Gass means by that term "ontological transformation" can be grasped easily from the example of the snowman. To stick a carrot in a properly shaped mound of snow and thereby finish building a snowman does not change anything in the carrot itself. It does not alter, add, or delete any characteristics from the carrot: its color, shape, size, texture, weight, etc., all remain the same. Thus, to become a snowman's nose the carrot does not undergo any "ontic" modification whatever, as Gass (or Heidegger) would say. Yet by being placed in a new context of connections and significations, in understanding which we also come to understand—and literally to see and experience—the carrot in an altogether new way, the carrot has undergone a complete transformation in its "being," rather than its characteristics or properties, a thoroughgoing "ontological" transformation, as opposed to any "ontic" one.

Indeed, to undergo such total ontological change even *requires* that the carrot remain ontically altogether *un*-changed. Gass puts it well by noting that it is only "[b]ecause of its natural shape," to take the feature of the carrot that is key for making a snowman's nose out of it, that, thanks to the "new relations it has entered" when we place it in the mound of snow, the carrot can undergo such a profound ontological transformation that "the carrot does not simply stand for or resemble a nose, *it literally is a nose now*—the nose of a specific snowman."

Before leaving Gass and his snowman, it is also important for my present purposes to note that making what we can call, following his usage, an *ontological* mistake is very different from making any mistake of an *ontic* sort. For example, as I wrote years ago when discussing Gass's remarks in a different context in *The Stream of Thought* (pages 7-8):

> Failing to see that a carrot is a snowman's nose (ontological) is not like confusing one thing with another—mistaking cherries for grapes, for example (ontic). In the second case, the mistake can be corrected through closer observation or, in general, through obtaining new information. In the first case, however, no new information about carrots and snow can possibly correct the error. It can only be corrected by learning a new context for the evaluation of the available information.

The sort of "mistake" that allows Ruth to be an inmate in Auschwitz for six full months before finally coming to see and understand just what Auschwitz *is*, or the "mistake" Speer makes by the account of Hety S., Primo Levi's German correspondent, which lets Speer go about his business without ever letting himself know just what sort of a murderous business he is really about, is an ontological, not an ontic, mistake.

What is more, it is the very mistaking of just what sort of mistake is at issue in such cases—a sort of second-order mistake in which one mistakes the difference between an ontological mistake and an ontic one—that itself first makes such ontological mistakes not merely *possible*, but even, at least within certain limits, inevitable, which is to say *necessary*. It is not just sometimes and in some places that we can become "discornered dunces." Rather, *in time*—taking that phrase at full face value, so that it means, "insofar as we are 'temporal' at all"—we are all always and everywhere such dunces. And we can and must everywhere always come to the truth only through recovery from our ontological mistakes.

It is exactly by making a sort of second-order mistake, that is, a mistaking of the difference between two very different ways of making mistakes—namely, in this case, "ontically" and "ontologically," to use the terminology of Gass and Heidegger (at least the early Heidegger)—that is at issue when contemporary American historian and trauma theorist Dominick LaCapra warns against confusing what he calls "historical trauma" with what he calls "structural trauma." By the former, LaCapra means a trauma that can be traced back to a datable occurrence, such as a train wreck, to use Freud's example, or such as the attacks on the World Trade Center on September 11, 2001. In contrast, what LaCapra calls structural trauma is trauma that cannot be reduced to the effects of any single datable occurrence or, in fact, even any series of such occurrences, but that, as the name implies, somehow belongs to the very structure of human experience as such, either universally or in some more limited frame of consideration.

According to LaCapra, it is important not to confuse one of those two sorts of trauma, historical or structural, with the other. To reduce the one to the other is, as he puts it in *Writing History, Writing Trauma,* (page 82), to commit one of two possible errors. On the one hand, one can fall into error by coming "to generalize structural trauma so that it absorbs or subordinates the significance of historical trauma." On the other hand, instead of reducing historical trauma to structural trauma, one can commit an opposite and equal error by trying, "on the contrary, to explain all post-traumatic, extreme, uncanny phenomena and responses as exclusively caused by particular events or contexts.' 'When structural trauma is reduced to, or figured as, an event,' he writes, 'one has the genesis of myth [in the negative sense of that term whereby a myth is a sort of 'false story'] wherein trauma is enacted in a story from which later traumas seem to derive (as in Freud's primal crime or in the case of original sin attendant upon the Fall from Eden)." LaCapra adds that this second error, that of reducing structural trauma to something historical, involves 'what one might term *reductive contextualism*," of which he uses as an example "deriving anxiety in Heidegger's thought [where it plays a major role, at least in *Being and Time* and other early works] exclusively from conditions in interwar Germany."

LaCapra prefaces his discussion of these two equal but opposite errors, both of which involve confusing structural with historical trauma, by remarking that "[t]he belated temporality of trauma and the elusive nature of the shattering experience related to it render the distinction between structural and historical trauma problematic," although, he adds, they "do not make it irrelevant." Yet, so far as I can see, LaCapra himself nowhere specifies clearly just *how*—and *where*—the distinction must be *problematized*, in order adequately to accommodate the two factors he mentions (the "belatedness" of trauma and its "shattering" quality).

In my judgment, fellow American trauma theorist Paul Eisenstein is more helpful than LaCapra on that score. In *Traumatic Encounters*, which I've cited before, Eisenstein insists—correctly, I am convinced—that what LaCapra calls "historical" trauma *presupposes* what LaCapra calls "structural" trauma. In effect, to put Eisenstein in my own words, what makes any datable occurrence traumatic in the first place is that it focuses, both revealing and concealing at once, a *structural* fault or gap that pervades and disrupts experience itself "from within," as it were, to use the way Taylor puts the point in the passage I cited above, about time in its three dimensions.

We might also profitably put the point by using Freud's well-known notion of the "screen memory," though introducing an ambiguity into that term that is not present, or at least not obviously so, in Freud's own usage. That is, we might well say that any datable occurrence can come to be *traumatic* precisely and only insofar as it functions as a "screen" for the underlying structural trauma, in a *double* sense of "screening." By the first of the two senses at issue, a "screen" would be something that *masks, dissembles,* or *covers-over* whatever it provides a screen for, screening it off from view. But by the second sense of the term, a "screen" would be, rather, something that served as a sort of *projection surface*, as a movie screen provides such a surface for projecting filmed images.

Putting all the pieces together, I would argue that, to paraphrase Spinoza, nothing is ever traumatic, save screening make it so. Precisely *because* of its in-dissociable "belated" and "shattering" qualities, to use LaCapra's own terms, what he calls "structural" trauma must and can *take place*—literally: make and hold a place for itself—only by *screening* (i.e., maskingly projecting) itself as a specific image—screening itself, in short, *as* "historical" trauma. In turn, "historical" trauma is not a *kind* of trauma distinct from "structural" trauma as another kind. Rather, historical trauma is the *taking place of* structural trauma itself. Only insofar as some datable occurrence has the features that make it suitable for being so employed, that is, for serving as such a screen in the double sense at issue, can such an occurrence, when "taken over" by a structural fault for so screening itself, be traumatic.

After all, what is traumatic for one person may not be so for another. For example, sometimes the break-up of a marriage or other long-term relationship will leave one or both parties no more affected, at least visibly, that a scraped knee, whereas for another couple it is more like a heart attack or a stroke. The difference is no more a matter of the ontic properties of one occurrence compared to another, than it is a matter of such ontic properties that differentiates a carrot ready for eating from one already in use as a snowman's nose. Just as what makes the carrot into a nose is a matter of ontological, as opposed to ontic, transformation, to use Gass's way of putting it, so is what makes an occurrence traumatic the same sort of transformation. In both cases, carrot-nose and occurrence-trauma, what is at issue is establishing a new set of crossed contexts and significations, as Gass puts it.

Of course, it is only thanks to its ontic properties that a given datable event will offer itself to serve as such as place for structural fault to take its own place. In the same way, it is only thanks to its ontic properties that a carrot is suited to become a snowman's nose, but a cabbage or a leaf of lettuce is not. Not every surface is equally suitable to become a screen.

LaCapra writes in *Writing History, Writing Trauma* (page 84) that structural trauma 'may not be cured but only lived with in various ways. Nor,' he then adds, 'may it be reduced to a dated historical event or derived from one." But, to speak paradoxically, neither can an "historical" trauma be "cured," nor can it 'be reduced to a dated historical event." To put the paradox most sharply, we can say that a *dated* historical event is as such no longer an *historical* event at all! History is not, in that sense, a series of datable events. It is never just 'one damned thing after another.' If it were, then it would altogether lose its *event*-ful-ness, the very quality whereby not everything that happens is as such an "historical" event, but only those things the happening of which is genuinely "an event." Becoming "historical" is itself a matter of ontological, not ontic, transformation.

A lesson from Heidegger that we can profitably apply is that the very distinction between what, following him and Gass, I have been calling "ontic" and "ontological" is one to which the *masking* of that very distinction, the *confusing* of the two, a confusion wherein the ontic and the ontological keep getting mixed up with one another, is itself essential to the very distinction—in the active or verbal sense of actually distinguishing, of drawing or accomplishing the task of differentiating between the one and the other—itself. That is, the only way in which the distinction—now in the nominal sense—between the two can get drawn is in setting underway the ongoing distinction in the verbal sense, that is, the ongoing struggle to sort the one out from the other, a struggle that can never end, without simply eradicating all distinction (nominal sense) whatever.

That, in turn, allows me to return to the passage from Mark Taylor that I cited before (from page 119 of his book *After God*): "*The present, understood both temporally and spatially, is always gift or present pre-sent by (the) nothing that is (not) present.*" Significantly, a few lines later Taylor draws the connection between this idea of a unique absence that alone makes presence itself possible, but only in such a way that such absence continues always to disrupt the presence of any present, with the idea of representation and the unrepresentable. Observing that what can never be present, as that absence definitive of presence can never be, also cannot, for that very reason, be represented (that is, literally, *re*-presented, with the *re*- taken in the sense of "again": what cannot ever be presented in the first place can hardly be presented *again*), Taylor concludes that representation itself "includes, as a condition of its possibility, 'something' that remains irreducibly urepresentable." Then he draws a connection that is especially important for my present purposes: "Expressed in terms of figuration: inasmuch as figuring can never be figured, every figure is always disfigured as if from within."

"Figuring," in the sense at issue in Taylor's remark, is the sketching or projecting of something in a figure. It means, then, in that sense, representing in an image, a "representation" in the nominative sense. We can thus rephrase Taylor to say that, since representing as such can never be represented, every representation (that is, every image) is always *mis*-represented "as if from within."

This disfiguration in every figure, which is to say the misrepresentation in every representation, "as if from within," points to the key relationship between trauma and figure—that is, representation, or image. In brief, the relationship between the two is such that every trauma, every traumatic event, as such, projects itself into and as some representation, some figure or image, that, precisely as such a projection, simultaneously both discloses and hides the very event so projected. To *take place* at all, a traumatic event *must* project itself in a representation, a figure or image. Yet that representation, that figure or image, cannot but cover over and conceal the very same event, *denying* it any *place to take*.

Riven by the Freudian belatedness definitive of it, trauma never "presents" itself. Instead of ever "presenting" itself, trauma can only "*re*-present itself," in a sense related to, but different from, Taylor's use of that term. It can *only* present itself "*again*," yet without every having presented itself for a "first time." To be trauma, it can never present itself "in person," but, rather, can only present itself through a "representation," in the sense of an image or figure, that functions as a "representative" in the sense of a "stand in," someone or something that "stands for" some other one or thing in some aspect or relation, to borrow Charles Sanders Peirce's definition of a "sign."

Furthermore, any such representation functions as an archive in which what has figured, sketched, or traced itself there—left a trace of itself there—is preserved, and from which it can be recalled by activating that archive, that trace. Any representation or figure in which trauma projects itself is just such a trace. As such, it is a *memory* of the trauma that traces itself in and into that image or figure.

However, insofar as any such representation or figure always necessarily *mis*represents or *dis*figures what it represents or figures, it is always a covering over and hiding of what it represents or figures. Consequently, every such memory image wherein trauma projects itself is of necessity simultaneously a "cover-memory." In short *every* memory of trauma is a "*screen memory.*"

Any representational image or figure in which trauma projects and traces itself serves that same archiving function. The photographic accuracy of the representation does not matter. That is, whether the memory is "true" or "false" in *that* sense is altogether unimportant. Indeed, if anything, the more photographically accurate the memory of a trauma may be, the greater becomes its potential to keep attention focused on itself, and to confuse trauma with its own figure or image—a sort of idolatry of the sign.

Scanning the Screen

In *Writing History, Writing Trauma* Dominick LaCapra follows up his remark, cited earlier in this chapter, about what he calls "structural" trauma not being curable—and thereby also suggesting that for him what he calls "historical trauma" *is* somehow 'curable" — by commenting (on page 83) on a view he sees as common to various other contemporary American historians. According to LaCapra, the other historians at issue seem to take it for granted that "once there was a single narrative that most Americans accepted as part of their heritage," but which has more recently been shattered into a multiplicity of diverse stories (one story for white Americans, another for black; one for men, another for women; one for straights, one for gays; etc.). LaCapra critiques such an idea as being "close to reductive contextualism . . . in which the proverbial past-we-have-lost becomes the metanarrative we have lost." Against such an idea, LaCapra expresses doubt that any such common American metanarrative ever really existed. Rather, "one might argue,' he writes, 'that there never was a single narrative and that most Americans never accepted only one story about the past."

But, *pace* LaCapra, one might also argue that the other historians at issue could be taken to be sharing, with one another and with unspecified "others," what amounts to a *screen memory* in the sense I have been trying to articulate. In that case, one would not be dealing in the first place with any simple "empirical" claim that a grand American metanarrative once existed, a claim that others might then deny (as LaCapra denies it). One would be dealing, instead, with a truth the "truth" of which was itself *traumatic*, in effect. The issue of determining the "truth" of the screen memory at issue would then no longer consist of checking for correspondences between the empirical claim that there once was such a common American metanarrative, on the one hand, and "what really happened" empirically, on the other. Rather, determining the "truth" of the widespread assumption that there once was such a metanarrative would consist of carefully unknotting the various interconnections of disclosure and concealment at play in that very notion. Accordingly, what would be required would be to treat that idea as symptomatic, in effect, of the very traumatic "structural" fissures that have indeed fractured and fragmented American society throughout its history—those very divisions that the notion of a common metanarrative both hides and reveals at one and the same time. To "understand" the idea of such a common American metanarrative would require that we "read" it in terms of that traumatic subtext, just as a Freudian analyst would "read" a slip of the tongue, for example. To remain fixated on the question of the degree of photographic "accuracy" of the idea of a common American metanarrative, and to think that one could dispel that idea by pointing out its "inaccuracy," as LaCapra tries to do, would then be to fall prey to the same sort of ontological confusion as Gass's "discornered dunce" who fails to grasp the context that establishes a carrot as a snowman's nose.

To cite another important example that raises the same underlying issues, in the 1990s verbal battles in the media and culture in general, as well as legal ones in the courts, broke out in the United States over a series of sensational, highly publicized cases in which criminal charges were brought against various defendants on the basis of purported victims' "recovered memories" of theretofore supposedly "repressed" experiences of childhood sexual abuse. The focus of nearly all public debate at the time and since has been on whether the supposedly "recovered" memories at issue were "true" memories—that is, empirically accurate memory images of something that empirically "really happened"—or whether they were, instead, "false" memories—images presenting themselves as memories but that had been somehow unintentionally (or at least presumably so) "implanted" in the minds of those who eventually leveled the charges of abuse, to which, however, no actual past occasion of abuse "really" corresponded.

Both sides to the debate—those, for example, who called upon everyone to "believe the [at least erstwhile] children" who claimed to "remember" having been abused, on the one side, and those who developed the concept of "false memory syndrome" and promoted the idea that most if not all of the charges in the most highly publicized cases of the time were made by persons who suffered from such a syndrome, on the other side—continued to operate with an understanding of memory in accordance with which the "truth" or "falsity" of a memory image is taken to be a matter of the image more or less photographically corresponding, or failing to correspond, to "reality," to "what really happened." For the most part, what was and has continued to be lacking in the entire debate has been any consideration of what I have been trying to articulate here as the "screen" nature of *all* memories of trauma, *regardless* of how photographically "accurate" or "inaccurate" they may be. However, it is just that *screening* relationship between trauma and the images in which trauma figures or represents itself that must be fully considered in any final assessment of what is at issue in all cases such as those infamous childhood sexual abuse ones of the 1990s.

What is needed for such an assessment is an analysis of the "memories" at issue in terms that proceeds along the same lines as Michael Pollack follows in a different but closely related context—that of assessing the testimonies of Auschwitz survivors—in his *L'expérience concentrationnaire*, which I have already cited before in this chapter (for the story of Ruth, the Jewish

Auschwitz survivor from Berlin). In a lucid discussion of his own methodology in the introduction to the second part of his book, Pollack reflects upon the methods adopted by many other researches addressing the same material, namely, testimonies from Holocaust survivors.

Knowing that every testimony is subject to doubt with regard to its "accuracy," many researchers conclude that any testimony must therefore be treated with suspicion to arrive at an "objective" assessment of its veracity and value. Accordingly, it is standard for such researchers to follow procedures to eliminate the supposedly "subjective" aspects of the testimonies with which they are concerned.

As a good example of someone who adopts that approach, Pollack himself cites fellow Holocaust researcher Miriam Novitch, from her book *Les Passages des Barbares*, a study on the deportation and resistance of Greek Jews during the Second World War. Novitch writes (page 5, as cited in Pollack, page 181): "Knowing that all testimony is subject to caution, we strove to interrogate several people on the same subject and to verify the facts recounted by means of other sources."

"In so proceeding," Pollack comments, after citing Novitch's line, "one eliminates what cannot be confirmed by a multiplicity of sources, toward the end of reconstructing the hard core of what really happened. But one risks by the same token occluding the tension, constitutive of testimony on the deportations, between what can be spoken, and what is unspeakable [*entre dicible et indicible*]." He then contrasts such a procedure with what he and his colleagues adopted as the methodology for their own work. Contrary to the approach such researchers as Novitch adopt, Pollack writes, the "problematic" for him and his fellow interviewers in their own work was based on the supposition "that every document has a sense, on condition of restoring the system for locating this sense." That is, in their own procedure he and his colleagues were not focused on the supposed "historical accuracy" of the accounts their interviewees gave, but, rather, on coming to an understanding of the *sense* or *meaning* of what they recounted or recalled *as it functioned in the context of their own ongoing endeavor to "maintain their social identity*," to put it in terms of the subtitle Pollack gives his book ("an essay on the maintenance of social identity").

Pollack's own approach, then, is basically the same as that of Dori Laub when, in a passage I have already cited and discussed in an earlier chapter, he responds to a group of historians who want to discount an Auschwitz survivor's recollection of multiple Auschwitz crematoria smokestacks being destroyed during the *Sondercommando* inmate rebellion at Auschwitz. The historians Laub was addressing wanted to dismiss that survivor's testimony because "in reality" only one crematorium smokestack was destroyed during the incident in question. However, Laub responds that what he calls the genuine "historical truth" of the testimony is expressed by the very supposed "mistake," insofar as, in the circumstances of Auschwitz, *any* act of rebellion among the inmates there was as such—independent of its "success" by ordinary ways of measuring such things—a complete success in terms of revealing the total vacuity of the Nazi claims of superiority and domination upon which the whole camp system was based. The genuinely historical truth of the supposedly "inaccurate" memory was that it altogether "accurately" reflected what the mere fact of there being a rebellion at all at Auschwitz demonstrated beyond doubt—namely, in effect, to use the relevant line from the fairytales of Hans Christian Anderson, that "the emperor had no clothes."

What is necessary, to grasp "historical truth" itself, in Laub's sense of that term—which is in fact the only sense that makes any sense, if we are to let history itself happen, rather than flattening it down to the level of some idiotic story of "one damned thing after another"—is to follow the procedure that Pollack recommends. "Rather than concentrating attention on the content of what is said," he writes, we need to attend to the various conditions that shape the given content of a given testimony, in order to recreate the set of crisscrossing connections that allow us to discern the *sense* of that content.

That does not at all mean that independent verification, comparison of accounts from diverse sources, and, in general, efforts carefully to sort out "what really happened" at the level of surface information that might have been registered by cameras, tape-recorders, or other such archiving devices, is not relevant. What it means, however, is that all such information, however accurate and exhaustive it may be in its own terms, is never more than raw data, as it were, that must be *interpreted* properly, if it is ever to yield genuine insight into what really *did* "happen," in the strong sense of that term—what really "made history" rather than just being one more link in the endless chain of "one damned thing after another."

The issue that confronts us in assessing testimonies of trauma is finally the same as that which confronts the psychoanalyst in addressing the symptoms of neurosis in verbal slips, physical tics, and dreams—the same issue as that to which Lacan points when he says that the unconscious is structured "like a language." One way we might make the point required here is to say that all such phenomena as "Freudian slips," neurotic tics, or dream-images—*or trauma testimonies*—function as *symbols*, in the sense that, for example, Paul Ricoeur captures in *The Symbolism of Evil*.

As Ricoeur uses the term, a "symbol" is not a "conventional sign," as it is in C. S. Peirce's threefold division of signs into "icon, index, and symbol." Rather, as Ricoeur uses the term, "symbols" are (page 18), "analogical meanings which are spontaneously formed and immediately significant, such as defilement, analogue of stain; sin, analogue of deviation; guilt, analogue of accusation." Ricoeur's examples (defilement, sin, guilt) are drawn from the domain with which his book is concerned, the domain, as the book's title indicates, of the symbols wherein humanity expresses its experience of evil, or "fault," as Ricoeur often prefers to put it. With regard to evil or fault, a few pages before the definition of *symbol* just cited Ricouer makes an observation that, as his own subsequent remark indicates he realizes, applies in general to the "spontaneously formed and immediately significant" symbols with which human beings articulate their own self-experience. "In short," he writes (page 9), "the preferred language of fault appears to be indirect and based on imagery." Then, in the very next sentence he broadens his focus to include all symbols, so defined, and not just symbols of evil: "There is something quite astonishing in this: the consciousness of self seems to constitute itself at its lowest level by means of symbolism and to work out an abstract language only subsequently, by means of a spontaneous hermeneutics of its primary symbols."

The images in which trauma fixes itself, those same images that trauma survivors then recall and recount in their testimonies, are just such "primary symbols." Embedded in the testimonies of trauma, however, those traumatic images, are subject to a *double distortion*, as my earlier discussion of two sets of remarks, one from Mark Taylor and the other from Michael Pollak, already suggests. First, as Mark Taylor observes, at the very heart of figuration itself there is a sort of distortion or disfiguring. That is perhaps most clearly evident precisely in the symbols—that is, remembering Ricoeur's definition, the "spontaneously formed and immediately significant" images or representations, including purely verbal ones, wherein those struck by trauma articulate their own self-experience, as so struck—of trauma. Following Ricoeur, we might call this level of distortion of the images that emerge in trauma testimony *primary distortion*, since it occurs at the level of what Ricoeur calls "primary symbols."

In turn, to this first or primary distortion is added a second one. That is the *secondary distortion*, we might call it, introduced by the play of the conditions under which the later testimony is called forth, and in which the primary symbols of trauma, already subject to a primary distortion, are integrated into *narratives of trauma*. Since, as Ricoeur himself insists, "primary symbols" themselves never occur in a vacuum, but are, instead, only encountered *within* more or less explicit narratives that are finally no less "spontaneously formed and immediately significant" than the primary symbols they contain and contextualize, these narratives, too, are themselves symbolic. Therefore, they too can only be "read"—and thereby *understood*—by a scanning that focuses, as we can put it, combining insights from Pollack and William Gass, not on the degree of some sort of quasi-photographic "accuracy" of the images taken at the level of their "contents," but, rather, on restoring the set of crisscrossing connections that alone allow us to "locate [their] sense" (Pollack).

To "read" the doubly distorting symbols of trauma requires us, accordingly, to scan them alert *for* the distortions they introduce, and then to follow, in effect, the "drift" of those very distortions. To come to understand the testimonies of trauma, then, we must let ourselves, as it were, be carried away by and in the drift *of* the very distortions, both "primary" and "secondary," that those testimonies themselves effect. Those distortions are not to be thought of as needing or even being subject to any possible "correction" that would, even if only "in theory" and not "in fact," somehow *eliminate* those distortions to yield some no longer distorted, "accurate" image or representation.

With regard to what I have called primary distortion, that is, the disfiguration at the heart of all figuration, all fixing—all bringing-to-stand-and-putting-into-play—in a figure, to "eliminate" the distortion would to abandon representation, figuration, as such. Or, if figures and figuration are still to remain somehow, it would be tantamount to giving up the whole attempt to *understand* the remaining figures or representations at all. To paraphrase closely Ricoeur's closing remark in his introduction to *The Symbolism of Evil* (page 24), anyone who wished to escape such primary distortion and to stand apart from the game in the name of some non-distorting "objectivity" would "at the most know everything but understand nothing." Indeed, as Ricoeur adds: "In truth, he would seek nothing, not being motivated by concern about any question."

Similarly, to attempt to "correct" the secondary distortion that occurs with the embedding of the primary symbols of trauma in testimony-narratives is to miss altogether what is most distinctive about such narratives—their own status as "second-order" symbols themselves. Once again, any gain in supposed clarity that one might thereby gain would be purchased at the price of all possibility of discerning the very meaning of what is so clarified. What one would have left might be clear, but it would no longer have any meaning.

Ricoeur writes at one pivotal point (page 235) in the second part of *The Symbolism of Evil*, the part devoted to reflection on the narrative myths in which, at the level of second-order symbolism, the primary symbols of evil are put in play, to understand such myths "it must be well understood *from the outset* that, for the modern man who has learned the distinction between myth and history," the events narrated in such myths "can no longer be coordinated with the time of history and the space of geography as these have been irreversibly constituted by critical awareness." That remark harkens back to something Ricoeur discusses earlier, in the introduction to Part I, where he characterizes "the modern man" as having "reached the point where history and myth become separate." He then writes (pages 161-162):

"This 'crisis,' this decision, after which myth and history are dissociated, may signify the loss of the mythical dimension: because mythical time can no longer be co-ordinated with the time of events that are 'historical' in the sense required by historical method and historical criticism, because mythical space can no longer be co-ordinated with the places of our geography, we are tempted to give ourselves up to a radical demythization of all our thinking." However, he continues, "another possibility offers itself to us: precisely because we are living and thinking after the separation of myth and history, the demythization of our history can become the other side of an understanding of myth as myth, and the conquest, for the first time in the history of culture, of the mythical dimension." Thus, if anything is lost in abandoning the pretense in accordance with which myths are taken to be attempts to "explain" how present actuality actually came about—the pretense that myth has any "etiological" value, to use the term Ricoeur often uses here—then what is lost is at most "the pseudo-knowledge, the false logos of the myth." What we gain, however, "when we lose the myth as immediate logos," is the possibility for the first time truly to "rediscover it as myth."

All of that can be carried over without change to apply to the narrative testimonies wherein the memory images of trauma occur: We must lose those testimonies as pseudo-transcriptions of past processes, and the memories of trauma as pseudo-photographic reproductions of some datable event that once happened but is now over and done with, precisely in order to rediscover them as the self-articulations of the experience of trauma itself. Only so can they be genuinely "understood" as trauma recollections and trauma narratives at all, in fact, rather than being flattened out and stripped of all relation to trauma in the very endeavor to understand them.

Conclusion: From the Sovereignty of the Image to the Image of Sovereignty

In her recent book *Trauma and Grace: Theology in a Ruptured World*, theologian Serene Jones writes of John Calvin (pages 45-46): "When he approached the Bible, he did not see before him a set of simplistic propositional claims from which he could extract doctrinal truths about God. Rather, he called the Bible 'a lens which we put on' and through which we look at the world. For Calvin, sacred Scripture was, in effect, a pair of eyeglasses that Christians wear to view reality."

Thus—at least by Jones's portrait, which runs counter to the popular image of him—Calvin was anything but a "literalist" in his own reading of the Bible. In effect, to return to the language I have been using throughout this chapter, Calvin, as Jones presents him, did not grant sovereignty to the representational content of Biblical images, but instead strove to grasp what, following William Gass, we might call the set of crossed contexts that gives those images sense as figures of the sacred.

We need to approach testimonies and other narratives of trauma the same way that Calvin, by Jones's account, approached the Bible. Nor is that accidental, if Jones is right. She argues—along with Calvin, by her interpretation, but in different terms, since Calvin, of course, never used the language of "trauma"—that at least one of the things the Bible is, is a library of tales of trauma, all bound together as a single book telling one overarching tale of trauma, the tale, namely, of God's traumatic entry into history, at least as it is told to have taken place with and through the self-experience of Jews and, later, Christians.

At any rate, as I read it the history of the concept of trauma itself is a story of struggle to overcome the same temptation to which those who read the Bible "literally" succumb. That is, in short, the temptation to grant sovereignty to the *image*, specifically taken as a *representation* of some supposed "actual"—or at least "potentially" so—occurrence, object, or state-of-affairs. Toward the end of explaining and justifying my claim, I will consider two examples that are themselves "representative," as it were, in a different but essentially related sense of that term—representative, namely, of the countless cases, in the history of the concept of trauma, where succumbing to the claim to sovereignty of the representational image unfortunately did occur.

My first example is the notorious wave of court cases involving alleged child abuse in the United States during the 1990s, the reaction to which also engendered, among other things, the movement that formed around the idea of a supposed "false memory syndrome." The problem with the "guilty" verdicts that came out of many of those cases—all too many, as it turned out (though I am more than sympathetic to the thesis that even one single such instance would already be all too many)—was not what the proponents of "false memory syndrome" claim. Indeed, the underlying problem involved was one to which the "false memory" movement also fell prey, and continues to fall prey.

The problem was not that the courts rendering "guilty" verdicts in the cases at issue made the mistake, in effect, of heeding the bumper-sticker advice to "believe the children." The problem was, rather, that those courts misunderstood what "the children"—who were often adults by the time they testified—were telling them. However, just so, too, did "the children" themselves misunderstand their own testimony, and the ultimate sense of their own memories.

To put the point briefly, the problem was not that the memories at issue *were* false, as the accused and their advocates among the "false memory syndrome" crowd claimed. Rather, the problem was that the interpretations all three parties to the cases—in effect, the accusers, the accused, and the courts, each along with their sympathizers and proponents—gave to those memories or memory images *turned them into* falsehoods.

That distortion of truths into falsehoods occurred whenever the memories of abuse were taken more or less, to borrow and adapt a phrase from Walter Benjamin, as "mechanical reproductions" of past event—taken, that is, as though they were like photographic images, to be assessed in terms of their accuracy of reproduction of datable, "actual" past occurrences. But by taking them that way to support "guilty" verdicts, the courts, as well as their opponents among the advocates of "false memory syndrome," were being "discornered dunces," to borrow again William Gass's playful phrase. That is, those who took such images that way had *not* "grasped the set of crossed contexts which establishes the figure," as Gass puts it (*The World Within the Word*, page 288)—establishes, that is, the images at issue themselves, *as* the very images they in truth *are*, *in* that very context.

That is my first example, then, from the history of the concept of trauma, of the mistake of submitting to the claim to sovereignty of the image as representation. My second example is from Freud himself, the very father of the modern concept of trauma.

At a relatively early stage of his career, in his famous/infamous "seduction theory," Freud interpreted the memories, dreams, and other symptomatic images of sexual abuse recounted by many of his female patients as representations of earlier "actual" episodes in which their fathers or other male father-figures had molested them sexually. On the basis of that interpretation he went on to assert that there had to be an alarmingly high rate of incidence of such abuse in the middle-class European (or at least Viennese) families of his day.

Freud eventually recanted that specific claim, and the specific interpretation of the reported memories of his patients on which it was based. After that, instead of interpreting such memories of abuse as more or less accurate representations of prior datable occurrences wherein fathers "actually" molested their daughters, he began to interpret them as "wish-fulfillments" of the repressed sexual desires those daughters had for those fathers—cases, in effect, of his female patients wishing, in an unacknowledgeable and therefore repressed wish, that sex acts with their fathers *had* been "actual." By that later interpretation, rather than fulfilling directly and "in reality" the all too blatant incestuous desires of abusive fathers for their daughters, the supposedly "recalled" images fulfilled indirectly and symbolically the repressed sexual desires of those daughters for their "actually" blameless fathers.

However, both before and after recanting his "seduction theory," Freud continued, in effect, to wander, sans identifying dunce-cap, outside his corner. That was so insofar as *both* the earlier "seduction" theory *and* the later "wish-fulfillment" theory granted sovereignty to the images themselves, taken precisely as representations of at least potentially "real" occurrences. Either those images were taken to be accurate reproductions of sexual contacts that "really did" occur (Freud's original seduction theory) or they were taken to be unconscious projections, driven by repressed desires, of such images *as though* they were "real." In either case, the images at issue were taken to be *representations*, in the sense of quasi-photographic "likenesses," of at least possibly (that is, imaginably) actual occurrences. It is just that in the first case, that of the seduction theory, the represented occurrences were taken to have "actually" happened, whereas in the second case, that of the wish-fulfillment theory, they were taken not to have "actually" happened, but only to have been repressed as "wished for." Nevertheless, and as a necessary presupposition, the *representational content* of the images remained the same in both theories.

Even more crucially, both theories continued to focus on that very content as such, rather than attending to the context, the set of crossed connections, as Gass puts it, that let that content *make sense*. Thus, in both stages of his career Freud failed to make exactly the sort of shift that Michael Pollack, whose way of putting the point I have just borrowed, saw needed to be made in dealing with recounted memories of trauma survivors (in Pollack's case, testimonies from Auschwitz survivors): the shift of focus from the representational *content* of the images at issue, and to the *sense* of that very content *in the context* of the "memory" or "testimony" wherein it occurred. In my own terms, what Freud did in both cases was to submit to the claim to sovereignty of the representational image.

What somehow especially both dunces and dis-corner -ers, so to speak—not just Freud and the various parties to the debate about "false memory syndrome," but also most if not all of our first reflections on the images whereby and wherein trauma survivors spontaneously, once given a chance, articulate their own traumatic experiences—*miss*, is trauma itself. As theologian Serene Jones, whom I cited to open this chapter-concluding section, which I will now close by citing her again, observes more than once in *Trauma and Grace*, by way of her own twice-repeated citation (first on page 20, then again on page 30—with an acknowledgement in a note that she is taking her citation from yet another, earlier one by another contemporary scholar)

from the dissertation of the seventeenth century physician Johannes Hofer, trauma is "a disease that is essentially due to *a disordered imagination.*"

I would amend that slightly, but still, I think, in accord with both how both Jones and Hofer understand things, to say that trauma does the very disordering. That is, I think it is better to say that the disordering of the imagination is due to trauma, rather than that trauma is due to such disordering. Put either way, however, what remains is that trauma and the disordering of the imagination are inseparable: Whatever else it may involve, trauma involves a disordered imagination.

Above all, the traumatic disordering of the imagination distorts how the imagination imagines itself, as it were. It distorts the self-understanding of the imagination, leading the imagination to imagine itself as no more than a sort of mechanical recording device, a place for the storing of photograph-like images. Thus, the traumatized imagination imagines itself as subject to what I have been calling the sovereignty of the image.

In that very process wherein the traumatized imagination subjects itself to the sovereignty of the image, however, the imagination projects a distorting image not only of itself, but also of sovereignty. Or, rather, the disordered imagination projects sovereignty itself *as* such a distorted image. What I mean is that it projects the pure image—now in the sense of being "no more than" an image, of being a "mere" image, an "illusion"— *that there is such a thing as sovereignty at all.* The sovereignty of the image, which is to say the reign of the representation, becomes inextricably intertwined with the image of sovereignty, which is now to say the illusion that there is any such thing as sovereignty—and that includes, most especially, any sovereignty supposedly vested in what is called, revealingly, "representative" government.

Thus, the sovereignty of the image opens out into the image of sovereignty. In this chapter I have focused on the former. It the next chapter, the second I am devoting to the exploration of the general topic of "Trauma and Representation," I will turn to the latter.

Chapter 5

TRAUMA AND REPRESENTATION II:

The Image of Sovereignty

Modern political theory—whether in the form of the "social contract" theories of classic liberalism from Thomas Hobbes, John Locke, and Jean-Jacques Rousseau in the seventeenth century to John Rawls in the twentieth, or in the form of reactions against liberalism, especially in such decisionistic theories as, emblematically, that of rightwing twentieth century legal theorist Carl Schmitt —consistently grounds sovereignty in trauma. Like the great, ancient myths of cosmic creation, modern political theory, in both its social-contract and its decisionistic forms, tells a story in accordance with which evil is older than good. Evil is there at the very beginning. Or, rather, it is there even before the beginning, at least if the beginning is taken to mean the point at which the story of modern sovereignty starts to be told.

In turn, the story of the emergence, expansion, and eventual crisis of sovereignty in the modern form, the very sovereignty for which both social contract and decisionistic theorists attempt to provide rational grounds, is inseparable from the story of the nation-state in its rise, development, and eventual decline, or at least apparent decline, in the face of the spread of global capitalism. Trauma is no less there at the very beginning of the nation-state than it is at the beginning of modern sovereignty. It is to the former, the inaugural, inaugurating relationship between trauma and the idea of the nation that I will turn first in this chapter.

Founding Trauma and the Birth of the Nation

In "Notes on the Memory Boom: War, Remembrance and the Uses of the Past," one of the essays in the collection *Memory, Trauma, and World Politics* (pages 58-59), historian Jay Winter quotes Ernst Renan, from a series of lectures Renan gave in Paris in 1882, entitled 'What is a nation?' Renan answers his own question as follows:

> A nation is a soul, a spiritual principle. Two things, which, in truth, are really one, constitute this soul, this spiritual principle. One is in the past, the other in the present. One is the possessing in common of a rich legacy of memories, the other is the present-day consent, the desire to live together, the will to continue to value the individual heritage one has received . . . To have the glory of the past in common, a shared will in the present; to have done great deeds together, and want to do more of them, are the essential conditions for the constitution of a people . . . One loves the house which one has built and passes on.

'Such ideas and images were commonplace in late nineteenth century Europe,' comments Winter on that passage from Renan. 'What was much newer,' he continues, 'were powerful means to disseminate them.' According to Winter, in the 19th century '[w]riters on memory reached a much wider audience than ever before,' precisely because '[t]he expansion of the print trade, the art market, the leisure industry, and the mass circulation press allied to developments first in photography and then in cinematography, created powerful conduits for the dissemination of texts, images and narratives of the past in every part of Europe and beyond."

At any rate, at least when they relate to what Indian psychoanalyst Sudhir Kakar calls "founding traumas," an idea I already used in an earlier chapter and will discuss further shortly, the sorts of "collective" or "community" memories at issue in Renan's original remarks and in Winter's reflections on those remarks become *falsifying* memories in a special sense that sets them apart from the sort of "screen memories" discussed in the preceding chapter, and most especially from the sorts of memories that come under attack by the proponents of so called "false memory syndrome." Unlike screen memories or those at issue in the controversy around "false memory syndrome," the sorts of "memories" Renan spoke about in 1882 are based on and involve the *manipulation* of memories of trauma and of the emotions those memories can trigger—a manipulation for some purpose formulated by the manipulator, however "collective" that manipulator may be, and irrespective of whether the manipulation is deliberate or not.

For ease of reference, I will call the sorts of memories—or at least the sorts of images that give themselves out as memories—with which Renan was concerned "national" memories, because of the role Renan and others attribute to them, the role of being midwives to the births of nations. *In contrast* to such national memories, screen memories, properly so called, *issue from* trauma itself, as part of the mechanism of joint, simultaneous presentation-repression. As I discussed in the preceding chapter, such memories "screen" in the double sense of (1) *hiding* or *covering-over* (repression), while at the same time (2) providing a surface, as it were, upon which trauma may project and thereby *reveal* itself (presentation).

Sometimes, paradoxically, and as was also touched upon in the preceding chapter, the very phenomenon of a sort of *hyper-real* image of a traumatic occurrence compulsively recurs to those who have been traumatized. Such recurrence of such images is, in fact, a common sign of the "dissociation" so often reported as accompanying traumatic experiences. Such hyper-real images, however, do not constitute a counter-example to screen memories. Rather, as compulsively recurring yet in all their recurrence remaining inseparable from dissociation, they continue, precisely as hyper-real, to fulfill the double role of screen memories, by both *masking* and *indicating*, at one and the same time, the underlying trauma. What gets effectively masked *by* the hyper-reality of the images is the very *traumatic*—the disturbing, *emotion-ladened*—character of the traumatic event they present themselves as imaging. The very vividness of the images, their being so real and more than real, fosters the dissociation whereby one remains blinded and numbed in the face of what otherwise would be, or is at least feared to be, altogether overwhelming.

The key distinction that needs to be drawn here is that between *repressing* the trauma and *manipulating* it. Therein lies the difference between screen memories, on the one side, and national memories on the other. To be precise, the differentiation at issue need not involve two different sets of images. Rather, one and the same image can come to serve both masters. That is, one and the same image—let it be an image of two people holding hands and jumping to their deaths from the Twin Towers on the morning of Septmeber 11, 2001, after the attacks took place—can serve as a screen memory when it vividly and compulsively recurs to someone who was traumatized by the attacks on the Towers; but it can also serve at the same time as something to be directly and even cynically manipulated, say by a politician with a vested interest in using it to justify pursuing a "war on terror."

Trauma memories that are supposedly "false", in the sense at issue in so called "false memory syndrome," are more properly viewed as a form of "screen" memory in the double sense of simultaneously hiding a traumatic event yet providing a surface upon which what is thus hidden can project and thereby reveal itself. So, too, are the supposedly "accurate," hyper-real memory images that recur, for example, in nightmares or "flashbacks" experienced by those who have been traumatized.

The sort of collective memory—or collective use of memory, if one is dealing with such an example of one and the same image functioning in two different yet interconnected ways, only one of which ways is that of "collective memory"—Renan describes, however, is *not* any such "screen." Rather, it is *manufactured* as a supposedly *collective* memory, through a process of production involving the *manipulation* (whether conscious or not) of trauma and the images of it for external ends of the manipulator.

It should come as no surprise to anyone who has read to this point that I consider the use of the images of 9/11 for the sake of justifying the American invasions of Afghanistan and Iraq to be examples of just such manufacturing and manipulation of supposedly collective images. However, for my purposes here it does not matter whether I am right in that judgment or not. All that matters is that the conceptual distinction between the two very different possible ways of deploying a memory image, or at least of what presents itself or is presented as a memory image, in relation to trauma be granted. That is, all I ask here is that one understand the difference between a memory image (or even pseudo-memory image, if one likes) that functions both to conceal and to reveal, at one and the same time, a trauma undergone by the person to whom that image occurs, on the one hand, and, on the other, the manipulation, consciously or unconsciously, of an image of trauma and of the fear and insecurity engendered by it, to achieve goals of the manipulator external to the processes of traumatization itself.

The latter, the at least unconsciously manipulative use of images of trauma and the emotions those images trigger for the sake of creating, sustaining, and heightening collective identity, is central to what Sudhir Kakar calls "founding traumas" in *The Colors of Violence*, his insightful and influential analysis of Hindu-Muslim violence in his native India. Especially important for my purposes here is Kakar's idea of how such "founding traumas" function in establishing religion-based cultural identities in conflict with other such identities based on the very same "founding trauma," only vastly differently interpreted. To give another example to add to his own Indian one, I would argue that it is just such a shared "founding trauma" interpreted two very different ways that is at work in the way "September 11, 2001," functions in the conflictual genesis of both Arab "Jihadist" and American "anti-terrorist" extremist identities. At any rate, what Kakar has to say about Hindu-Muslim violence in India clearly has relevance for the analysis of other cases elsewhere as well.

From my perspective—which considerably overlaps Kakar's own, in my judgment — it is important to make explicit that the (no doubt largely unconscious) use of trauma to serve as the foundation for such religious/ cultural identity-formation as Kakar addresses is actually a matter of the *manipulative avoidance* of trauma, as opposed both to the dissociative repression of trauma and to the potentially healing overcoming of that repression in subsequent processing. It is, in short, a coercive move to block trauma from traumatizing—and, therefore, a reactionary effort at forestalling the transformative and healing action that can occur only by letting such traumatization work itself through.

"Cultural identity, like its individual counterpart,' writes Kakar (page 150), 'is an unconscious human acquirement which becomes consciously salient only when there is a perceived threat to its integrity. Identity, both individual and collective, lives itself for the most part, unfettered and unworried by obsessive and excessive scrutiny." Yet what if identity, either cultural or individual, is itself something that must, so to speak, be *struck* in the first place—in the same sense as one "strikes" (that is, mints) a coin—by the trauma at issue, such that the appearance of identity having already been there all along (but only "unconsciously," as "lived") becomes visible *as a fiction*: a fiction founding identity, a founding fiction that itself *forms* identity in the first place?

Kakar himself, it seems to me, touches on something of the sort when, after making the remark cited above, he immediately continues as follows: "Everyday living incorporates a zone of indifference with regard to one's culture, including one's language, ethnic origin, or religion." What is such indifference, if it is not indifference toward one's "cultural identity"? And if it is that, then it would be an indifference toward, precisely, an "identity' one is somehow given but that one experiences still as really *not one's own*— which is to say an identity that is, paradoxically, *not* one's identity at all. Then only in and as reaction to trauma would any "cultural identity," any self-identification, any identifying of one's self *with* one's "culture," form— get cast or created: *fictioned* in the original sense of that term—at all. Then "cultural identity"—or, for that matter, even "*individual* identity"—would be a reactive formation designed to *ward off* the 'founding' trauma at issue. And then, too, only the *collapse* of that reaction, that reactive formation or fiction, would at last *let the trauma traumatize*: let the truth that flashes there "materialize."

As already noted in an earlier chapter, in *The Colors of Violence* Kakar draws a useful distinction between "community" and "communalism." What is crucial to what Kakar calls communal*ism* is the explicit *assertion* of belonging to some community. Communalism is, in effect, a matter of yoking one's own sense of personal identity with membership in a given community. It is irreducible to simply belonging to a given community, being a member of it. Instead, it is the elevation of such membership to the status of what defines one for oneself as the individual one is. Communalism is literally self-identification — that is, the locating of one's own personal identity or 'selfhood'—in terms of belonging to a given community. As Kakar nicely puts it, in communalism "[t]he 'We-ness' of the community is . . . replaced by the 'We *are*' of communalism." As such, communalism is a sort of identity with a chip on its shoulder, always asserting itself and ever alert to the smallest perceived slight to the community to which one belongs, which gets taken as a personal insult.

Kakar himself uses a model developed by his colleague Oscar Peterson of the stages through which someone 'identifying with his or her ethnic group' in such a way must go. According to that model, the first stage of a "change from community to communalism" is to "declare to all who share the crisis with me that I am one of them—a Hindu, a Muslim [or whatever]." Thus, for Kakar, the explicit *assertion* of membership in *such* communities is itself preceded and grounded on an antecedently explicit *awareness of* that very membership. That awareness of belonging to such a community is itself, by the model he is using, triggered by the occurrence of some traumatic event that is *antecedently shared* with other members of that same community. In effect, the fact that the trauma is already *shared* with other members of the community to which one has belonged all along, but without express awareness of such membership or any felt need to assert it—that antecedent sharing of the trauma is what allows the explicit awareness of group membership to surface, which in turn grounds the experience of a need explicitly to assert that membership—and, of course, to defend the group itself against perceived threats originating from "outside" the group, in one sense or another of "outside." First comes membership in some group, then comes a trauma that galvanizes group members into becoming aware of their membership, then comes the assertion of solidarity with the group in the face of ongoing threat of one sort or another.

But what if the process actually occurs in a very different way, with a very different order of stages? What if the very awareness of being a member of the community at issue—what if one's very cultural or communal self-identification in terms of membership in the community—does not in fact *precede* the assertion thereof, as Kakar maintains, but *results from* it, by a certain, far from universal or "natural" process? What if the whole idea of an antecedent awareness of a supposedly still earlier condition of belonging to the community is itself a retrospectively cast myth or fiction of the origin of the community, membership in which is being asserted? What if the very constitution of the ethnic group itself as a distinct "we" is just another retrospective projection—in this case, the retrospective projection of group-identity as already having been there all along, when in fact it is first *constituted* only in a defensive response to trauma?

Kakar mentions the "individual who, *as a consequence of a shared threat*, is in process of self-consciously identifying with his or her ethnic group" (page 191, emphasis added). But what if the very constituting of a threat as a "shared" one in the first place does not precede the trauma, but first comes about only *through* it, insofar as the trauma is *communicated*, in the very sense of being *shared with others*. It is worth noting, in that connection, the German term for "communication." That term is *Mitteilung*, from *mit*, with, and *teilen*, to share or apportion, that is, to break into parts or portions—"shares"—and to give each of a group a part: To share the shares, we could say. That is the sense of "communication" at issue in, for example, the Christian Eucharistic ceremony, wherein bread is broken into parts and each "communicant" is given a piece. In such cases, it is only the act of communication itself, *the act of sharing*, that first establishes something as shared. What is more, the community of those who have shared the same thing is established *by* the very act of sharing, rather than preceding that act. The sharing of what is shared gives rise to the community of the sharers, rather than that community already being there and then, as a community, having something happen to it, either collectively as something that happens to the community as such, or distributively as something that happens to each of the individual community members.

It is just such communities—those constituted through and in the very sharing with one another of a trauma, rather than constituted in retrospect as already having been there all along and prior to the trauma—that are at issue in Rebecca Solnit's idea, also already discussed in an earlier chapter, of what she calls "disaster communities," communities of "mutual aid" that form spontaneously of themselves among those struck by the same traumatic event, such as an earthquake or a hurricane. Communities constituted in that way, through the sharing of trauma with one another among those traumatized by some event, are not concerned with patrolling community borders for the sake of insuring community identity. They do not demand any sort of "credential," as it were, attesting to group membership. Rather, constituted by trauma itself, they are open to all the traumatized, without exception or qualification. Such communities are accordingly open and inclusive.

In contrast, the sorts of communities that Kakar discusses are those in which the community constitutes itself as having already existed prior to the traumatic event, and as being, precisely *as* the community it takes itself to be, the *target*, in effect, *of* the traumatic event. For example, insofar as the attacks of 9/11/2001 were cast as "attacks on America," the latter—America as a community, or the community of all Americans—was construed as having already existed prior to the attacks and, indeed, as having been targeted *for* such attacks precisely *as* just that same pre-existing community, and *because* it was that community, that community and no other.

For ease of reference, I will call the first-mentioned sorts of community—those constituted only by and in the sharing of some trauma—*communities of trauma* or *trauma-communities*. In contrast, I will call the sorts of communities Kakar discusses especially—those claiming an identity prior to, and open to being targeted for, trauma—communities *invested in trauma* or *trauma-invested* communities.

Now, to apply that distinction to the concept of a nation or nation-state, it is clear that *a nation or nation-state is a trauma-invested community.* The nation-state literally has a vested interest in trauma, an interest that the nation exploits for its own profit. The nation traffics in trauma.

Nations profit from trauma in two intertwined ways. One way uses trauma to justify aggressive courses of action on the part of already constituted nations. The other uses it to justify the nation itself—that is, the claim to national sovereignty as such. In the next section of this chapter I will address the first way in which nations profit from trauma, before turning to the second way in the section after next.

War-Profiteering in Trauma

It has often been noted that nations can, and frequently do, use traumatic events to legitimate their own aggressive actions, and to maintain popular support for them. In such cases, trauma conveniently serves the nation — after the fact, as it were—for claiming legitimacy and demanding support for aggressive national actions. Colin Davis captures well the mechanism employed. First the spokesperson for the national interest casts the traumatic event as an attack on the nation by some national enemy (which it may well be, as in the Japanese attack on Pearl Harbor on December 7, 1941), then casts aggressive action against that enemy as the only appropriate response to that attack, and claims ongoing support for whatever further acts are taken to be necessary for securing the nation against future attack. "By projecting the violence of society onto an identifiable group of criminals [or the equivalent, such as a "rogue" state or, in general, some supposed enemy of the nation, one should add]," as Davis sums the whole process up in his post-9/11 book *Haunted Subjects: Psychoanalysis and the Return of the Dead* (page 34), "the forces of order can assure the intelligibility of evil, deny their own responsibility for it, and indulge their inclination to violence in eradicating it."

One example of such a case is how the United States under President Franklin D. Roosevelt used the already mentioned Japanese attack on Pearl Harbor on December 7, 1941, to justify declaring war on Japan, and then fanned the flames of Americans anger and resentment—and, for that matter, racist prejudice—after the attack, to help keep support for the war effort high. The point is not that the attack was somehow fabricated and never really happened. It certainly did. The point, however, is that that attack was immediately de-contextualized in such a way as to obviate any consideration of what part the United States itself may have played in the events leading up to the Japanese action, and any need or desire to pursue any other course of response short of war. Then recurrent appeal to that "day that will live in infamy," as President Roosevelt famously called it in his address to Congress requesting a declaration of war against Japan the day after the attack, served to justify the United States in the aggressive prosecution of that war, down to and including dropping nuclear bombs on Hiroshima and Nagasaki to bring Japan to unconditional surrender.

"Such an experience is hardly unusual," as Robert J. Lifton notes in *Super Power Syndrome* (page 152), already cited in an earlier chapter, "and could be the experience of any national leader" faced with something similar to the attack on Pearl Harbor in 1941. "The danger a leader faces," writes Lifton, "is that of equating a sense of debt to the dead with fierce, amorphous retribution." Of course, we should note, from the point of view of such a leader, "fierce amorphous retribution" will rarely if ever appear as a "danger." Instead, it will appear as the only appropriate response, and very often even as an important opportunity to consolidate both national and personal power.

At any rate, by Lifton's analysis the United States, four decades after Pearl Harbor, made just such a use of the attacks of September 11, 2001, to legitimate American invasion first of Afghanistan and then of Iraq, and to try to build support for those actions not only among American citizens themselves, but also among the governments and citizens of its allies and beyond. As Lifton observes, the Bush administration and its many supporters took the idea that after 9/11 the entire nation owed a "debt to the dead, and to the immediate survivors representing them," and "instantly transformed [that idea] into a strong impulse toward retaliative action." The rush into war against Afghanistan and then against Iraq amply confirms Lifton's diagnosis.

What is more, such manipulation of trauma for justifying subsequent national decisions and actions often also bolsters itself by analogizing the most recent trauma with earlier ones that had been successfully manipulated for similar purposes in the past. So, for example, in his editor's introduction to the collection of essays that make up *Memory, Trauma, and World Politics*, cited earlier, international relations scholar Duncan Bell calls attention to how this occurred after 9/11. As he writes (page 14): "In post 9/11 [American] public life memories of both Vietnam and the attack on Pearl Harbor have been invoked repeatedly and for multiple and often contradictory reasons." As a demonstration, Bell goes on to cite President George W. Bush in a speech delivered to the cadets at the

United States Air Force Academy in Colorado Springs on June 24, 2004, almost three years after the 9/11 attacks. "Like the Second World War,' said Bush on that occasion in Bell's citation, 'our present conflict began with a ruthless surprise attack on the United States.' Then he drew an implicit parallel between his administrations response to the 9/11 attacks and the Roosevelt administration's earlier response to the Japanese attack on Pearl Harbor by adding: 'We will not forget that treachery and we will accept nothing less than victory over the enemy.' He then even proceeded to conflate the 9/11 attacks with *state*-sponsored violence, such as, for example, the Nazi genocide against Jews: 'Like the murderous ideologies of the 20th century, the ideology of terrorism reaches across borders, and seeks recruits in every country. So we're fighting these enemies wherever they hide across the earth."

Later in Bell's collection of essays, K. M. Fierke, another scholar of international relations, follows Hannah Arendt's well-known analysis in *Eichman in Jerusalem* in arguing that Israeli prime minister and national hero David Ben-Gurion similarly used the Eichman trial in 1961 to reinforce the idea that there was a direct and unbreakable connection between the Holocaust and the founding of the state of Israel. So, Fierke observes (page 127): "The experience of the Holocaust was woven into Israeli identity, rather than [Ben-Gurion and Israel] distancing it [that is, the Holocaust] in the past."

Ironically, Ben-Gurion's use of the Holocaust thereby follows the model of Hitler himself, who, in his manipulation of the widespread "stab in the back" myth popularly subscribed to by many Germans at the time, "called on the trauma of [German] defeat in the first World War and the humiliation of the Versailles treaty, in mobilizing an existential threat to German society, to the end of making Germany great once again." As if to confirm again the frequency with which such manipulations of trauma occur, and how they continue to recur all too frequently in recent history, rather than being relegated to earlier epochs, Fierke prefaces her remark about Hitler with one about how Slobodan Milosevic used the very same sort of manipulation of memories of trauma to justify Serbian aggression during the 1990s.

The example of the Nazi exploitation of the myth of the "stab in the back" is worth a bit more reflection. According to that myth the Germans were supposed to have lost World War I not through any lack on the part of the German military or the leadership of the Wilhelmine Reich in general, but by being subverted from within by the Social Democrats and other leftist forces, those very figures to whom fell the responsibility to declare and then uphold what came to be known as the Weimar Republic after the German collapse and surrender in November 1918. Unlike the Japanese attack on Pear Harbor twenty-three years later, which actually did take place, no such "stab in the back" ever occurred. The whole thing was indeed no more than a manufactured "myth," in the sense of a false story. That the whole thing was made up, however, proved to be an advantage, not a disadvantage, for the right wing elements in German politics and society, including especially the Nazis. The idea of such a "stab in the back" was not a claim based on evidence in the first place. It was, rather, solely a symptomatic expression of the very anguish, resentments, and fears upon which it played. As with any such delusion, any evidence adduced against it was automatically reinterpreted and converted into yet further confirmation of the pseudo-thesis at issue. Not based on evidence to begin with, such a delusional idea can never be refuted by any appeal to contrary evidence. Accordingly, it can be freely exploited by any interest able to adapt it to its own purposes, as the Nazis easily adapted the myth of the stab in the back to gain and hold power.

Furthermore, it is common knowledge that, once in power, Hitler was also not in the least averse to inventing new myths of traumatic attacks upon Germany whenever necessary to justify his aggressions. The ramp-up to what became World War II was full of examples of such a process, which culminated in the Nazis trumping up the fake border incident of a Polish attack on a German radio installation as a pretense for invading Poland at the beginning of September in 1939. Thus, traumatic events are so useful to a political leader's pursuit of national or even personal goals that, if chance does not present one, the leader will have to invent one, as the President in the film *Wag the Dog* fakes a war to boost his popularity and secure his own reelection.

Even if the traumatic event diverted to serve such extraneous ends "really happened," as did the Japanese attack on Pearl Harbor, drafting that event into public service by what presents itself as the national interest has the effect of transforming the event into a myth. In that sense, even such otherwise egregiously offensive claims as Iranian President Mahmoud Ahmadinejad's that the Holocaust is a "myth," touch on a truth—the truth, namely, that employing trauma to serve power is itself already a falsifying distortion, a fiction-spinning and myth-making. By shanghaiing it for service in what they take to be the national interests of the state of Israel, for example, Ben-Gurion and the other Israeli leaders perverted remembrance of the Holocaust into a mere myth even before Ahmadinejad and other Holocaust deniers came along. Indeed, the already accomplished perversion of the traumatic truth of the Holocaust into a state-justifying myth actually helped to open, and still helps keep open, a door through which those who would deny the reality of the Holocaust can come.

That transformation of the trauma of the Holocaust into no more than another sorry story of the exercise of the power of the state exemplifies the second, and indeed decisive, way in which the nation-state turns a profit on trauma. The first way, that in which an already established state uses a serendipitous traumatic event—that is, one occurring by a chance that is fortunate at least for the state—to justify state-enacted violence, has been the focus of this section of the current chapter. The second, decisive way, in which trauma is used not to justify aggression by already constituted states but, rather, to justify the foundation of the state in the first place, will be the topic in the next section.

The Myth of the State, the State of the Myth

Some of the examples of state profiteering in trauma mentioned earlier can serve to introduce what is now at stake in this new section of the current chapter. One such example is Hitler's recurrent use of the myth of the "stab in the back" to justify the Nazi *Machtergreifung* ("seizure of power") in the 1930s. Another is Ben-Gurion's and other Israeli leaders' recurrent use of the recollection of the Holocaust to justify Israeli national policy after World War II. The third is Slobodan Milosevic's recurrent citation of old, remembered traumas to justify Serbian aggression in the 1990s. In all three cases trauma is made to serve a founding role exceeding that of legitimating decisions and actions taken by already constituted nations falling prey to the temptation Robert J. Lifton mentions, that of transforming trauma "into a strong impulse toward retaliative action" against national enemies made to bear the blame for the trauma.

Beyond that reactive way of forcing trauma to serve the purpose of the nation-state, the three cases at issue involve the even more radical use of trauma to justify the very formation of a state or regime in the first place. Thus, Hitler and the Nazis used the German defeat in World War I to justify the very foundation of the "Third Reich." Ben-Gurion and other Israeli leaders used the Holocaust to defend the very creation of the modern state of Israel. And Milosevic used the recollection of long-past violence perpetrated by Moslems against Christians in the Balkans to legitimate the breaking away of Serbia from the former Yugoslavia, to constitute Serbia as an independent state of its own. In all three instances trauma served the nation not only by providing a foundation for specific acts or ranges of action, but also by providing one for the very formation of the nation in the first place.

Above all, the idea of "founding trauma," as I have formulated it following Sudhir Kakar, means trauma used in this second way, to legitimate not just actions taken by already formed nation-states, but the very formation of those nation-states to begin with. In such cases, the nation-state has a vested interest in trauma not just to justify even the widest range of its actions. Rather, the interest the nation-state invests in trauma is for the very sake of establishing itself as a nation in the first place, or at least of providing justification after the fact for its establishment. It is not merely the decisions and acts *of* or *by* a sovereign nation that are at issue. At issue is, instead, the very constitution of the *sovereign nation* in the first place.

At first glance, such cases of the exploitation of trauma for founding a nation-state would appear to contrast with others in which such a state seems to found itself on what looks at first to be the very opposite—namely, the repression and avoidance of any explicit reference to a trauma without which the state at issue would nevertheless, in fact, never have emerged. The paradigmatic example of what I have in mind is the creation, out of the ruins of the German catastrophe at the end of World War II, of the Federal Republic of Germany —"West" Germany as opposed to "East" Germany, the German Democratic Republic (the dynamics of the founding of which embodied an at least superficially different relation to the devastation of Germany by allied bombs and armies than that embodied in the foundation of the Federal Republic).

In 1997 German novelist and literary scholar W. G. Sebald delivered a series of lectures in Zurich about the strange silence in almost all postwar German literature concerning the overwhelming devastation visited upon Germany by the allied policy of heavy aerial bombing of civilian centers of German population such as Berlin, Hamburg, Munich, Cologne, Nuremberg, and, no doubt most famously, Dresden. Sebald later revised his Zurich lectures for publication, along with a related, shorter piece of literary criticism, under the title *Luftkrieg und Literature.* The lectures appear in English under the title of "Air War and Literature" in *On the Natural History of Destruction*, where they constitute the first and longest of a collection of three of Sebald's interrelated literary studies.

What I want to take from Sebald's lectures for now is a single insight—just one of many, but a crucially important one. The insight at issue is into the relation between, on the one hand, the state which eventually emerged from the German devastation—to become, in 1949, under the leadership of Konrad Adenauer, who became its first Chancellor, the Federal Republic of Germany—and, on the other hand, the trauma of that devastation itself. Referring to what came to be known as the West German *"Wirtschaftswunder,"* or "economic miracle," for which the government of the Federal Republic served simultaneously in various roles, including those of architect, overseer, and heir, Sebald notes early in his first lecture (page 7 of the English translation):

From the outset, the now legendary and in some respects genuinely admirable reconstruction of the country after the devastation wrought by Germany's wartime enemies, a reconstruction tantamount to a second liquidation in successive phases of the nations own past history, prohibited any look backward. It did so through the sheer amount of labor required and the creation of a new, faceless reality, pointing the population exclusively towards the future and enjoining on it silence about the past.

A few pages later (pages 11-12) Sebald follows up with this observation:

The almost entire absence of profound disturbance to the inner life of the nation suggests that the new Federal German society relegated the experiences of its own prehistory to the back of its mind and developed and almost perfectly functioning mechanism of repression, one which allowed it to recognize the fact of its own rise from total degradation while disengaging entirely from its stock of emotions, if not actually chalking up as another item to its credit its success in overcoming all tribulations without showing any sign of weakness.

The German self-image Sebald depicts in those two early passages is of a sustained forward march of German—at least West German—history after World War II, a collective march "eyes front," in effect, in which the devastated German society as a whole is so focused on the future that it cannot take time even to acknowledge its own past, the very past the utterly devastating nature of which requires just such single-minded devotion to the building of a supposedly new future, to rise over the very ruins of that past.

Such a picture of a resolutely forward-looking historical progression contrasts poignantly with the very different picture that emerges from the passage with which Sebald ends his Zurich lectures, at least in their published version, before he goes on to write a postscript to them. In that closing passage to his second lecture, Sebald first asks whether the destruction of Germany does not finally constitute (page 66) "irrefutable proof that the catastrophes which develop, so to speak, in our hands"—that is, the hands of humanity in general, culminating in the humanity at whose hands the horrendous events of 20th century history took place, including both the German genocide against the Jews and the devastation wrought by the Allied air war against Germany in World War II—"and seem to break out suddenly are a kind of experiment, anticipating the point at which we shall drop out of what we have thought for so long to be our autonomous history and back into the history of nature."

A few lines later (on page 67), Sebald goes on to suggest that among postwar German authors "even the most enlightened of writers" can look back at the scenes of the destruction of the writer's home country by the Allied bombers only "with the horrified fixity of Walter Benjamin's 'angel of history,' whose 'face is turned toward the past.'" Sebald then closes his somber reflections by citing the rest of the passage containing that famous image from Benjamin's "Theses on the Philosophy of History," in *Illuminations* (pages 257-258):

> Where we perceive a chain of events, he ["the angel of history"] sees one single catastrophe which keeps piling wreckage upon wreckage and hurls it in front of his feet. The angel would like to stay, awaken the dead, make whole what has been smashed. But a storm is blowing from Paradise; it has got caught in his wings with such violence that the angel can no longer close them. This storm irresistibly propels him into the future to which his back is turned, while the pile of debris before him grows skyward. This storm is what we call progress.

Benjamin's angel faces backward and longs to restore what has been ruined by the progress of the storm of history, against which, caught in the draft of that very storm, the angel is impotent to mount any resistance. In contrast, whatever angel—we might call it the "angel of progress," to fit as a counter to Benjamin's "angel of history" (and we should remember that some angels are *"fallen"* angels)—presided over the establishment of the German Federal Republic turned its back on the ruin that is the German Nazi past and marched in lockstep, face fixed forward, into the appallingly and violently desolating future Benjamin's angel longs impotently to avert.

The betrayal of the past, filled with its dead, by the always-forward march of progress, makes use of the very names of its victims to justify and reinforce itself. Not infrequently such manipulation of memory even goes so far as end up justifying the perpetrators of the very abuses that have crowded the past with so many victims in the first place.

In an essay aptly titled "Remembering to Forget/Forgetting to Remember," from the already mentioned collection *Memory, Trauma, and World Politics*, political scientist Maja Zehfuss analyses the process involved. At issue are the different ways of remembering and memorializing trauma and its victims. Zehfuss points to the expropriation of victims' memories by, and the exploitation of those same memories to salve the conscience of, those same victims' very victimizers, the perpetrators of the same abuses at issue.

Though in the case that Zehfuss uses as a prime example (and that I will give in a moment), the process of expropriation and exploitation was presumably unintentional and not deliberate, there are no doubt all too many other cases that can be adduced in which it was fully intentional and deliberate. There are, as well, cases in which one is uncomfortable either attributing full intention to the expropriators and exploiters of victims' memories — making them perpetrators who in full knowledge rob the memories of the dead, thus compounding the damage the original trauma has already inflicted — or attributing exculpating inadvertence and igno-rance to them, as seems to hold for the case Zehfuss discusses. That is, there are cases in which, I would suggest, there is indeed an entry of ignorance and inadvertence into the equation, but the ignorance at issue itself turns out to be all too motivated, as it were, and the inadvertence all too planned.

One clear example of such an all too motivated ignorance is that of the 'good' Nazi doctors at Auschwitz, as analyzed in Robert J. Lifton's book on that topic — doctors among those responsible for making the 'selections' at Auschwitz who, while sending so many to the gas, nevertheless showed decency and even collegiality towards individual inmates with whom they interacted in carrying out their other medical tasks in the camp. Another example might be, at least by a generously charitable interpretation, the Bush administration's recurrent references of various sorts in various venues to the memory of the victims of "9/11" to justify invading Iraq, conveniently forgetting clear evidence that Iraq had no connection to the attacks on September 11, 2001, as well as forgetting the *lack* of any clear evidence that Iraq was hiding "weapons of mass destruction." In such cases there is at least the strong suggestion that the forgetting and ignorance involved are all too willful—or at least not entirely unrelated to one's own interest, and one's own will to realize that interest.

At any rate, to return to Zehfuss, the case she discusses in "Remembering to Forget/Forgetting to Remember" pertains once again—echoing Sebald—to the Federal Republic of Germany, or 'West' Germany. Whereas Sebald addresses the forgetting of the Nazi past, a forgetting with which the Federal Republic was established near the beginning of the so called Cold War, Zehfuss addresses a later episode of questionable West German memory, one that occurred during the waning years of the Cold War. As Zehfuss recounts (page 215), on May 8, 1985, the anniversary of German surrender in 1945, forty years earlier, "Federal President Richard von Weizsäcker—urging incidentally that 8 May 1945 should be seen as liberation—cited the cabbalistic saying inscribed at the Yad Veshem memorial [to Holocaust victims, in Israel]: 'Wanting to forget prolongs the exile, and the secret of redemption is remembering.' ' As Zehfuss observes, following the view of Helmut Dubiel, a German critic who wrote about the incident not long after it occurred, it soon became clear 'that Weizsäcker's discussion had not been differentiated enough.' The Yad Veshem dictum, as Dubiel had written, 'had been 'stripped of its Jewish origin' and strangely referred to 'the possibility of a moral emancipation of the perpetrator through memory of guilt'.' To add further reinforcement of her point, Zehfus goes on to note that Klaus Naumann, another German critic writing at the time, also criticized von Weizsäcker for seeming 'to be unaware that the caballa [from which the Yad Veshem slogan derives] deals with 'the victims of historical injustice,' not the perpetrators."

A bit further on (page 219), Zehfuss tells her readers how, a few years later, in 1988, in his acceptance speech for the Peace Prize of the German book trade, novelist Martin Wolser criticized what he called "a 'monu-mentalization' of German disgrace" in the "planned [German] Holocaust memorial." Zehfuss goes on to inform us that, along the same lines, the same memorial "has also been called a '*Kranzabwurfstelle*' (a place to drop wreaths).' She then sums up by articulating the general significance of such examples as von Weizsäcker's 1985 remarks and the German Holocaust memorial. What such examples show, as she observes, is that, far from hon-oring the dead in memory, 'official commemoration may actually conceal forgetting: the dropping of wreaths by politicians creates no more than an illusion of remembering."

What is at issue in the critique of such cases is not, according to Zehfus (page 214, quoting from Andreas Huyysen 's *Twilight Memories: Marking Time in a Culture of Amnesia*), "'whether to forget or to remember, but rather how to remember and how to handle representations of the remembered past.' The argument 'against forgetting', with its implied imperative 're-member', is a move in the struggle over what it is to remember." Clearly, what is also at issue is the whole claim to sovereignty that a state or regime is advancing in such recurrent acts of dishonoring the dead under the very guise of honoring them.

The conjunction of Sebald's example of the founding of the West German state with Zehfuss's of the abusive use of memorials by the same state decades later, helps to make clear an important point. That is the point that the underlying mechanism of state cooptation and manipula-tion of trauma for the state's own extraneous purposes remains the same, regardless of whether the state stakes its claim to sovereignty on explicit, recurrent reference to the supposed memory of some trauma, or by invok-ing the need to turn one's back on such memory in order to focus on a fu-ture that can only be won by such cultivated forgetfulness. Hitler's Third Reich claimed sovereignty in Germany in 1933 by a movement of the first sort. Rising some sixteen years later on the ruins of that Reich some years later, Adenauer's Federal Republic claimed sovereignty by a movement of the second sort. However, only to a superficial analysis does the example of West Germany, founded on the active refusal of its own desolated past, and therefore on the betrayal of all those who lie dead among the ruins the march of progress leaves behind it as it passes, stand in contrast to the example of Hitler's earlier German Reich, which founded itself on the explicit, recurrent recall of the German collapse at the end of the First World War. Both states, first Hitler's and later Adenauer's, served themselves through the same manipulative cooptation of the memory of trauma, at the expense of its victims (which is not to suggest that the two regimes are morally equivalent—that Adenauer's Germany was no better than Hitler's).

As Zehfuss argues, such manipulation of trauma in the very name of the dead actually serves the opposite of remembrance. It feeds forgetting. What is more, the forgetting at issue is of an especially devastating sort, since it strikes at the roots of the very possibility of genuine recollection. Deployed as part of "a politics of trauma"—to use K. M. Fierke's apt phrase in her already cited contribution to *Memory, Trauma, and World Politics* (page 130), designed for the manipulative exploitation of the memory of trauma to bolster claims to political sovereignty—what occurs is a thoroughgoing regimentation of all memories of trauma and its victims. As in the Nazi *"Gleichschaltung"* —"equalization," used to name the process, after Hitler's rise to power, of bringing all German institutions, from the family to the university, industry, and labor into conformity with Nazi ideology: thus, in effect, the progressive Nazification of the whole of German society—all memories of the trauma on the recurrent citation of which the state seeks to found itself are made to conform to the single interpretation of the traumatic event that the same state imposes as obligatory.

Fierke is careful to distinguish between the denial of the memory of trauma at work in such a politics of trauma, on one hand, and the psychological phenomenon of denial, as in Freud's concept of it, on the other. 'In the political world,' she writes (in Bell, page 131), 'denial, rather than a function of unconscious repression [as it is in Freud and the psychological use of the term], can be understood as a political act for the purpose of creating a unity of interpretation . . . which require[s] the suppression of alternative memories."

Such politically motivated *sup*-pression, then, is not at all comparable to the *re*-pression at work in denial in Freud's sense of the term. The political suppression of any alternative to what gets promulgated as the only officially recognized interpretation, and psychological repression belonging to the very process of traumatization, are two very different things. Referring to the political suppression of all but the officially sanctioned interpretation of a traumatic event, Fierke writes (still page 131): "While this process involved an element of repression, it did not require psychological denial. What is repressed is difference, debate or alternative narratives of the past." Such a process, however, will not be called *re*-pression at all, if we confine that term to its psychological sense, as I think is wise, to avoid confusion. It is simply *sup*-pression, as Fierke expresses it herself in what I already cited a moment ago, at the end of the preceding paragraph.

"Individuals," writes Fierke to end the paragraph in which she makes her remarks about the difference between political and psychological denial, "may be inclined, in a repressive situation [which by my suggestion above might be called for clarity's sake an *op*-pressive and *sup*-pressive situation, rather than *re*-pressive one], to adopt an *interpretation* akin to that of the authorities, in order to survive or avoid conflict, but this is not the same as repression an in unconscious." It most certainly is not.

The suppression directly intended by a "political act" enforcing the universalization of a single, state-sponsored interpretation of trauma is, in fact, a manipulative exploitation *of* the very repression and denial that are an inseparable part of psychological trauma. Thus, for example, President Bush was already calling for a moment of silence to memorialize the victims of 9/11 *even before the towers struck by two of the hijacked planes had actually fallen, and also before the two other hijacked planes had crashed, one in the fields of Pennsylvania and the other into the Pentagon.* Whether it was intentional on his part or not, what Bush was doing was seizing the earliest possible moment to manage reactions to the 9/11 attacks and channel them into a uniform, officially sanctioned interpretation that served the interests of his administration.

"While distorted," Fierke correctly notes (pages 127-128), in such cases "the salience of the discursive move is dependent on a context of past experience." That is, the exploitation of trauma is dependent upon the prior occurrence of the trauma itself and, even more crucially important for the purposes of exploitation, the psychological denial and deferment of affect that are definitive for the Freudian "belatedness" of trauma. Thus, as Fierke goes on to observe, "collective anxiety is never purely a product of elite intervention or manipulation, although there is an element of this," an element especially strong in such cases as the Nazi manipulation of the trauma of German defeat at the end of World War I, or the Bush administration's manipulation of the trauma of 9/11. Even in those cases, however, there must be an antecedent widespread anxiety of just the sort generated by shared trauma before manipulations such as Bush's can take hold. "The discursive moves" whereby such manipulation is accomplished "are only effective," as Fierke observes, "if they respond to deep and genuine social concerns in a time of general malaise, that is, a population has to be receptive to manipulation."

What is more, when carried to completion the sort of political manipulation of traumatic memory she describes even deprives those whose memories are being oppressed of all possibility of *articulating* that oppression clearly, and therefore even of the possibility of becoming fully aware of their own oppression themselves. When the very terms of public discourse are fixed by the same officially sanctioned, standardizing interpretation that manipulates the memory of trauma to secure its own sovereignty, then those who suffered the trauma are denied even any language in which to *name* their suffering. As that standard, standardizing interpretation progressively pervades the means and media of communication, suppression and oppression reach a maximum. At that point the circle of what Fierke calls the "politics of trauma" is closed, and along with it any gap in the circle through which the traumatized themselves might enter, to play a genuinely political role of their own, is also closed. In that way the closure of the politics *of* trauma becomes the exclusion of all trauma *from* politics. However, since *the political* itself is traumatic—a point to which I will be returning in the next chapter—that means that the closure of the politics of trauma is the paradoxical elimination of the political as such. The only questions left for "politics" to answer become questions of how best to "manage" what are claimed to be unquestionable and unalterable forms and forces. To cite what is in fact the prime example, the forces at work in "market economics" are held out as working their effects inevitably and inexorably, and the only questions left for supposedly "political" processes to answer are those of how, if at all, those forces can be channeled or directed to be given the maximum opportunity to provide for universal economic "progress"—in short, Francis Fukuyama's vision of the global spread of free-market capitalism and parliamentary democracy as the benign "end of history," after which things just keep on getting better and better.

At any rate, so useful is the exploitation of trauma to the state for establishing and securing itself as sovereign, and in the process curtailing and eventually eliminating the very possibility that any genuine political resistance to its claims to sovereignty might arise, that the state will not hesitate to invent a trauma, should chance fail to provide it with one. If fortune does not smile upon the state by bringing along a good traumatic event, the state will take over from chance and make up a trauma to suit its purposes. That process, and how it fits with Fierke's insight that the state can effectively manipulate trauma only if provided with a population trauma has already made receptive to manipulation, will be the topics with which the following section of this chapter will begin.

Making a Myth of Trauma

In her book *The Shock Doctrine*, Naomi Klein traces what she calls "the rise of disaster capitalism"—the subtitle of the book. As she recounts that rise, disaster capitalism really began to come into its own when the "free market" doctrine of conservative economist Milton Friedman and the entire "Chicago School" of economics that sprang up around him became, under Ronald Reagan's Presidency, the official, reigning, American economic ideology, a position it has since then not only retained but also expanded into eventual global dominance. As Klein argues, in that now globalized economic ideology—sometimes also called economic "neo-liberalism," in the classic sense of "liberalism" defined by such watershed publications as Adam Smith's *The Wealth of Nations*—economics is, in effect, liberated from anything approaching the genuinely political. The supposed laws of the market are elevated to the status of absolutes, no longer subject to question by, or subordination to, any supposedly independent political interests.

Indeed, the securing of the independence of the "free market" economy against the possibility of any genuinely significant external political intervention became the major goal of "the Chicago Boys," as they came to be called, in the interventions they and their local supporters began to make in Chile in the 1960s, and then proceeded progressively to extend. The model worked out in Chile was extended, first, to other South American nations during the 1970s and, especially, under President Reagan's seal of approval during the 1980s. Eventually it was expanded to apply to all "developing nations" around the world. In a note (on page 257 of *The Shock Doctrine*) to a chapter on how the model that was first developed in Chile was later applied in South Africa during the transition to majority rule, Klein discusses how the 'Chicago Boys' and their accomplices in Chile under the military dictatorship of Pinochet rigged the Chilean constitution and court system "so it was legally next to impossible to reverse their [that is, the Chicago School market ideologists'] revolutionary changes,' thereby, 'as Pinochet's young minister José Piñera put it, ensuring 'insulation [of the market economy] from politics.' "

According to what was by then already emerging as the official American economic dogma, any failure to heed the supposedly invariant laws of "free market" economics—the workings, as it were, of Adam Smith's all-powerful "invisible hand"—by attempting to direct the economy to extra-economic political ends, can lead only to economic collapse. Correlatively, however, it is precisely such moments of economic collapse or disaster that open the door of opportunity for the imposition of a newly refurbished, pure "market economy" on the heretofore economically foolish nations that have tried to circumvent the inexorable economic "laws" at issue. As a result, all that remains for any "politics" that can claim legitimacy in such a market-subservient society—any "politics," that is, not guaranteed by market "laws" to lead to even worse future economic disasters—is to acquiesce joyfully in the operation of those "laws," and vigilantly to eradicate, like a good gardener attentively weeding a garden, any recalcitrant weeds that might spring up to obstruct the natural flowering of the "free market."

Thus, we might say that "disaster capitalism," as Klein calls it, is the form capitalism takes when it learns to capitalize on disaster. For example, Hurricane Katrina in 2004, notes Klein near the end of her book (page 518), "was a tragedy, but, as Milton Friedman wrote in his *Wall Street Journal* op-ed [at the time], it was 'also an opportunity.' " From such an elevated economists' perspective, the radically de-politicized 'free market' economy can be seen to be open to what Friedman himself called "shock" capitalism, whereby "liberal market economies" can be imposed upon a nation after, and purportedly as the only effective response to, the disaster of an economic collapse. Such 'shock' or 'disaster' capitalism needs only to wait patiently, as it were, for the forces at work in the global market itself, aided by chance, to engender economic crises and collapses that such agents of disaster capitalism as the 'Chicago boys' can then exploit after the fact as golden opportunities to impose 'free market' economies on the survivors of the catastrophes at issue. 'Not so long ago,' as Klein goes on to remark a few pages later (page 522), "disasters were periods of social leveling, rare moments when atomized communities put divisions aside and pulled together. Increasingly, however, disasters are the opposite: they provide windows into a cruel and ruthlessly divided future in which money and race buy survival" — as her earlier cited example of Katrina all too clearly demonstrates.

In that most straightforward form, disaster capitalism simply waits for antecedent economic processes, combined with chance good fortune (good for the free market ideologues, that is), to engender disasters, which can then be capitalized upon after the fact. As Klein notes earlier in her book (on page 174), it was once again Milton Friedman himself who formulated the basic 'shock doctrine,' as Klein labels it. "Only a crisis—actual or perceived—produces real change,' Klein quotes Friedman as saying. 'When that crisis occurs,' he continues. 'the actions that are taken depend on the ideas that are lying around. That, I believe, is our [that is, Chicago School economists'] basic function: to develop alternatives to existing policies, to keep them alive and available until the politically impossible becomes politically inevitable."

However, Friedman's qualification that the opportune crisis may be either 'actual or perceived' already points toward the possibility for such free market economists as himself to take a much more active role in the whole process. As Klein details, beginning in the 1960s the economists and theorists in service to such capitalism often became too impatient just to wait for serendipitously exploitable crises to come along on their own. No longer content just to sit back and wait for opportune disasters to develop for their after-the-fact exploitation, the 'Chicago boys' and their ilk around the globe began intentionally to foster crises for the purpose of creating golden opportunities for capitalization. Klein (pages 222ff), cites a speech by American economist John Williamson at a by-invitation-only conference on January 13, 1993, in Washington, D. C., as the first time the transition was made from the idea of economic "shock therapy" as a matter of the exploitation of crises *when they occurred*—exploitation of the "opportunities" crises afforded for imposing otherwise unacceptable and impossible "neoliberal" (that is, "Chicago School") economic reforms such as privatization, massive spending cuts on social programs, and deregulation—to the idea of *actually engendering and/or fostering crises* for that purpose. By the dawn of the new millennium, the principle was already well established. It had by then proven itself globally through multiple experiments.

What is more, from the perspective of what Klein calls disaster capitalism, what is truly ideal is the sort of thing for which the attacks on the World Trade Center in New York and the Pentagon in Washington, D. C., on September 11, 2001, near the very beginning of the new millennium, provide a perfect example. In such a case fortuitous chance and deliberate manufacture coalesce all but seamlessly to create an inexhaustible wellspring for ongoing, ever expanding economic exploitation. All that is needed is a conveniently vaguely definable enemy ready to hand to blame for the disaster — the very vagueness, the final indefiniteness and in-definability, of which is crucial for the purposes at issue. In the case of the various measures that have been taken by the American government in the wake of 9/11, to stay with that example, Klein observes (page 380): 'Through all its various changes—the War on Terror, the war on radical Islam, the war against Islamofascism, the Third World War, the long war, the generational war—the basic shape of the conflict has remained unchanged. It is limited by neither time nor space nor target.' This lack of limit or definition—the impossibility of any clear-cut victory over such a multitudinous, limitless enemy identified with no nation or alliance of nations, but to be found everywhere and, therefore, nowhere in particular—is not a defect, from the point of view of the capitalism that knows how to capitalize on disaster. Such an amorphous and ill-defined status is, rather, the greatest virtue of such enemies. 'From a military perspective,' as Klein remarks, it is of course the case that such 'sprawling and amorphous traits make the War on Terror an unwinnable proposition.' Nevertheless, as she goes on to observe, 'from an economic perspective, they make it an unbeatable one: not a flash-in-the-pan war that could potentially be won but a new and permanent fixture in the global economic architecture.'

In that way, "terrorists" play the same role for the never-ending "War on terror" and all that goes with it that "the Jews" played for the Nazis in their seizure and holding of power in Germany for the twelve endless years of their rule. It is not *despite* the impossibility of clearly indentifying just who belongs to the enemy camp and who does not, but *because* of it that the struggle against such ubiquitous enemies as "terrorists" or "Jews" is so useful for those seeking to capitalize on trauma. Claims to power that are based on the purported necessity of defending those in whose name that power is exercised against the threats to security that come from such never eliminable enemies will never go wanting for apparent grounds and justifications. Even—indeed, especially—if that necessity is, as Friedman hinted, merely perceived and not at all actual, no more than an illusion, a fire fed only by flames of unconscionably manipulated fear, it is all that is needed to provide an inexhaustible source of justification for that sovereignty willing to base itself upon it. That, finally, means any sovereignty at all, as I shall return to below

At any rate, what is at issue in all such capitalization on disaster, whether in its patient form of waiting for fortune to bring felicitous crises its way for after-the-fact exploitation, its impatient form of actively helping to foment such crises, or its perfected form of the fomenting of the crisis of a perpetual fear of crises to come, is always the *exploitation of trauma* for profit. What Klein labels "disaster capitalism" is capitalism built upon such exploitation. As it unfolds, such capitalism institutionalizes the very trauma it requires to profit from its investment. The more advanced the process, the less market capitalism must *either* twiddle its thumbs, patiently waiting for fortune to bring a crisis its way, *or* find ways actively to hasten the processes of disaster along. Instead, a sort of permanent state of crisis—actual or only, even better, merely perceived—gets built right into the market itself. Thus, as Klein points out toward the end of her book (pages 540-541), "[g]iven the boiling temperatures, both climatic and political," that prevail today, "future disasters need not be cooked up in dark conspiracies" any longer, if they ever did need to be. Because they have now been built directly into the economic system itself, crises—at least *perceived* crises, which are all that is required, as Friedman saw — are always conveniently at hand, readily available for exploitation. 'All indications are that simply staying the current course,' as Klein goes on to observe, crises 'will keep coming with ever more ferocious intensity.' Conspiratorial shenanigans such as once were practiced by Americans in Chile prove no longer necessary today. 'Disaster generation can therefore be left to the market's invisible hand,' as Klein ironically says: 'This is one area in which it actually delivers.' Accordingly, she concludes, a 'new consensus is emerging. It is not that the market has become immune to instability, at least not exactly. It is that a steady flow of disasters is now so expected that the ever-adaptable market has changed to fit this new status quo—instability is the new stability.'

In a sense, what disaster capitalism, to use Naomi Klein's term, ends up doing when it bars the door against any political interruption of economic business as usual is really a matter of just coming back around, after a long journey, to the same point from which it and, in juncture with it, the twin ideas of the nation-state and modern sovereignty first started out, in the social contract theories of the seventeenth century. Only insofar as a mythical "state of nature" identical to a state of war, or at least the constant threat of war, in which each individual struggles with all others to claim ownership over limited resources, is postulated as "original," does any need arise in the first place for the contending parties to enter into contract with one another, establishing peace between themselves by voluntarily relinquishing some of their freedom and autonomy to create a common sovereign of one sort or another, whose charge it is to keep that peace. Thus, for the benefits of security against the rapacity of their fellows, each individual party to the contract gives up the free exercise of his or her own rapacity against those same fellows. As is the all too common and recurrent pattern, security trumps freedom in such a narrative.

The clear interest of whoever would claim sovereignty, or even just to be acting in sovereignty's name, is to convince those over whom the claim is made that their very security depends upon granting that same claim. That is, the interest of sovereignty is to keep its subjects persuaded that, save for that very sovereignty itself, they would be thrown back into a traumatic insecurity in which, as Hobbes said, every person is a wolf to every other, and in which, no matter how big a wolf one may be, there is always a bigger wolf on the way, at least in one's own wolfish imagination—which is all it takes, as Milton Friedman in effect saw with regard to what he called "shock" capitalism. That there really be wolves as the door is not necessary, in order to make the case for establishing and perpetuating sovereignty as supposedly the only sure way to keep the door barred against them. In fact, it is not even necessary that the subjects of the sovereign, whoever or whatever that sovereign may be (monarch, dictator, president, directory, political bureau, committee, parliament, "the people," God, etc.), *believe* that such wolves *are* at the collective door. All that is necessary is that they believe that wolves *would be* at the door, save for there being some sovereign keeping them at bay.

Franklin Roosevelt may have been right that there is nothing to fear but fear itself. However, that mere fear of fear itself, he might well have added—at least to himself, if not to those whom he was addressing, since to say it to them would have risked undercutting his own claim to Presidential authority—is more than enough fear, all on its own, for the purpose of keeping the powerful in power.

We might express the point by saying that it is not so much trauma itself that sovereignty exploits in order to justify itself, as it is the *fear of* trauma. Alternatively, we could say that sovereignty founds itself only *indirectly* on trauma, insofar as it founds itself *directly* on the *avoidance* of trauma. Sovereignty makes a myth of trauma for the very purpose of assuring that trauma never be allowed to carry itself to term, as it were—never be allowed to complete its *traumatization*. Sovereignty just cannot afford to let trauma really happen, to let it "take place," as we say. Most especially, sovereignty cannot afford to let trauma take over its own place and set itself up there, establishing its own occupancy of the space over which it contests with sovereignty itself.

As international relations scholar Jenny Edkins observes in "Remembering Relationality: Trauma Time and Politics," her contribution to *Memory, Trauma, and World Politics* (page 107), in a remark that fits well with Rebecca Solnit's analyses of what she calls "disaster communities," which I discussed in Chapter 1: "Trauma is clearly disruptive of settled stories. Centralized, sovereign political authority is particularly threatened by this. After a traumatic event what we call the state moves quickly to close down any openings produced by putting in place as fast as possible a linear narrative of origins." What Edkins' own discussion of that point suggests—although she does not go so far as to say it herself, at least in the same terms—is that the trauma that most threatens "sovereign political authority" is the very trauma of its own groundlessly violent birth. Sovereignty itself is founded in and as the 'putting in place' of a 'linear narrative' of its *own* origins, a narrative in which a fictitious trauma is, to put it paradoxically, retrospectively projected back before the emergence of sovereignty, creating the illusion that sovereignty arises as the only satisfactory response to such supposedly original trauma.

Structurally, the movement at issue is the same as that made by the abusive husband who attempts to "justify" abusing his wife by projecting blame for the abuse back onto that wife herself, who supposedly 'asked for it' by her own earlier non-compliance to his wishes. In both cases, the abusive husband justifying abuse or the ruling sovereign justifying rule, what occurs is really no more than the *rationalization* of an earlier act of violence. Indeed, that movement of rationalization actually compounds the violence further, by robbing those who have been violated of even the space to voice any protest. Thus, for example, Hobbes's tracing of the legitimacy of sovereignty back to the supposed need to defend against the trauma of the war of all against all, where "man is wolf to man," effectively not only masks the very violence whereby a supposed sovereign first imposes itself on its subjects—that it, subjects them to itself—but also subjects those same subjects to the illusion that their subjection is really for their own good, so that even any complaint about the whole arrangement just serves to demonstrate ingratitude, even in the plaintiffs' own minds.

At issue in such making-myth of trauma is the same thing that Paul Eisenstein argues allows us to align classic liberalism with fascism, as I discussed in an earlier chapter. As already mentioned in that earlier discussion, by Eisenstein's analysis liberalism shares with fascism the endeavor to *avoid* trauma—just as I have been arguing above with regard to modern sovereignty as such. The argument he advances is that both liberalism and fascism, especially in its German variant as National Socialism, end up "disavowing" the "traumatic kernel"—the Lacanian *point de caption* or "quilting point"—that is "internal" to any political order. Both disavow the "traumatic instability/inconsistency" that is internal to social order as such, by turning it into a definite historical something or other, rather than keeping cognizant of what Eisenstein calls its "transcendence," which is to say its structural role in the very constitution of any social order whatever. They both disavow the "transcendence" of that traumatic kernel of all social order by telling a story wherein that kernel is given (page 45) "a context, a history, from the beginning." Eisenstein makes that remark in discussing the example of "the figure of the Jew" in National Socialism, but his analysis makes clear that it applies just as well to such figures in classic liberalism as that of "the state of nature."

The Sovereign's Clothes

'Sovereign is he who declares the exception,' writes Carl Schmitt, the important and influential right-wing legal theorist who eventually used his thought to provide the Nazi state with legal justification. That is the famous opening line of *Political Theology*, first published in Germany in 1922. The exception at issue is to the ordinary norm to and in which the defining laws of the society at issue apply. Sovereign is whomever is vested with the power to declare a "state of exception" in which there is a suspension of the basic legal principles, the fundamental laws, that in all other, non-exceptional, "natural" and "routine" conditions are always in force and never to be abrogated—such laws as are embodied in the Bill of Rights amended to the United States Constitution, including the right of habeas corpus, for example.

In *Political Theology* (page 5), after his opening line defining sovereignty, cited already, Schmitt immediately goes on to observe that "[o]nly this definition can do justice" to a "borderline concept" such as that of sovereignty. "Contrary to the imprecise terminology that is found in popular literature," he continues, what makes such a concept a "borderline" one is not that it is somehow "a vague concept." Rather, it is a borderline concept because it is a concept "pertaining to the outermost sphere." That is, it is a concept that *fixes a border*.

Because sovereignty is just such a border-setting concept, the "definition of sovereignty must therefore be associated with a borderline case and not with routine." That is not at all to say, however, that the border established by the assertion of sovereignty—that is, the exercise of the definitive power to decide on the exception—is itself exceptional, in the sense of only coming into play under special, rare, or exceptional circumstances. Rather, it is the very decision that establishes the boundary between what is "inside" and what "outside" the community as such and, therefore, protected by the law. The exception is precisely what defines what is to count as the rule.

Thus, writes Schmitt, the exception, on the power of the decision and declaration of which sovereignty itself must be defined, "is to be understood to refer to a general concept in the theory of the state, and not merely to a construct applied to any emergency degree or state of siege." The border that the sovereign decision establishes between routine and extraordinary conditions is what alone determines the limits of very distinction between the inside and the outside of the "nation" or "national community" as such. As the drawing of the boundary between what is inside the nation and what is outside it, that decision is the establishment of a legal order as such.

"Like every other order," writes Schmitt a few pages after his opening definition (page 10), "the legal order rests on a decision not on a norm." Indeed, in Schmitt's way of thinking the norm itself can only be established *by* a decision that cuts the exceptional away from the normal. The sovereign is whoever makes that decision with regard to any "legal order," the very decision that establishes the norm in the first place (page 13): "Every general norm demands a normal, everyday frame of life to which it can be factually applied and which is subjected to its regulations. . . . For a legal order to make sense, a normal situation must exist, and he is sovereign who definitely decides whether this normal situation actually exists."

Three-fourths of a century after Schmitt, contemporary Italian philosopher Giorgio Agamben attempted critically to come to grips with Schmitt's analysis of the concept of sovereignty, and to combine that analysis with insights from Foucault. Above all in two works—*Homo Sacer: Sovereign Power and Bare* and its sequel *State of Exception*—Agamben combines elements from those two earlier thinkers to develop his own analysis of sovereignty.

From Foucault Agamben takes the notion of "biopower," power exercised directly over life itself, rather than only indirectly through the power over death, that is, the power to *take* life, the power to *kill*. According to Foucault, the difference between the "classical," monarchical sovereignty and sovereignty in a distinctively modern sense, lies precisely in the transition from sovereignty as the power to take life, to sovereignty as power exercised directly over life itself, which Foucault calls *biopower*. Agamben and others also develop that Foucauldian notion into that of 'biopolitics,' which would be the 'politics' that corresponds to sovereignty as the exercise of such 'biopower.'

With Schmitt, Agamben defines modern sovereignty as the power to draw the line between what falls under the norm—and therefore under the shelter of the law—and what falls outside the norm—and therefore also outside that shelter. Going beyond Schmitt, however, Agamben argues that, although sovereignty as Schmitt defines it may really come into its own only in the modern period, it grows from a seed planted long before modernity. That was the seed planted by the ancient Greeks, when they distinguished between *bios*, or life in the fully human sense—such as can be captured in "biographies": literally, "life-writings"—on the one hand, and *zoe*, or life in the purely "zoological" sense, which Agamben calls *"bare* life,' on the other.

In ancient Greek thought, most especially as formulated in Aristotle, *bios*, life in the supposedly fully human sense, is possible only within the *polis*, the political community of norm and law. In contrast, *zoe* is "bare" life, in the sense of a minimum where there is "just" life, life "and no more," the "mere" life human beings share with animals and even plants. It is to life in that minimal, less-than-human sense that those denied any place within the *polis* would be reduced, according to this Greek line of thought.

The sovereign as such, Agamben argues, is vested with the power to pronounce the *ban* whereby someone is cast out of the community and marked accordingly. Whoever is placed under such a ban and thus cast out of the community, is also thereby cast over the threshold separating genuinely human life from bare life. Accordingly, to be vested with sovereignty as Schmitt defines it, namely, the power to decide what will fall under the norm and what will constitute an exception to that norm, is to be vested with the authority to decide who will be granted the right to live a truly human life, and who will be denied any such right, and reduced instead to a condition of no more than bare life—without even any claim to keep that!

To be placed under the ban, that is, to be cast out of the community and deprived of all shelter under the laws of that community, is to be fully exposed to whomever and whatever one chances to encounter. Those reduced to the status of *bare life* can thus be counted as *barely alive* at all any longer, in the sense that even the minimum of life they retain when deprived of all legal status is thoroughly precarious, without human recourse or defense against whatever acts —however arbitrary—others may choose to commit against them. Their life—the minimum that remains to them of it—can be taken from them at any moment without any possibility of appeal. No longer even subjects of the sovereign, and so no longer citizens of the state—no longer members of the community the boundaries of which the sovereign alone can decide—they are cast completely at the mercy of those who remain such subjects and citizens, with all the rights that pertain thereto.

The status of such an outcast, Agamben argues, is that of *homo sacer*, "sacred man." That category was used in ancient Roman law to designate someone who, paradoxically, may be *killed*, but cannot be *sacrificed*. It is the status *within* the law of those who have been placed altogether *outside* the law. In effect no longer counting as human, they can also no longer be offered up to the gods. Such an offer would be a blasphemy, a violation, an affront, like offering the gods excrement or some other "unclean" thing. Precisely because they have been cast outside the law, those reduced to the status of *homo sacer* can therefore not be sacrificed. However, again precisely for the same reason, there is no legal stricture against taking *from* them the bare life that alone remains *to* them. Thus, designated as unholy and therefore not to be sacrificed, they are by the same stroke marked as those who can be killed without legal consequence, but simply at whim and will by anyone who chooses to do so, and has the means to do it.

The power that defines sovereignty is, accordingly, the power to decide who becomes *homo sacer*, and when. Furthermore, Agamben argues, the status of *homo sacer* is exactly that of the prisoner inmates in the Nazi extermination camps. According to his analysis, the condition of bare life outside any protection of the law finds its ultimate instantiation in the *Muselmänner* ("Muslims") of the camps. The *Muselmänner* were those inmates who have been so reduced by the abuse to which they had been subjected that they became a sort of living dead. They were those who had lost all active will to live, and to whom all that remained was passively to receive whatever treatment was dished out to them moment by moment. They were so traumatized by their ordeal that they were no longer capable of any degree of effective agency in their own lives, including that of trying to avoid the abuse inflicted upon them. At most, they could merely cower before their abuser, like beaten dogs.

In *Homo Sacer* (page 181) Agamben sums up his "provisional conclusions" in three theses:

1. The original political relation is the ban (the state of exception as zone of indistinction between outside and inside, exclusion and inclusion).
2. The fundamental activity of sovereign power is the production of bare life as originary political element and as threshold of articulation between nature and culture, *zoe* and *bios*.
3. Today it is not the city [that is, what the Greeks called the *polis*] but rather the camp that is the fundamental biopolitical paradigm of the West.

Thus, by Agamben's analysis the emergence under the Nazis of the camp system was no anomaly. Rather, the Nazi camps represent the culmination and flowering of the whole Western concept of sovereignty as such. What is more, he argues, insofar as everyone today is subject to such sovereignty, everyone today is at least potentially, by virtue of the decisions of whomever has been vested with the power of sovereignty over one — that is, the decisions of whomever has been designated "the decider,' as George W. Bush notoriously identified himself as President of the Unites States after September 11, 2001—a *Muselmann*.

All reservations about the details of Agamben's argument aside, his account has the great merit of highlighting just how *paradoxically precarious* the situation of all who are subject to "modern" sovereignty (however ancient the institution of such sovereignty may prove to be) must always remain. The precariousness of the subject of sovereignty is *paradoxical*, precisely because the very claim on which sovereignty founds itself is the claim that sovereignty is necessary in order to *avert* an otherwise inescapable precariousness or insecurity: As Hobbes first argued, only the institution of sovereignty—that "leviathan"—can offer those who contract with one another to establish that institution escape from the condition in which "man is a wolf to man," and in which there is never any security against the "war of all against all." What Agamben helps us see is that if, in the very name of security, one subjects oneself to a sovereign, one thereby actually exposes oneself to an even more radical *in*security—the constant threat that "the decider" may at any time decide to declare one outside the law, that is, outside the normal state in which the law holds sway, having somehow entered, instead, into a state of exception where, by law, the law itself no longer holds.

Ultimately, however, the decisions of the sovereign, "the decider," can come into effect only if those to whom they are to apply *regard* them as so applying. That is, to have any effect the claim to sovereignty must be *acknowledged* by those very "subjects" *over* whom sovereignty is to be exercised. That acknowledgement may be more or less explicitly made, through some public ceremony of investiture, for example. But even such explicit investiture itself always remains essentially *symbolic* and, therefore, dependent upon something implicit that can never, in fact, become fully explicit, without undoing sovereignty itself.

In a note to the third section of the first chapter of *Capital*, Karl Marx comments that one man is a king only because other men hold themselves to be his subjects, but that, on the contrary, those other men imagine themselves to be subjects because he is a king. That is, the sovereign is not sovereign by some trait or quality of his being, but only insofar as he is *treated as* a sovereign, in effect.

To be a sovereign, however, is to be so treated not only by others—namely, by the sovereign's "subjects," those over whom the sovereign has been invested with the power to rule—but also, and indeed above all, by one's own sovereign self. For a sovereign to think otherwise, for a king to think, for example, that he is somehow a king by nature, and not by symbolic investiture, is to succumb to madness, as Slavoj Žižek puts the point in *The Ticklish Subject*. Žižek cites (page 274) "Lacan's well-known dictum according to which a madman is not only a beggar who thinks he is a king but also a king who thinks he is a king (i.e. who perceives his symbolic mandate 'king' as directly grounded in the real of his being)."

Sovereignty constitutes itself at the point of intersection between two different intersections, as the differentiation of two different differentiations, as it were. On one hand, there is the de-cision, in the literal sense of the cutting apart, that draws the border or cut between the normal state and the state of exception. Sovereignty, in that regard, establishes itself at and as the intersection, the border or crossing point, by crossing which one comes under or outside the norm, and the law that shelters that norm. On the other hand, there is the symbolic investiture whereby sovereignty –the very right and authority to decide the exception (and therewith the norm)—is instituted, and wherein the claim to rule on the part of the one who would be sovereign intersects with the acquiescence to that claim on the part of those who, in that very acquiescence, become that would-be sovereign's subjects.

The authority to decide the exception is vested in the sovereign by the bestowal of symbols of power, recognized as such by those who, in that very recognition, subject themselves to the very sovereignty that is dependent upon that same recognition in order to exist at all. In that regard, the distinction between sovereignty itself and the individual person or persons— all the way up to and including even "the people" as a whole, if it is in "the people" that sovereignty is vested (as in that "government of, by, and for the people" touted by Lincoln at Gettysburg)—who hold or carry that sovereignty at any given time, functions in the same way as the distinction between the phallus and the penis as Žižek draws it. Indeed, the phallus is itself the Lacanian "Master-signifier" the bestowal of which symbolically invests with power the one upon whom it is bestowed. Fundamentally, *all* symbols or power are, as such, "phallic symbols" in a strong sense—whoever carries, by investiture, a symbol of power, "has" the phallus.

Žižek discusses the issue in similar passages in a variety of his books. Thus, in 1999 in *The Ticklish Subject* he writes (page 383) about what a "crucial point" it is to

> distinguish between the penis (the erectile organ itself) and the phallus (the signifier of potency, of symbolic authority, of the—symbolic, not biological—dimension that confers authority and/or potency on me). [I have moved the closing parenthesis in this line from right after the phrase "and/or potency," where it occurs in the printed original, to the end of

the sentence, where it seems to me to belong.] Just as (. . .) a judge, who may be a worthless individual in himself, exerts authority the moment he puts on the insignia that confer his legal authority on him, the moment he no longer speaks only for himself, since it is the Law itself that speaks through him, the individual male's potency functions as a sign that another symbolic dimension is active through him: the 'phallus' designates the symbolic support that confers on my penis the dimension of proper potency.

A few years later, in *Organs Without Bodies: Deleuze and Consequences* (page 87), Žižek writes, similarly, that "one has to think of the phallus not as the organ that immediately expresses the vital force of my being, my virility, and so forth but, precisely as . . . an insignia [of power], as a mask that I put on in the same way that a king or judge puts on his insignia—phallus is an 'organ without body' that I put on, which gets attached to my body, without ever being the 'organic part', namely, forever sticking out as its incoherent, excessive supplement."

Even more recently, in his *In Defense of Lost Causes*, Žižek expands upon the same basic idea of the inescapably symbolic nature of power, this time without explicit reference to the distinction between penis and phallus. In discussing how such a "pathetic figure" as, for example, Kafka's father (at least as Kafka presents him) could exercise the sort of dictatorial authority and power that he did (again, at least by Kafka's own account), Žižek writes (pages 86-87):

The answer would then be the socio-symbolic network that invests an empirical person with power . . . . From the traditional rituals of investiture, we know the objects which not only "symbolize" power, but put the subject who acquires them into the position of effectively *exercising* power—if a king holds in his hands the scepter and wears the crown, his words will be taken as the words of a king. Such insignia are external, not part of my nature: I don them: I wear them in order to exert power. As such, . . . they introduce a gap between what I immediately am and the function that I exercise (that is, I am never fully at the level of my function). . . .

. . . When the subject is endowed with symbolic authority, he acts as an appendix to his symbolic title, that is, it is [what Lacan calls] the big Other, the symbolic institution, which acts through him: suffice it to recall a judge, who may be a miserable and corrupted person, but the moment he puts on his robe and other insignia, his words are the words of the Law itself.

In *The Psychotheology of Everyday Life: A Reading of Freud and Rosenzweig* Erik Santner—strongly influenced by Žižek, who is in turn influenced by him—argues that all symbolic investiture, all conferring of authority and power through the bestowal of symbols, requires, precisely because of the "gap" Žižek identifies, the perpetually, recurring "citation" of the formulas of investiture. Such continual recitation—in the literal sense of re-citation: citing again—is needed to cover the very *lack of foundation* of power in the natural properties or qualities of the one who has been vested with power and authority, or in anything at all save the recitation or reiteration of the symbolic formulas themselves. Such recitation is a reenactment of investiture that can never be finished, demanding ever further reenactment, because the investiture of power is itself never accomplished as a fact: Žižek's "gap" is never closed. In that sense, the investiture of power is never sufficient to secure the claim to power supposed to be authorized by such investiture.

In the perpetual, perpetually insufficient reenactment of investiture in endless reiterations takes place the repeated laying claim to power or authority on the part of those who would have that claim honored. The claim to power and authority, and the demand that the claim be honored, are reiterated each time those who advance that claim and that demand once again display the symbols of power. The bestowal of those very symbols in acts of symbolic investiture *constitutes* the very power and authority they "represent" or "stand for." Thus, such symbols function the same way "sacraments" do in Christianity—as "effective signs," signs the making or bestowing of which *effects* the very condition or status they stand for.

Nor is that theological connection accidental. At least it is no accident within what Heidegger calls *onto-theology*, that tradition wherein to think and speak of beings as such and in totality is also inseparably to speak of the "highest being," the most in being of beings—God as the supreme being, *sovereign* over all other beings. Furthermore, Heidegger likes to cite one of Heraclitus's fragments, in accordance with which the Lord over the oracle at Delphi (namely, the god Appollo) neither says clearly what he means, nor merely hides his meaning, but gives, instead, a sign or "hint"— in Heidegger's German, the word *Wink*. And indeed, it is of the nature of sovereignty as such, not just of the sovereign divinity of the Delphic oracle, to communicate by hints, most especially, in fact, when it comes to the communication of the claim to sovereignty itself.

In translating Heidegger himself from German into other languages, translators will often leave some terms in the original German. That is most widely done with the term *Dasein*, which in everyday German means "existence" but which etymologically means "to be [*sein*] there [*da*]" and which Heidegger himself uses to designate the human being. However, it is also not infrequently done with the term *Wink* itself in translations of Heidegger's texts. So, for example, does contemporary French philosopher Jean-Luc Nancy leave it untranslated in his essay "On a Divine *Wink*" in *Dis-Enclosure*.

In that essay, a critical reading of Heidegger, Nancy gives thought to the connection between: (1) the concept of the *Wink* or hint; (2) *translation*, which *winkt* or hints when it makes an exception for an "untranslatable" word (such as *Wink* itself in the title of Nancy's own essay, of course); and (3) *sovereignty*, most especially insofar as, following Schmitt, it is defined as the power to declare "exceptions" to the presumed rule of law. As Nancy writes (pages 106) of those connections: "The exception of the untranslatable constitutes the law of translation. . . . Where there is exception, there is sovereignty. What is sovereign is the idiom that declares itself to be untranslatable." In the next paragraph (page 107) he continues: "Sovereign is the translator who decides to suspend the translation, leaving instead the word in the original." Then he proceeds to express a double connection between the *Wink* and sovereignty:

Thus we can establish, on the one hand, that the *Wink* is sovereign, and on the other, correlatively, that the sovereign *winkt*. . . . Nothing is more specifically characteristic of sovereign majesty than the frown, the wink, the expression said to be 'imperceptible,' the reply to which is called a 'sign of complicity,' in the sense that, in that complicity, connivance precedes and exceeds understanding, in the sense that complicity has already understood whatever it is that has not been openly offered up to the understanding, but is expected. The *Wink* opens an expectation at the same time as an impatience to which the decision to understand without waiting, in the twinkling of an eye, responds.

In his essay on the *Wink* Nancy connects Heidegger's notion of "the last God" as the God who *winkt*, with Derrida's *différance,* the ordinary spelling of which, in French as in English, uses an *e* where Derrida writes, instead, an *a.* Nancy notes that the *a* in *différance* is itself a *Wink.* The very difference to which it calls attention can only be indicated in writing, since as pronounced in French there is no difference between the sound of the word written with an *a* and the same word written with an *e.* As spoken, the difference between *"différence"* and *"différance"* passes by unnoticed—just as Heidegger says his "last god" passes by, and *is* the last god only in so passing. In that connection of multiple connections itself, Nancy sees a *Wink* that opens upon "another sense"—a sense other than that of sovereignty. Since, as Derrida taught in *Speech and Phenomena*, there can be no "meaning" without "indication," which is to say without any *Winken* that opens the space for "signification," that would also be a sense other than that of the sovereignty of "meaning" itself—of *that* very sense of *sense.*

That topic, however, no longer belongs to this chapter on the image of sovereignty. I will take it up, instead, in the next chapter, which is devoted to an initial exploration of what lies on the far side of sovereignty—and, therefore, the far side of that effort to avoid trauma upon which sovereignty itself is based.

Chapter 6

TRAUMA AND THE REMNANTS OF POLITICS

W hat is the politics of trauma?

That is, for one thing, in what ways and within what limits can politics be played with trauma, as the Bush administration played politics with the trauma to so many Americans of "9/11," to countenance the American invasion of Afghanistan and then Iraq, and the curtailing of civil liberties through the Patriot Act and other means? What can politics do with trauma?

But also, what politics does trauma itself elicit? What would a politics grounded in trauma itself—in the acknowledgment of it, in letting the trauma traumatize, rather than avoiding and denying it—be like? What does trauma do to politics?

I will begin this chapter on the politics of trauma with some further reflections on the topic of the preceding chapter, the topic of sovereignty and its relations to trauma.

The Sovereign Fetish

The sovereign is a fetish.

That, at least, is what Slavoj Žižek's way of handling the concept of fetish suggests. In his recent book *In Defense of Lost Causes*, Žižek differentiates between a fetish and a symptom. As he presents it, the fetish, like the symptom, involves (page 282) "a gesture of transference (onto the fetish object)." However, in the case of the fetish this transference "functions as an exact inversion of the standard formula of transference (with the subject supposed to know)," which applies to the symptom. By Žižek's account, "a symptom embodies a repressed knowledge, the truth about the subject that the subject is not ready to accept." In contrast, "what the fetish gives body to is precisely my disavowal of knowledge, my refusal to subjectively assume what I know." The fetish is defined by such "refusal-to-know," he says.

A few pages later (page 296) Žižek elaborates a bit on his treatment of the distinction between symptom and fetish, in applying it to the analysis of "ideology" and arguing in favor of "opposing the *fetishistic* mode of ideology, which predominates in our supposedly 'post-ideological' era, to its traditional *symptomal* mode, in which the ideological lie which structures our perception of reality is threatened by symptoms *qua* 'returns of the repressed,' cracks in the fabric of the ideological lie." He then continues:

> The fetish is effectively a kind of *envers* of the symptom. That is to say, the symptom is the exception which disturbs the surface of false appearance, the point at which the repressed Other Scene erupts, while the fetish is the embodiment of the lie which enables us to sustain the unbearable truth. Let us take the case of the death of a beloved person: in the case of the symptom, I "repress" this death, I try not to think about it, but the repressed trauma returns in the symptom; in the case of a fetish, on the contrary, I "rationally" fully accept this death, and yet I cling to the fetish, to some feature that embodies for me the disavowal of this death. In this sense, a fetish can play a very constructive role by allowing us to cope with the harsh reality. Fetishists are not dreamers lost in their private worlds, they are thoroughly "realist," able to accept the way things effectively are—since they have their fetish

to which they can cling in order to cancel the full impact of reality.

Ironically, however, by the rest of what he says about the fetish as opposed to the symptom, the way in which the fetish allows us to "cope" with whatever "harsh reality" is at issue is precisely by *refusing to cope with it at all*: the way the fetish makes us "able to accept the way things effectively are" is by the very "refusal-to-know" anything at all about how things are. We might put the point by saying that the only way that the fetish let's us accept the way things *effectively* are is by altogether denying how things *affectively* are. But, after all, such a traumatic blow as "the death of a beloved person" *is* a traumatic blow in the first place only insofar as one is affected by the loss of that person; if I really don't "feel" anything when the other person dies, then that death is no more than the death of an acquaintance with whom I had no special bond, and not the death of a *beloved* person at all. As Žižek writes two pages yet further on (page 298):

> *This* is a fetish at its purest: a tiny stupid object to which I cling and which allows me to endure all the dirty compromises of my life. Do we not all have, in one or another form, such fetishes? They can be our inner spiritual experiences (which tell us that our social reality is mere appearance which does not really matter), our children (for whose good we do all the humiliating things in our jobs), and so on and so forth.

Another distinction Žižek draws in some of his earlier works is of use here, with regard to clarifying the current distinction between fetish and symptom. That is the distinction Žižek adopts from Jean-Pierre Dupuy's *Pour un catrophisme éclairé* between *knowledge* and *belief*. In *The Puppet and the Dwarf: The Perverse Core of Christianity* (pages 159-160) Žižek uses Depuy's distinction to explicate a passage from Henri Bergson's *Two Sources of Morality and Religion* (*Les deux sources de la morale et de la religion*, pages 166-167), a passage in which Bergson describes his own subjective experience at the onset of World War I in August, 1914. What follows is my own earlier discussion of the issues involved, from my article "9/11 Never Happened, President Bush Wouldn't Let It: Bob Dylan Replies to Henri Bergson."

In the passage from the *Two Sources*, Bergson depicts how he reacted on the occasion of the actual outbreak of declared hostilities between France and Germany, on August 4, 1914. By his own account, he experienced the pending war as "*simultaneously probable and impossible*" (emphasis added). In a closely related passage from "The Possible and the Real" ("*Le possible et le réel*," page 111) that Žižek also cites in his own discussion (and of which I will use his translation), Bergson goes on to elucidate such a "complex and contradictory notion" (as Bergson himself calls it) pertaining to the notions of possibility and actuality, and to how unforeseeable events retroactively project their own possibility behind them, as it were. Bergson is concerned to clarify his position, and to distinguish it from the idea—one that, as Žižek will later observe, belongs in the domain of science fiction—that current events could somehow change how the past itself "really was." Bergson writes:

> I never pretended that one can insert reality into the past and thus work backwards in time. However, one can without any doubt insert there the possible, or, rather, at every moment the possible insert[s] itself there. Insofar as unpredictable and new reality creates itself, its image reflects itself behind itself—in the indefinite past: this new reality finds itself all the time having been possible; but it is only at the precise moment of its actual emergence that it *begins to always have been {possible}*, and this is why I say its possibility, which does not precede its reality, will have preceded it once this reality emerges.

In a remark parts of which have already been noted above, Bersgson writes that, before the actual declaration of war between his country and Germany, war appeared to him as "simultaneously possible and impossible: a complex and contradictory notion that persisted to the end," that is, till war actually broke out in the declaration of hostilities on August 4. Using Depuy's analysis of the global ecological catastrophe pending today, almost a centrury after Bergson and the First World War, Žižek writes that such events as either global ecological catastrophe today at the beginning of the 21st century, or global war early in the 20th century, are "always missed," the bypassing or missing of such events taking one of two basic forms, in accordance with which "either it [the event] is experienced as impossible but *not* real (the prospect of a forthcoming catastrophe that, however probable we know it is, we do not believe will really happen, and thus dismiss it as impossible), or as real but no longer impossible (once the catastrophe happens, it is 'renormalized,' perceived as part of the normal run of things, as always-already having been possible)." He then goes on to call explicit attention back to Dupuy's distinction by remarking that "as Dupuy makes clear, the gap that makes these paradoxes possible is the gap between knowledge and belief: we *know* the catastrophe is possible, even probable, yet we do not *believe* it will really happen."

Thus, to stick with the example of Bergson at the outbreak of World War I, Bergson did indeed *know* that war was not merely possible, but even probable, as he says himself. Yet, as he also says, he continued to relate to that same war as *im*-possible. That is, at the level of his everyday life, in common with most of his countrymen and, indeed, most of the populations in the other European countries about to be drawn into the carnage of the "Great War," Bergson's conduct, thought, and emotions bore no evidence of that very knowledge that war was coming. If by *belief* we mean precisely that which underlies and expresses itself in our conduct—and there is certainly ample ground and precedent for such usage —then it is exact to say that Bergson and all the others of that time did not *believe* what they perfectly well *knew*.

To return to the concept of the fetish, as Žižek later articulates it in *In Defense of Lost Causes* (and where he also cites again, after his discussion of the fetish, the same passage from Bergson), a fetish is something by fixating on which I can *block* what I know from having any effect on what I believe. It is a bar to the door through which any restructuring of my belief might come from events that exceed my capacity to accommodate

or understand them, a sticking to my already entrenched patterns of going about my days. The symptom, in the psychoanalytic sense, marks the
spot where I *am* affected by an event that cannot be processed by my old
set of beliefs—the spot where the lightning *has* struck. In contrast, the
fetish tries to *efface* the mark and *block* the affect, keeping everything in
the dark. Žižek points in this direction himself in *Lost Causes* when he
writes (page 300—just before repeating nearly verbatim what he wrote
comparing transference in the fetish and the symptom back on page 282,
cited above):

> Fetishism does not operate at the level of "mystification" and
> "distorted knowledge": what is literally "displaced" in the
> fetish, transferred onto it, is not knowing but *illusion itself*, the
> belief threatened by knowledge. Far from obfuscating "realistic"
> knowledge of how things are, the fetish is, on the contrary,
> the means that enables the subject to accept this knowledge
> without paying the full price for it [that is, precisely, without
> letting it change one's "belief"—without letting it *affect* one!]:
> "I know very well [how things really stand {in brackets in
> original}], and I am able to endure this bitter truth because of
> a fetish (a hamster, a button . . .) in which the illusion to which
> I stick is embodied." [So I "endure" the truth only by making
> quite sure I will have to endure none of its impact upon me
> affectively!]

The two strategies, in effect, that Žižek mentions in *The Puppet and
the Dwarf* for warding off any chance that new knowledge might strike
changes at the level of genuine belief—the two ways that, according to
him, epoch-changing events are "always missed"—are the two sides of
one and the same fetishizing mechanism. Fixation on the fetish is, on one
side, the denial of "reality" to the event at the fully affective, experiential level, the level of "belief" as contrasted with "knowledge. In short,
the event is denied any event-ful-ness. That denial is coupled, on the
other side, with the reduction of the event to the status of "nothing really

new" after all, but just the actualization of a possibility that was already inscribed in the conditions that preceded the event, and that are now asserted to have caused or produced it. In that reduced form, the event, denied reality *as an event*, which is to say at the affective level of belief, can nevertheless be granted reality at the merely notional or informational level of "knowledge."

So fetishized, the event both did and did not occur, and the unacknowledged slippage between the two very different senses of occurrence at issue is what allows one to go on acting "as if nothing had happened" after even the most shattering trauma.

If the sovereign is a fetish, with the latter being understood as "a tiny stupid object" (Žižek) by clinging to which we can avoid letting what we "know" affect what we "believe," just what knowledge is it, against which we are insulating ourselves by fetishistically designating, then clinging to, some tiny, stupid person or thing as a sovereign? In general, social contract theory might suggest it to be the knowledge that we live in a Hobbesian "state of nature" tantamount to a state of war of all against all: By fetishizing someone into a sovereign we would, by such an interpretation, be allowing ourselves to go on living despite knowing that we are caught, with no exit possible, in such a horrifying condition. So understood, the fetish of sovereignty would institutionalize our refusal affectively and fully to acknowledge the general, inescapable rapacity that we nevertheless know perfectly well characterizes all human relationships and, therefore, our very own life. That is, understood as a fetish within the context of general social contract theory, sovereignty would be the security blanket by clinging to which we could narcotize ourselves against our own knowledge that *there is no security*. There are problems with that suggested identification of the knowledge against which the fetish of sovereignty is supposedly designed to protect us, however.

In *On Populist Reason* (page 88) Ernesto Laclau, repeating a point he made earlier in "Why Do Empty Signifiers Matter to Politics?", one of the essays in *Emancipation(s)*, captures the beginning and the heart of the social contract tradition—namely, in Hobbes—this way:

[W]hen people are confronted with radical *anomie* [radical social instability—that is, radical lack of social order], the need for *some kind* of order becomes more important than the actual . . . order that brings it about. The Hobbesian universe is the extreme version of this gap: because society is faced with a situation of *total* disorder (the state of nature), whatever the Leviathan [that is, the one(s) designated as sovereign] does is legitimate—irrespective of its content—as long as order is the result.

That, at least, is the story a sovereign, any sovereign no matter who or what, would have us believe—that someone or something must be vested with sovereignty, to avoid us all lapsing back into the traumatic condition of the state of nature, and that subjection to even the worst and most arbitrary sovereign is preferable to such relapse. Here, then, there is no effective notional acknowledging of a traumatic truth by way of clinging to a fetish that insulates us at the affective level against that very truth. Rather, there is the claim that the trauma at issue (the trauma that is the Hobbesian state of nature) can be altogether *cured*, and any future recurrence of it *avoided*, if only we will pay the price of subjecting ourselves to a sovereign—one sovereign or another, it doesn't really matter which, since any sovereign at all, no matter how brutal and capricious, is better than the state of nature into which we would immediately and inevitably lapse without a sovereign.

However, as the recurrent critique I have already embraced of the entire social contract tradition argues, the idea of a Hobbesian state of nature equivalent to a state of war of all against all, a state in which man is wolf to man, is itself a myth generated after the fact by the very institution—sovereignty—it supposedly legitimizes. It is neither an empirically actual, historical condition, as earlier social contract theorists can—and often have been—taken to have maintained, nor a theoretically necessary sort of transcendental construct, as, say, Rawls reworked the idea. The Hobbesian state of nature is, rather, a retrospective illusion that sovereignty casts behind itself to justify its own claim to be necessary and desirable. It is an origin myth, in the negative sense of the term *myth*.

So if the sovereign is a fetish that allows us to cling to some illusion, the illusion at issue turns out not to be the illusion that, thanks to having a sovereign, we are safe, secured at last against the rapacity of our fellows, from which the state of nature provides us no protection. Rather, the illusion to which our fetishistic attachment to a sovereign allows us to cling at the level "where we live," so to speak, that is, the level of affective "belief," clinging to it despite all our "knowledge" to the contrary, turns out to be the very illusion on which sovereignty itself is based—the illusion, in short, that we need a sovereign at all, lest we regress to a traumatic state of nature.

Thus, the illusion to which we cling in our clinging to some manner of sovereign, no matter which, is the illusion that, until our sovereign came along, we were in desperate straits, ready prey to all our voraciously preying neighbors. To put it paradoxically, the trauma against the full impact of which the fetish of sovereignty insulates us is, then, *the trauma that there is no trauma*—no trauma, at least, from which only a sovereign could save us now.

In turn, that illusion is based on a confusion—a highly motivated confusion, as it were. To put the point in the terms that Holocaust historian Dominick LaCapra uses, the confusion at issue is that between "structural trauma" and "historical trauma"—or, to be more precise than LaCapra's categories permit, between conceiving of trauma as such, and thus as a necessary, "structural" matter, and conceiving of it as it manifests itself at a datable, passing moment "in history." In the Heideggerian terms Ernesto Laclau, whom I quoted a little while ago, himself uses, sovereignty bases itself upon a certain confusion of the "ontological" level with the "ontic" one. We might combine the two terminologies and say that, in founding itself upon the myth of an originally rapacious, Hobbesian state of nature, sovereignty obfuscates the distinction between trauma conceived as a necessary *ontological structure* definitive of all human experience, and trauma conceived as a specific *historically datable ontic* condition or occurrence.

Only the latter would be something that could possibly be *avoided*, and by confounding unavoidable ontological-structural trauma with an avoidable ontic-historical traumatic event, sovereignty–any old sovereignty of whatever sort—can not only justify itself, but call out and rely upon feelings of loyalty and devotion from those "subjects," to the status of which the sovereign reduces everyone else, everyone not the sovereign him/her/itself. That subject-ive attachment to—that is, the sovereign's subjects' own affective investment in—sovereignty, is motivated, in turn, by the strong interest those subjects themselves have in maintaining their own willful ignorance (John Hawkes's "stupidity") about the inescapability of "ontological" trauma. That is to say, the interest at issue is one in maintaining the illusion that, if only a certain "ontic" occurrence can be avoided, then trauma itself can be vanquished, and we can be saved from all real wounding, all genuine traumatization.

Hence, the paradoxical character of what I said above, that sovereignty insulates us from having affectively fully to acknowledge that *the trauma is, there is no trauma*, can be discharged: Sovereignty allows us to maintain the illusion that there is some one, datable, potentially avoidable traumatic event such that, if we can only succeed in avoiding it, we can avoid trauma altogether. The traumatic truth of the matter, however, is that there is no such trauma.

To flip that paradox over, while still retaining its paradoxical quality, we could also say that the trauma against the full occurrence of which sovereignty insures us is the trauma of actually believing, not just notionally knowing, that 'God's in His heaven, all's right with the world,' as the good, old cliché has it. After all, if 'there is no trauma,' then indeed there is nothing so horribly broken that it calls out before all else to be fixed, and we appear to be left to heed that other old cliché about not bothering to fix what isn't already broken. Nor, to borrow a phrase from one of the missives of madness Nietzsche sent out from Turin after his mental breakdown there in January of 1889, is there any excuse any longer for not being content, and praising the God who has created all this.

However, a God who merited so to be praised would be an altogether other God than that old, familiar *sovereign* God of usual worship—a topic to which I will turn next.

A Symptomatic God

If the sovereign is a fetish, a sovereign God is an idol. What God is there, however, beyond God the Sovereign?

Jean-Luc Nancy has addressed some of his own reflections to that question, as I already indicated at the end of the preceding chapter, in his essay "On a Divine *Wink*" in *Dis-Enclosure: The Deconstruction of Christianity*. To recapitulate: Nancy first establishes an essential interconnection between sovereignty and the sort of "sense" or "meaning" that pertains to the sign and to indication, the sense of "sense" at play in the *Wink*, a term that has importance for the latter Heidegger and which could be translated by "hint," "indication," "reference," or even "sign" itself, were it not often left sovereignly *un*-translated— as Nancy leaves it himself, to help make his point. But then, in that very connection to which he has just called attention, the connection between sovereignty and the referentially indicative significant hint, most especially in the *passing* quality of all such reference, indication, signification, and hinting—a reference that was not a "passing" reference would be no reference at all, but something more, or at least other than, any mere "reference"—Nancy himself sees a *Wink*, a hint, an indication, a passing reference, that gestures toward and opens upon "another sense"—a sense of sense other than the sense of sovereignty, with all its frowns, winks, and grimaces, all its signs, hints, indications, and references.

Thus, in the very passing by of the signs of sovereignty in all its senses, Nancy discerns the first signs of the emergence of a sense of "meaning" or "sense" itself that is, as I already put it at the end of the preceding chapter, "other than that of the sovereignty of 'meaning' itself—of *that* very sense of *sense*." This "other sense," Nancy writes (page 113), "is not the sense of the other or of an other"—such as in, say, Levinas, or, through him, still in Derrida. Rather, this "other sense" that hints at itself beyond the sovereignty of hints and the hints of sovereignty is

the other of sense and an other sense, an always other sense
that begins freely—if freedom consists in the beginning,

and not in the completion, of a new series of events, a new sending back and forth of sense. This inaugural and never terminal freedom accedes to that excess of sense—which is its sense, which is to say also *the sense of being*—as if to a climax, a supreme or a sublime that we cannot (and this is precisely the point) call 'supreme being,' and that corresponds rather to the suspension of the supreme or of the foundation by which sovereignty declares itself.

What is at issue is the emergence of a sense in an altogether different sense of "sense." It is another sense of "sense" that consists, to use the title of the next essay in *Dis-enclosure*, in which Nancy reflects on a notion from Roland Barthes, of "an exempting from sense." Nancy observes (pages 125-126) that to "exempt" is "to relieve of an obligation, to free, to exonerate from a duty or debt." Thus, "an exempting from sense" requires (to *make* sense) that, to begin with, "first sense must have been posited at the level of an obligation, an injunction of some sort . . . an imperative.' If we are to be exempted on occasion from making sense, we must first have been placed under standing orders 'to make sense and produce sense, or else produce ourselves as sense."

Just a bit later (still on page 126) Nancy adds a connection between the old demand that everything make sense, on the one hand, and the contemporary rise to dominance—to an all but unquestionable, unchallengeable claim to sovereignty—of neoliberal global market economics, coupled, as it has so clearly come to be, with the equally peremptory demand for the universal recognition of 'human rights,' on the other. As Nancy articulates it, "the formally sublime dignity of the 'person'" that is enshrined in such presumed rights, on the one side, and the 'anonymous monetary circulation,' the sacrosanct free flow of money, that defines global market capitalism, on the other, are but the two sides of the single coin, the very coin of the realm of what sets (itself) up (as) the sovereign.

The "other sense" Nancy discerns in or through the passing by of the sense that belongs to the *Wink* would circulate a very different sort of coinage, however. It would make an altogether different sense from whatever

sense the globalization of neoliberal market economics, especially as con-
joined with the universalization of "human rights," makes—or, rather,
"has" to make, is enjoined or required to make by the imperative always
to make sense in a certain sense of sense, the very imperative from which
Nancy's "other sense" would be "exempted."

As Nancy goes on to observe, *meaning* anything at all, *making sense*
at all, in the only sovereign sense of meaning something and making
some sort of sense, is always a matter of *mastery*. It is always a matter of
speaking what Lacan calls the discourse of the master. In French, *to mean*
is *vouloir dire*, which is literally *to want to say*: To ask what a given word
'means' is to ask what that word 'wants to say.' Accordingly, Nancy
writes (still on page 126) that the 'meaning,' the 'wanting-to-say' (*vouloir dire*), that is 'commanded by sense" — that is, commanded if one is
to make sense at all, as sovereign sense commands one to do — 'always
consists, in sum, in a wanting-to-have-said ('I have said' is the word of
the master).'

Against this wanting-to-say, this mean-ing, that always seeks mastery,
there stands—or lies, perhaps—the other way in which what has been exempted from sense and the demand to make sense wants-to-say or means.
"An exempting from sense, by contrast, designates a wanting-to-say [a
mean-ing] in which the wanting melts into the saying and gives up wanting, so that sense is absent and makes sense beyond sense." This other sense
would be the sort of sense that corresponded to the will to give up willing that Heidegger addresses in *Gelassenheit*, for example. It would be a
wanting-to-say in which the wanting stilled itself in, and into, the saying,
which then could sound and resound of itself, without any wanting at all
any longer.

Indeed, in the end, it is only such sense beyond sense that actually allows any sense to emerge at all, if, as Nancy has already written at the very
beginning of this essay on Roland Barthes and on the idea of an exemption
from having to make sense, 'There is no sense that is not shared." On the
last page of that same essay, Nancy returns to that opening observation to
the effect that only a shared sense makes any sense at all, and writes: 'Sense
is shared or it does not exist.'

Because it breaks such sharing, the sense that we are commanded to make, and from the making of which the other sense of sense exempts us, ends up paradoxically depriving us of all sense. It does so precisely by claiming to secure saying in what has already been said—that is, in reducing meaning from something shared, and therefore inexhaustible, to something clear and clearly delimitable, something that can be expressed in terms of general equivalences, in effect—and more than in effect.

It reduces sense or meaning to something that can be *owned*—that is, to *property*.

Thus, Nancy at the end of his essay on the sense that comes from the exemption from having to make sense, after writing that an unshared sense does not exist, writes: 'The contrasting couple of the exclusive ineffable and the general equivalent, or, if you prefer, of negative theology and monetary ontology, is the result of the disintegration of sharing itself, in which each of the two senses falls to a single side. Unique sense, in sum, is always unilateral, and no longer has any sense for that very reason.' A unique sense is no sense at all, if all the sense of sense is to be shared. 'Nor is it a question of juxtaposing multiple senses,' as though there were a plethora of different unique senses, one sense to each sharer, that might sometimes be all rolled up together.

So what's the point? Nancy answers:

> Here's the point: What *makes sense* is *one person speaking to another*, just as what *makes love* is someone making love to someone else. And one being the other by turns or simultaneously, without there being an end to these comings and goings. The goal—if we must speak of a goal—is not to be one with sense. It is not even mutual understanding: it is to speak anew.

Then, at the bottom of the same page, he ends his essay on the sense that doesn't have to make sense — the senseless sense that is the very best sort of sense, we might add—with this observation: "And there we have, if I still dare use this word, an ethics for our time—and more than an ethics."

What "more" that might be, is expansive enough to include a theology of a God who no longer claims any sovereignty. It is in the very passing by of what Heidegger in the *Contributions to Philosophy: From Enowning* calls "the last God," the God who "passes by," that Nancy reads the signs of the emergence of an other sense, "other" than the sense of sovereignty, the sovereign sense of the hint or *Wink*. Yet any remnant of a God left behind, after the passing by of Heidegger's "last God," would no longer be a God who *winkt*. In Nancy's own spirit of keeping the talk going, we might even venture to say that the no longer, if ever, sovereign God who gets left behind when even the last God passes by, would be a God who only *hinkt*, to stay with German.

Appropriately, whereas *winken* cannot be translated—or at least isn't translated in the title of Nancy's essay on "The Divine *Wink*"—*hinken* can be translated easily enough. It means to limp or hobble. Used figuratively, it means to be lame, including as in speaking, for example, of a lame joke — which is all it may be, to talk of a God who *hinkt*, whereas some other, sovereign God *winkt*. At any rate, such a limping God would be a pretty lame God, to be sure. It would be an altogether *disabled* and *disempowered* God, a God stripped of all his abilities and powers.

It is toward just such a hobbled, lame, *hinkender* God that we might take Nancy himself to be hinting. And it is not only Nancy who can be read as giving indications in that direction—that is, who drops such hints or *Winken*. For example, although very different from Nancy in many other regards, Gianni Vattimo is like him at least in that one. In various works, especially *Belief* and *After Christianity*, Vattimo argues for a conception of God along lines already laid down in Christian *kenotic* theology, from the Greek word *kenosis*, "emptying."

First, according to kenotic theology, in the Incarnation, God the Father "empties" himself of his very divinity in order to "become man," as the Nicene Creed has it, in Jesus. In turn, Jesus as God the Son "empties" himself before God the Father, not claiming "equality" with the Father, as he would have every right to do, but humbling himself in obedience to the Father's will—obedience "even unto death on the cross," as the formula familiar from the letters of Paul has it.

Vattimo argues that this trajectory of *kenosis*, of self-emptying, fulfills itself in the very secularization—indeed, in the complete depletion of meaning constitutive of *nihilism* itself—whereby God relinquishes all claim to power or potency, and becomes wholly powerless, altogether im-potent. For Vattimo, that final "weakening" even of God into divine impotence, is the very "destinal essence," the *Wesen* (essence) in the Heideggerian sense of the *Geschick* (destiny) toward which the cast or throw of *Geschichte* (German for "story" and "history," and deriving from the same root verb, *schicken*—to send, to set underway toward or to—as does *Geschick*) is cast. The "destinal essence" of something is that toward which that of which it is the essence is tending (as in, for instance, Thomas Wolfe's final line in *You Can't Go Home Again*, about that "land more kind than home, more large than earth . . . toward which the conscience of the world is tending," and to find which "a wind is rising, and the rivers flow").

Although neither Nancy nor Vattimo mentions him (nor do they especially mention one another, at least not in the discussions at issue here) in what I am reading as their shared gestures toward an impotent, disabled, disempowered God, the evangelical Protestant German theologian Gerhard Sauter can also be read as pointing in the same direction. In *Questions of Meaning: A Theological and Philosophical Orientation*, Sauter contends that the very search for *meaning* (German, *Bedeutung*, which is also often translated as "significance") arises only with the breakdown of *sense* (German, *Sinn*). Sauter uses that latter term in the sense of *sense* that insists on keeping current what is involved when we talk of "the five senses," or of the "sensory" in general, as what is accessible to and/or though the senses.

We could say, supplementing Sauter, Vattimo, and Nancy, that what "makes sense" in the sense of *sense* at issue, say, in the five senses is just what makes *no* sense in the first, sovereign sense of *sense*, where it means (wants to say) only and always that sense that *must* be "made," to master what some master-speaker means (wants to have said) in making some gesture or giving some sign. The sense of what the senses have to say is nothing that they just *have* to say (*must* say: are under orders to say), but is, rather, that which is always an unnecessary—even if unavoidable—addition to what *must* be said—always in excess of it, excremental in relation to it: what's left over in what's said when all the meaning's been wrung out of it.

If the God to whom belong such things as the oracle at Delphi neither speaks out nor hides his meaning, but, as Heraclitus says, gives a sign, then the God who remains when all the signs have been assigned and signed away has *no* "belongings." Instead, the God who remains behind after even the last God has passed by is no more than a God of remnants, in both the "objective" and the "subjective" senses of the preposition *of*: a God who God-self *is* mere remnants, on the one hand, and a God who is also God merely *for* remnants, on the other. The remnant of God left behind after even the last God has passed by is thus a remnant-God for remnants.

Or, to say the same thing yet a bit more sensibly—at least in Nancy's "other" sense of *sense*, that other sense that Sauter takes to be the original, originating one—such a remnant-God/God of remnants is a God of dung, who literally *reeks* of whatever sense that God makes. Thinking of Nietzsche's remark about the horrible stench that the corpse gives off after the death of God, the God of what Heidegger later comes to call "ontotheology," it is perhaps only fitting that the remnant that's still left behind even after the passing by of Heidegger's "last God" should be a *reeking* God.

It is also a God who no longer serves as a fetish to guard the Hawkesianly stupid, willful ignorance with which we surround our knowledge lest it have any effect on what we actually believe. Instead, that of which the remnant-God would reek would be the pus of belief itself, festering up to break, and break out at, the surface of our ignorance of what we still know all too well despite all our efforts to ignore it. To experience the "sense" of that reeking remnant-God would thus be to follow the scent that marks the very spots at which, despite all our clinging to festishes, including especially the fetish of God (that is, God as a fetish), what we would willfully ignore still breaks through all our stupidity, changing us and everything. A reeking, remnant-God would thus be God as symptom, rather than as festish, using those terms as Žižek uses them.

Such a symptomatic, remnant-God would also be fitting to a sort of politics very different from that to which any fetishistic, sovereign-God, any old "God of power and might," would be appropriate. If Carl Schmitt has outlined the "political theology" of sovereignty—that is, the politics grounded in, and in turn enacting, the theology of a fetish-God as the Supreme Being—then just what politics would go with a reeking remnant-God, a "God of dung"?

We will turn to that issue in the next section of this chapter.

The Politics of Remnants

At the end of *The Shock Doctrine*, after almost six-hundred pages exposing the workings of what she calls "disaster capitalism," and the politics that goes with it, Naomi Klein discerns the possibility of something different in the communities that spring up after such disasters as hurricane Katrina—what Rebecca Solnit a few years later in *A Paradise Built in Hell* calls 'disaster communities.' Thus, Klein ends her book with a few accounts of how some natural-disaster survivors have taken reconstruction and recovery into their own hands—to learn, as one Katrina survivor Klein quotes (page 586) puts it, "to say, 'What can we do right now to start to bring our neighborhoods back in spite of the government, not because of it?' " A little later (on pages 588-589), Klein sums up her reflections on such cases:

> Uniting all these examples of people rebuilding for themselves is a common theme: participants say they are not just repairing buildings but healing themselves. It makes perfect sense. The universal experience of living through a great shock is the feeling of being completely powerless in the face of awesome forces. . . . The best way to recover from helplessness turns out to be helping—having the right to part of a common recovery.

As the disaster has been shared, so is the recovery from that disaster to be shared. Indeed, the recovery *must* be shared, if it is to be a true recovery at all. That is because it is only sharing as such, in the sense of sharing and the sharing of sense that Jean-Luc Nancy helps us envision, that answers or responds to, *makes any sense out of*, the trauma that evokes a response, demands to be made sense of, in the first place—made sense of, in just such a sense of *sense* as Nancy hints at, a sense beyond any pretense to mastery. Precisely because "the universal experience" of trauma is, as Klein has it, "the feeling of being completely powerless in the face of awesome forces," anything less than the abandonment of all claim to mastery is a movement of avoidance, rather than recovery. It is a movement into the fetishistic ignor-ance of what trauma gives those who share it to know, which is their common helplessness, powerlessness, and lack of all mastery.

Sharing a trauma is, in the *sovereign* sense of the term "sharing"—where it means to have something in common with others of the same kind, something that differentiates all things of that kind from all other kinds of things—no sharing at all. The only thing all those who share a trauma have in common, in *that* sense of "having in common," is that they are all different. Indeed, what is above all traumatizing in trauma is exactly that it breaks through all the ordinary connections one has all along, without even knowing it, been relying upon—all those connections to "others," both individual and institutional, upon which one has always counted, without ever even taking explicit account of the counting. As reduction to helplessness, the traumatization in trauma consists, for one thing, in the casting of each one traumatized back upon that one's own radical lack of all resource to "deal with" the trauma. In that regard, any trauma that anyone undergoes is equivalent to death, as Heidegger presents it in the famous analysis of death in the first chapter of the second division of *Being and Time*: It dissolves all "relationality," all ways in which others may stand in for me, "representing" me, and radically individualizes me, casting me back solely on my own resources—or, rather, upon my own *lack* of all resources in the face of my death/traumatization.

The only "community"—that is, the only being "with and for" one another, as Paul Ricoeur puts it in *Oneself as Another*, on the basis of what all have "in common"—that is possible for the traumatized is the community of those who are *alone together* before, or in the face of, the traumatic event. The community of all those who share in a traumatic event is the community of those who no longer have anything in common, except being alone in the face of what faces each alike, with no prospect for interchanging anyone for anyone else, for one standing in for or representing the other.

Indeed, trauma as such is just the revelation to each one traumatized that she or he has nothing in common any longer with anyone else, upon which to rely for any hope of rescue. It is the bringing of each one face to face with that one's irremediably being *alone* before the disaster. To share a trauma is to share this— that here, where trauma strikes, no sharing, in the sovereign sense of having something in common, is any longer possible.

Sharing *that*, however, is the only possible way of coming fully into the sharing that alone can constitute a truly *universal* community. After all, the only thing we "all" really *have* in common is that we all are, each and every one of us, alone before death. *That*, we might well say, is the *traumatic truth*: the truth the very laying bare of which constitutes "trauma" itself. Only a community built on that truth is truly "universal," open to all, without exception—and, therefore, we might well add, without need for any sovereign to declare the exception.

One of the jokes Groucho Marx liked to tell was that he never wanted to belong to any club with entry standards so low that it would accept him. Communities built on trauma—communities built solely "on the basis of vulnerability and loss," as Judith Butler puts it in *Precarious Lives: The Powers of Mourning and Violence* (page 20)—avoid Groucho's problem by having no entry standards at all. All are welcome, with no qualifications required. As Solnit emphasizes, it is characteristic of what she calls "disaster communities"—the communities of "mutual aid" that spring up of themselves, with no need for any "authority" to institute them, after such disasters as the San Francisco earthquake early in the 20th century or hurricane Katrina early in the 21st—that they offer aid to all, no questions asked. No one is required to prove traumatization or need, to verify any claims to have been affected by the disaster. Whoever comes to receive, is given freely whatever is available. No distinction is drawn between "us" and "them," such that only "we" are entitled to receive aid, whereas "they" are not.

Indeed, as Solnit elaborates repeatedly for the cases she examines, that is one of the clearest ways in which the distribution of aid through such trauma communities differs from aid-distribution through government bureaucracies or even through organized private "charities." In responding to disasters, governmental relief programs, from local to international levels, as well as relief efforts conducted by independent charities or other non-profit organizations, are alike in their constant concern to assure that aid go only to those who "qualify" for it, and not just to anyone who happens to request it. At least that is the ideological commitment, however it may be "corrupted" in practice. And when it is corrupted, there is always the search for someone to blame for it, the corruption thus being relegated to the status of the results of individual moral shortcomings.

In contrast, communities of mutual aid that spring up after disasters among disaster victims themselves typically give no concern to the practice of such careful discernment. They remain blithely unconcerned with documenting the "qualifications" of those who come for aid. Rather, whoever asks, is given.

Accordingly, if, as Carl Schmitt insists in *The Concept of the Political*, the fundamental "political" distinction, the distinction that establishes politics and the political as such in the first place, is that between *friend* and *enemy*, then by definition trauma communities—those communities constituted solely in and by the sharing of trauma, built on no more than Butler's "loss and vulnerability"—are not *political* communities at all. If the distinction between friends and enemies is definitive of politics as such, then the response to trauma embodied in the community of trauma has no direct political relevance; and insofar as it just such community that trauma calls forth, trauma itself would evoke no special politics.

Schmitt's definition of the political in terms of the distinction between friend and enemy, "us" and "them," is broadly accepted, even if the acceptance is often hidden beneath explicit professions of pious disagreement or, as is perhaps more often the case, simply goes unmentioned. Wherever politics is taken necessarily to involve struggle or contestation—as it is, for example, even if not stated in those terms, in the oft-cited idea that politics is always a matter of "compromise," in the practice of the "art of the possible"—Schmitt's fundamental categories of friend and enemy remain in play.

So does sovereignty, which is always what the struggle between friend and enemy is all about. As far to the left of the standard political spectrum as Schmitt is to the right, Ernesto Laclau, whom I already cited earlier in this chapter, is still in agreement with Schmitt on that point. Whether in the recent, explicitly populist rendition of his thought in *On Populist Reason*, from which that earlier citation came, or in his now classic work with Chantal Mouffe, *Hegemony and Socialist Strategy: Towards a Radical Democratic Politics*, Laclau casts the political as essentially the struggle for hegemonic dominance, which is defined by "antagonism" between the struggling parties. In the earlier work, Laclau and Mouffe even read the struggle for dominance back into the very structure of their fundamental concept of "discourse," effectively "politicizing" even it. Thus, they write (page 112): "Any discourse is constituted as an attempt to dominate the field of discursivity, to arrest the flow of differences, to construct a centre." As Jean-Luc Nancy ties the very meaning and sense of signification to the Schmittian sovereignty that declares the exception, so do Laclau and Mouffe tie discourse—and, therewith, not only language but also the social as such—to the struggle over just such sovereignty.

For Laclau and Mouffe, as for Marx, there is no sovereign "by nature," as it were, and the struggle for sovereignty is accordingly never at an end. Sovereignty and, with it, "society" is never achieved once and for all. Instead, the "arresting" of the "flow of differences" that constitutes the struggle is always only "partial," to use their terminology.

"We will call the privileged discursive points of this partial fixation," they write, *"nodal points."* Within parentheses, they go on to link their idea of such "nodal points" with Lacan's "concept of *points de caption,* that is, of privileged signifiers that fix the meaning of a signifying chain." Then they close their parenthetical remarks with this observation: "This limitation of the productivity of the signifying chain establishes the positions that make predication possible—a discourse incapable of generating any fixity of meaning is the discourse of the psychotic."

Perhaps what we really need, however, is just such psychosis—at least if we are trying to find our way to Nancy's "other sense," in which all claim to mastery is abandoned. Perhaps what is called for is letting go of meaning or sense as something "fixed," something that could ever be "secured," in effect.

It does not matter whether the fixation and securing of sense and sovereignty singles out some one figure or group of figures—some one leader, one archon, or some segment of society, whether a class, a party, clan, family, or whatever—for hegemony, or whether, as with Laclau, it is "the people" themselves who come to rule, and even if that is in the form of "democracy." Laclau, for example, formulates democracy itself as belonging to the struggle for hegemony. Democracy arises from the establishing of "equivalencies" between a variety of different—often very different—demands, articulated from a correspondingly wide variety of subject-positions, but united in their "antagonism" to some one opponent. As Laclau conceives it, "radical democracy" must be "populist," meaning that it must fix the identification of the "people" by articulating a single antagonism shared by diverse subject-positions presenting diverse demands, a shared antagonism against some one common opponent. Thus, democracy, the rule of "the people," can emerge, and then, once emerged, continue to maintain itself, only by making the same differentiation in terms of "friend" and "foe" or "enemy" which, according to Carl Schmitt, defines the very concept of the political as such.

The problem is that, so conceived, democracy becomes no more than just one other way in which people themselves—actual, historical, concrete, singular human beings (or "human animals," if one wants to follow Alain Badiou's way of speaking, to which I will return eventually)—are cast aside in the name of some ideal, supra-temporal abstraction imposed upon them as a rule—a rule in relation to which people themselves, as the very singularities they are, always constitute an exception. To put the same point a bit differently, such democracy is just another way in which real people are reduced to the status of mere byproducts of the political process, the excess left over by that process, the un-processed, un-processable remnant left over to be discarded at the end of the whole thing—in short, no more than the excrement, the "shit" to which the inmates of the Nazi death camps were reduced, just as Giorgio Agamben has argued, and as Terrence Des Pres long ago graphically documented in *The Survivor: An Analysis of Life in the Death Camps*.

Essentially, Žižek makes the same point about "the people," who are supposed to rule in a "democracy." Thus, Žižek writes (*In Defense of Lost Causes*, page 281): "In the same way that Laclau likes to emphasize that Society does not exist, nor does the people." However, as he adds and as Laclau's own discussion makes abundantly clear, in populism "the people *does* exist." Even more to the point, "the People's existence is guaranteed by its constitutive exception, by the *externalization* of the Enemy into a positive intruder/obstacle." Accordingly, for Žižek, "far from standing for the political as such," as Laclau would have it, populism (and, I would add, the very hegemony that the "friend/enemy" polarity itself exercises in both Laclau and Schmitt, despite the great political gulf between them) "always involves a minimal *de-politiciza-tion*, 'naturalization,' of the political"—the very de-politicization that Laclau and Schmitt themselves complain of, with regard to parliamentary liberalism.

It is interesting to note that Michel Henry, a very different sort of thinker than Žižek, also says much the same thing about "democracy" and "politics," conceived as Laclau (who is not at issue in Henry's discussion) and many others conceive them. In *Du communisme au capitalism* he reflects upon the notion of "the political" that is operative in the ruling political discourse of our day.

Before discussing Henry's critique of that discourse itself, it is worth remarking just how dominant the discourse at issue has become. That discourse has today, more than twenty years after the fall of the Berlin wall, so thoroughly succeeded in establishing its hegemony, to use Laclau's terms, that it no longer even needs explicitly to assert its claim to dominance. Instead, today that discourse almost everywhere appears to be the only and obvious way to speak of things, the only discourse "transparent" to the truth of how things simply, really are. As Henry himself acutely observes, the effect of such unquestioned, no longer even visible dominance is actually a radically effective, heretofore un-exemplified form of *censorship*. Thus, Henry writes (page 211):

> We today are subjected to the most extraordinary censorship that has ever existed. For in the time of the king of Prussia, of Stalin, or of Hitler, at least one knew that there was censorship, while today, under the reign of freedom, one no longer knows that. Thus does the formidable ideological conditioning of the totality of society accomplish itself at each instant, in the bombardment of the media and publicity which imposes on everyone the quasi-totality of one's mental contents, even to one's desires and fantasies, in everyone, even infants, without criticism, without any power to contest it having the possibility to manifest even its simple existence.

Talk about *totalitarianism*!

At any rate, in the everywhere so dominant, totalitarianly censorious discourse at issue, the very concept of "the political" is tied, writes Henry (page 178), to the notion that there exists some one thing that is *"a general affair"* (*"une affair général"*: the emphasis is Henry's own)—some one "common" or "public thing," which is the literal meaning of "republic," from *res publica*, a phrase the echoing of which in the talk of "our thing," *cosa nostra*, among and with regard to participants in "organized crime" is far from accidental or innocuous.

For Henry, the idea of such a "general affair" is finally no more than an abstraction that, once made, sets itself up as reality itself, and imposes itself *as* reality upon everyone in the society over which that abstraction has come to hold sway. That occurs, however, without any genuine regard to the actual differences that concretely define the lives of those individuals upon whom that reigning abstraction has been imposed, those very individual people whose interacting interests and demands alone give sense to the idea of the political in the first place. Consequently, the rise to dominance of *that* sense of "the political" actually entails a radical *de*-politicization of the genuinely political, which now gets treated as *outside* the entire political domain.

That process of de-politicization of the genuinely political in the very name of "the political" itself did not occur, according to Henry, only in the communist countries of the former East block, over the corpses of which the self-styled "Western democracies" crowed victory at the end of the "Cold War." Rather, exactly that same process also—and, indeed, especially—takes place at the heart of the very *democracy* that claimed such victory, as Henry goes on to articulate. His discussion culminates in a passage (page 198) in which he starts off by saying the same thing Žižek will later say, using the very same terms—namely, that "the people," in the sense at issue in populism and the dominant discourse of democracy, "does not exist":

> In a democracy it is the people who govern. Unfortunately the people does not exist: it is no more able to govern than to work a field or sow it with seeds. The concept of democracy is thus a lure, the most extraordinary ever invented by men [*les hommes*] to abuse themselves or others. That this lure rings like a bell before the stupefied regard of all nations that together make up Europe changes nothing of the ontological mystification on which it rests, but only makes it more dangerous.

For Henry what today counts as the political—that is, "the political" defined as it is in the dominant "democratic" discourses of our day—must be subordinated to the concerns of concrete, individual life. Only so can the political in any *genuine* sense of that term count at all.

In *Du communism au capitalism* furthermore, Henry links his critique of such de-politicization in the very name of the political, on the one hand, to a critique of capitalism in its modern, "techno-economic" form, where the economy is cut loose from its grounding in life itself, on the other. According to Henry, the last mentioned — concrete human life itself—is precisely where Marx himself saw the economic to be grounded. Many years before *Du communism au capitalism* Henry had already argued directly and in great detail to that effect in his two-volume work on Marx. In *Du communism au capitalism*, he extends his earlier against-the-grain analysis of Marx to write as well against the grain of the capitalist-democratic triumphalism of the (still) current times, as expressed perhaps most famously/notoriously in Francis Fukuyama's *The End of History and the Last Man*. In that book Fukuyama argued that with the going global of the "free market" economy and the "liberal democratic" form of government, with its "universal human rights," the very goal of world-history is at last reached.

Against all such valorization of 'free-market' capitalism, especially as yoked together with parliamentary democracy, Henry argues that such capitalism and such democracy uproot economic processes from their grounding in the only context that allows them to make human sense, the grounding in concrete human life itself. It is just such uprooting and casting loose of the economic from the soil of life that results in a world where goods are over-produced everywhere, while in the very midst of such overflowing abundance, global poverty not only continues but even exponentially worsens, as those who most need the very goods that are so abundantly produced are denied the money necessary to buy them. Specifically with regard to the concept of democracy, Henry insists (page 108 of *Du communism au capitalism*) that "the only conceivable and real equality" that is possible is that "which exists between individuals ineluctably different." However, the global economicization of all human life at issue in the rise to dominance of what Henry alls 'techno-economic' capitalism militates against all such real equality—and against any genuinely autonomous politics that could not be reduced to the status of a handmaiden for the global market economy, any politics that would work to establish real equality.

It is worth noting that the "techno-economics" Henry attacks is the same as the "neo-liberal" economics that Milton Friedman and the Chicago School preached so effectively—and so disastrously for so many actual people, including all the workers in the United States cast into long-term, if not interminable, unemployment by the Great Recession that began in 2008 and the dating of the end of which remains debatable. Thus, Henry's critique of the techno-economy links up with Naomi Klein's withering critique of "shock capitalism" in *The Shock Doctrine*, bringing us back around again to where we began in this chapter-section on "The Politics of Remnants."

Politics After the War on Terror

I began the preceding section on "the politics of remnants," with a reference to Naomi Klein. I then in effect traced the intertwining of two different but related paths of reflection on the idea of sovereignty. In terms of the authors who entered into my discussion, one of those two paths led from Klein to Rebecca Solnit, then Jean-Luc Nancy, Martin Heidegger, Paul Ricouer, Judith Butler, Slavoj Žižek, and Michel Henry. As their voices entered my discussion in the preceding section (though not at all necessarily when regarded in other contexts), all those thinkers might be said to travel along a common path that brings them also to share a common "antagonism"—to use a term important to Ernesto Laclau—to a way of thinking that travels along a different path, at least in terms of the idea of sovereignty as I was considering it in the preceding section.

That *second* path is one that lets sovereignty keep its throne, so to speak. For that reason we might call those who go by that path "loyalists," in the sense of being loyal to the sovereignty of the very idea of sovereignty, without regard to whether sovereignty is to be exercised by a monarch or by the People. The roll-call of the loyalists in the just-mentioned sense of the term includes not only Carl Schmitt but also Ernesto Laclau himself—two figures who, by virtue of the great differences between them (despite their common loyalty to the idea of sovereignty), can serve to define the right and the left ends of the political spectrum, respectively.

In contrast, we might call the camp of the fellow-travelers along the way of the *first* of the two paths mentioned above the camp of the "dis-loyalists." In terms of my discussion in the preceding section, Klein, Solnit, Nancy, Heidegger, Ricoeur, Butler, Žižek, and Henry are dis-loyalists.

To balance things up a bit (eight dis-loyalists against merely two loyalist may seem a bit unfair), I will add that the loyalist ranks include not only Francis Fukuyama, whom I did mention in the preceding section, but also untold others I easily might have mentioned—namely, everyone, willy-nilly, who speaks the language of the masters of the market today, which in turn includes the heads-of-state of all the current world's nations. Thus, given the numbers of all those "untold others," if there is any unfairness of balance, it is all to the loyalist side, not the dis-loyalist one. But since the notion of justice as fairness is most closely associated with the name of John Rawls, one of the foremost contemporary theoreticians of loyalism, in the sense I have given that term, there would seem to be nothing surprising in that.

At any rate, there is really no question of balance at all at issue here, because there is, in effect, no common scale for weighing the two "quantities" involved, since those two are finally not even commensurable with one another. Any common scale on which we might think we could weigh the two relative to one another is, so to speak, always already rigged—and *infinitely* so: *all* the weight always remains, in effect, on one side of the scale, leaving nothing to weigh on the other side at all. Any supposedly common scale is always rigged absolutely to favor the loyalist side, the side of sovereignty as such.

To vary the metaphor: If we are required to rely on the concept of authority in all our measuring, then all the authority always already belongs to one and the same side in the purported "antagonism" at issue: All the authority is on the side of "authority" itself, we might say—that is, the side of the master, of fixed sense, of secured sovereignty.

Indeed, insofar as the issue of sense or meaning is itself cast in terms of the "fixing" or "securing" of stationary points of signification at which an otherwise unimpeded, ever ongoing "flow of differences" between signifiers is "arrested," just such a fixation, securing, and arresting has *already* taken place. The struggle for hegemony has *already* been won, and *one* understanding of the very sense of sense has already established its own hegemonic sovereignty over all other understandings.

Fortunately, however, to paraphrase Jean Baudrillard, writing in *Le Monde* not long after the traumatic event that has come to be known simply as "9/11," no sooner is hegemony established than it is contested. "Allergy to any definitive order, to any definitive power, is—happily—universal," Baudrillard wrote in that article, eventually reprinted as the title piece of

The Spirit of Terrorism (page 6). In fact, in all four essays that comprise that book, Baudrillard in effect argues that the truth of the trauma of "9/11" lies in its opening—or, more precisely (and fully in accordance with the structure of trauma as such), its *re*-opening—of a new space for thought and action, a space *outside* that of global market capitalism.

For Baudrillard, the very collapse of the Twin Towers of the World Trade Center on 9/11 /01 reopened that space. The Twin Towers were chosen for attack in the first place precisely because of their symbolic importance, by virtue of which they stood for the whole complex system of what Baudrillard calls "global power," which, in turn, he defines (page 92) in terms of the interweaving of "the supremacy of positivity alone and of technical efficiency, total organization, integral circulation, [and] the equivalence of all exchanges."

However, it is important to remember that the spectacular collapse of the Twin Towers was in no way part of the plan of the attackers themselves. It was nothing foreseeable for them, any more than for anyone else. It altogether exceeded even the most grandiose expectations on the part of those who planned and executed the attacks, as it certainly exceeded any expectations that viewers of the event worldwide via "real-time" simulcasts were able to form while watching it actually unfold. It was just that excessive, unforeseeable—indeed, *unimaginable*, at least at the level where, to use Depuy's terms, "knowledge" becomes "belief"—dimension of the collapse that constituted the traumatic core of 9/11 as such.

What concerns Baudrillard is not the question of the legitimacy or illegitimacy of the terrorist attacks. One can emphatically agree with Derrida, Habermas, and the overwhelming majority of intellectuals in the advanced industrial West in condemning the terrorists and denying them any possible justification for their acts, yet still maintain that something unprecedented happened on 9/11, something theretofore unthinkable, the opening of some new, up-till-then impossible possibility.

That is just what Baudrillard maintains, and he is not alone in doing so. Habermas, for one, also holds that something new emerged on 9/11. In a conversation with American philosopher Giovanna Borradori not long after the 9/11 attacks, which Borradori later published as part of

Philosophy in a Time of Terror: Conversations with Jürgen Habermas and Jacques Derrida, Habermas responded to Borradori's opening question (page 25) of whether he considered 9/11 to be "an unprecedented event, one that radically alters the way we see ourselves." After remarking (page 27) that only (what Hans-Georg Gadamer dubbed) the eventual "effective history" (*Wirkungsgeschichte*) of what occurred on 9/11 can "adjudicate its magnitude in retrospect," Habermas went on to suggest at least two ways in which 9/11 may indeed have been an "unprecedented" event. The first involves it being "[p]erhaps the first historic world event in the strictest sense" insofar as it was the first such occurrence to be simultaneously broadcast worldwide on television while actually happening: "the impact, the explosion, the slow collapse—everything that was not Hollywood anymore but, rather, a gruesome reality, literally took place in front of the 'universal eyewitness' of a global public." The second and, for my purposes here, more important way in which something new took place on 9/11 is a matter, according to Habermas, of the "intangibility" (page 29) of the exact focus (that is, the clear "identification of the opponent") and goal (what the terrorists were aiming at or hoping to achieve) of the 9/11 attacks.

With regard to that second feature suggesting that something unprecedented indeed did occur on 9/11, Habermas remarks (page 34) that what distinguishes "the global terror that culminated in the September 11 attack" from earlier forms of terrorism is that it

> bears the anarchistic traits of an impotent revolt directed against an enemy that cannot be defeated in any pragmatic sense. The only possible effect it can have is to shock and alarm the government and population. Technically speaking, since our complex societies are highly susceptible to interferences and accidents, they certainly offer ideal opportunities for a prompt disruption of normal activities. These disruptions can, with minimum expense, have considerably destructive consequences. Global terrorism is extreme both in its lack of realistic goals and in its cynical exploitation of the vulnerability of complex systems.

After another question from Borradori, Habermas continues in the same vein by noting that

> a political transition can be hoped for only by terrorists who pursue political goals in a realistic manner; who are able to draw, at least retrospectively, a certain legitimation for their criminal actions, undertaken to overcome a manifestly unjust situation. However, today I cannot imagine a context that would some day, in some manner, make the monstrous crime of September 11 an understandable or comprehensible political act.

Significantly, the very same political incomprehensibility of the terrorist attacks on 9/11 that Habermas uses in his conversation with Borradori to introduce doubt into the idea that what happened on 9/11/01 is really of the "magnitude" of such an "unprecedented event" as the French Revolution, is precisely what, for Baudrillard, constitutes the genuinely unprecedented eventful character of what took place on that date. As Baudrillard depicts it, the very impossibility of comprehending 9/11 in terms of the till then exclusively dominant concepts of what constitutes something as deserving of being called "political," is exactly what points to the unprecedented character of 9/11 as the opening of an altogether new way of thinking of the political as such. For Baudrillard, it is by exceeding all terms of what theretofore had been taken to define the political, that 9/11 was able to rise to the status of a full reworking of all the *symbolic* coordinates involved in any such definition.

In Baudrillard's analysis, it is precisely that symbolic level that is the definitive one for what truly took place on 9/11. He agrees with Habermas that the attacks lack any "realistic" chance of changing anything about "global power." "If the aim of terrorism is to destabilize the global order merely by it own strength, by a head-on clash, then it is absurd," he writes (page 55), because "the relation of forces is so unequal." However, Baudrillard insists, what truly happened on 9/11 did not take place on any such "realistic" level to begin with. The significance of 9/11 is to be found not at the "realistic" level, but at the symbolic one: What took place then was a realignment of all the symbolic coordinates that until then had defined the whole global situation. The heart of the violence perpetrated by the terrorists on 9/11 lies, for Baudrillard, not at the level of the objectively "real" effects of the objectively "real" terrorist acts on that date, but at the level of such a shift of the entire taken-for-granted symbolic system in terms of which such "realities" are always processed. "The terrorist violence" of 9/11, he writes (page 29), "is not 'real.' In a sense, it is worse: it is symbolic."

In turn, Baudrillard points to the unforeseen, unforeseeable collapse of the Twin Towers, those dominant symbols of dominant "global power" itself, as "the major symbolic event" that took place that day (page 43). He views that literally incredible—unbelievable—collapse as though it were, in effect, the response of the towers themselves, and, therefore, of "global power" as a whole, to what truly *happened* in the attacks, exceeding all the intentions, hopes, dreams, dreads, and nightmares of those involved in it in all their various capacities as perpetrators, victims, and/or spectators. "Imagine," Baudrillard invites us (still page 43), that the Twin Towers "had not collapsed, or only one had collapsed: the effect would not have been the same at all." Indeed, the event as such—what most truly *did* happen that day—would *not* have happened.

But the Towers did collapse, and what happened in that collapse was, by Baudrillard's analysis, the revelation (page 74) of the "fracture and disarray—of [the] fragility—at the heart of [global] power itself." In their dominance of the skyline of the dominant city of the dominant nation in the whole deployment of "global power," the Twin Towers symbolized that power itself. Accordingly, in their collapse they symbolized the collapse of that same power. Or, rather, the collapse of the Twin Towers *was* the very collapse of global power, at the symbolic level where such power itself must be able to exercise hegemonic sovereignty, if it is to have any power at all. In truth, that is, in the final analysis, the only level at which global power is *vulnerable*—that is, open to wounding, to trauma. "This," according to Baudrillard (still page 74), "is the 'truth' of the terrorist act" on 9/11, a truth, it is important to add yet again, that altogether exceeded even and especially any intentions formulable by the terrorists themselves

Accordingly, if the towers had not collapsed, or even if only one of them had, then (page 43) "[t]he fragility of global power would not have been so strikingly proven" as it in fact was. "The towers, which were the emblem of that power," he writes, "still embody it in their dramatic end." Symbolically, therefore, that power itself collapsed in the collapse of the two towers.

Indeed, Baudrillard writes (pages 43-45) that the end of the towers, their collapse, "resembles a suicide":

> Seeing them collapse themselves, as if by implosion, one had the impression that they were committing suicide in response to the suicide of the suicide planes.

> Were the Twin Towers destroyed, or did they collapse [on their own accord, as it were]? Let us be clear about this: the two towers are both a physical, architectural object and a symbolic object (symbolic of financial power and global economic liberalism). The architectural object was destroyed, but it was the symbolic object which was targeted and which it was intended to demolish. One might think the physical destruction brought about the symbolic collapse. But in fact no one, not even the terrorists, had reckoned on the total destruction of the towers. It was, in fact, their symbolic collapse that brought about their physical collapse, not the other way around.

> As if the power bearing these towers suddenly lost all energy, all resilience; as though that arrogant power suddenly gave way under the pressure of too intense an effort: the effort always to be the unique world model.

> So the towers, tired of being a symbol which was too heavy a burden to bear, collapsed, this time physically, in their totality. Their nerves of steel cracked. They collapsed

vertically, drained of their strength, with the whole world looking on in astonishment.

The symbolic collapse came about, then, by a kind of unpredictable complicity—as though the entire system, by its internal fragility, joined in the game of its own liquidation, and hence joined in the game of terrorism. . . . [S]omewhere, it [the global power system] was party to its own destruction.

Thus, by imagining what it would have been like, had the towers not collapsed, we come to see that the collapse of the Twin Towers cleared the way, opened the space, for imagination to begin exploring altogether other possibilities, possibilities that theretofore, before the physical collapse of the towers and the symbolic collapse of the global power they symbolized, were *im*possible. And so, in their absence, the Twin Towers come to stand even taller than they ever could in their presence, as Baudrillard writes (pages 47-48):

They, which were the symbol of omnipotence, have become, by their absence, the symbol of the possible disappearance of that omnipotence—which is perhaps an even more potent symbol. Whatever becomes of that global omnipotence, it will have been destroyed here for a moment.

Moreover, although the two towers have disappeared, they have not been annihilated. Even in their pulverized state, they have left behind an intense awareness of their presence. No one who knew them can cease imagining them and the imprint they made on the skyline from all points of the city. Their end in material space has borne them off into a definitive imaginary space. By the grace of terrorism, the World Trade Center has become the world's most beautiful building—the eighth wonder of the world!

For Baudrillard, then, we could say that the "truth" of the terrorist at-tacks on 9/11—the *gift*, in effect, with which they unexpectedly "graced" us, if we can only accept it (even if only "for a moment," something to which I will eventually return)—is the opening of an altogether new, unheralded, heretofore impossible imaginary space. That space is "imaginary", not in the sense of a "mere fiction," a u-topia (a no-where), that can be imagined but is not real, but in the sense of a space in and into which we can build a new dwelling place to live "the good life, together with and for one another, in just institutions," to borrow a phrase from Paul Ricouer to which I have alluded before. We can use what Baurdrillard has to say in such passages as the one just cited, to go beyond what he explicitly says himself, which is directed to the omnipotence—the all-powerfulness, the absolute *sover-eignty*—of contemporary "global power," and extend it to apply to power and sovereignty in general.

For Baudrillard, what took place on 9/11 was not just "another" trau-ma. In an important sense it was, so to speak, *trauma itself* that took place. The trauma was that there could *still*, even now, be such trauma at all: *That* was the trauma. That *still*, in this epoch of the "global world order," a true event could happen, was what was so shocking. The epoch of the going global of "order" itself, ushered in with the fall of the Berlin Wall and the collapse of "really existing socialism," which was supposed to have signaled the end of the Cold War in the victory of "democracy" over Ronald Reagan's hated "evil empire," and therewith the dawning of the New World Order and the Pax Americana that Fukuyama would soon proclaim to be the glorious fulfillment and, therefore, end of history—that there could *still* occur, in this epoch of the going global of "order" itself, such shocking *dis*-order: *that* was what was most truly and fully traumatic and event-ful about "9/11."

"When it comes to world events," Baudrillard wrote sarcastically short-ly after 9/11, in the opening line of "The Spirit of Terrorism" in the book by that same name (page 3), "we had seen quite a few." He then gives the death of Princess Diana and the World Cup of soccer as examples of the sorts of pseudo-events that occurred during the decade preceding the attacks on the Twin Towers, pseudo-events the images of which were broadcast worldwide in the mass media as the real thing, and accepted as such in the popular imagination. In addition, there were "violent, real events, from wars right through to genocides," images of which were also broadcast worldwide. However, it is a very different matter "when it comes to symbolic events on a world scale—that is to say not just events that gain worldwide coverage," as so often did both such pseudo-events as World Cup soccer competitions and such real ones as the wars in the former Yugoslavia or the mass-murder in Rwanda, "but events that represent a setback for globalization itself." Such events are "world-events" not just because they are broadcast "live" worldwide in "real time" while they are happening—which is what Habermas, for one, pointed to as distinctive about 9/11, making it "the first world-event" in that sense. Rather, what Baudrillard means are events that, far more importantly, happen *to* the newly declared "one world" itself, the "globe" of globalization. World-events in *that* sense are events that break into that supposedly global world and break it apart: a trauma to the "world" itself, in effect. During the 1990's we had plenty of world-events in the sense that the death of Princess Diana was a world-event, but of world-events in the sense that interests Baudrillard, "we had had none." Indeed, with regard to any such genuine world-events, Baurdillard writes that "[t]hroughout the stagnation of the 1990's, events were 'on strike' (as the Argentinian writer Macedonio Fernandez put it)."

Before proceeding any further with Baudrillard, it is worth noting that the idea that "events" somehow went out "on strike," as he puts it, during the 1990's is an idea he shares with Slavoj Žižek. In his own analysis of 9/11 not long after that day, an analysis published in *Welcome to the Desert of the Real: Five Essays on September 11 and Related Dates*, the latter draws an unexpected comparison between the Cuba of the experiment in socialism under Castro, on the one hand, and "Western 'postindustrial' societies" that trumpet the triumph of the globalization of capitalism and the democracy with which that capitalism is supposed to be yoked, on the other. First Žižek notes (pages 6-7) how, "[m]aking virtue out of necessity," the necessity created by the long-standing American-imposed embargo against it, Cuba "heroically continues to defy the capitalist logic of planned obsolescence" insofar as "many of the products used there are, in the West, treated as waste—not only the proverbial 1950s American cars, which magically still function, but even dozens of Canadian yellow school buses (with old painted inscriptions in French or English, still completely legible), probably given as a present to Cuba and used there for public transport." From that observation, Žižek then goes on to remark that "[t]hus we have the paradox that, in the frantic era of global capitalism, the main result of the revolution is to bring social dynamics to a standstill—the price to be paid for exclusion from the global capitalist network." Then he makes the comparison mentioned above: "Here we encounter a strange symmetry between Cuba and Western 'postindustrial' societies: in both cases, the frantic mobilization conceals a more fundamental immobility. In Cuba, revolutionary mobilization conceals social stasis; in the developed West, frantic social activity conceals the basic sameness of global capitalism, *the absence of an Event . . .*" (ellipsis in the original, but I have added the emphasis).

Indeed, as both Baudrillard and Žižek suggest, the standardization of culture and the universalization of the system of general equivalencies that are inherent to globalization place the *avoidance* of trauma—and, therewith, of any true events—at the very heart of the whole process. Paradoxically, the vested interest of the very "world" that goes worldwide or global with the triumph, at the end of the Cold War, of everything that is symbolized under the name "America," lies in *keeping the very events that allow a world to occur in the first place—allow world itself "to world," as Heidegger likes to put it—from happening.* Thus, it is far from accidental that just when order itself goes global after the end of the Cold War, events as such "go on strike," to return to Baudrillard and his way of putting the point.

With the events of 9/11/01, "the strike is over," according to Baudrillard (pages 3-4): "Events are not on strike any more. With the attacks on the World Trade Center in New York, we might even be said to have before us the absolute event, the 'mother' of all events, the pure event uniting within itself all the events that have never taken place." Moreover, since "fundamentalism" of whatever stripe, as well as the "terrorism" such fundamentalism can engender, are themselves not throwbacks to some supposedly pure condition that existed prior to all the processes tied up under the idea of "globalization," but are themselves, rather, products of those very processes, inseparable from the very globalization of "Western values" against which fundamentalists take themselves to be resisting, the "pure event," "'mother' of all events," that came to be known as "9/11" was no "clash of civilizations," as Samuel P. Huntington famously dubbed it. Thus, Baurdillard writes a few pages later (pages 11-12)—in a passage that is reminiscent of Derrida's analysis of 9/11, in his interview with Borradori, in terms of what Derrida likes to call "autoimmune" processes—that what is truly brought into issue by 9/11 is not

> a clash of civilizations or religions, and it reaches far beyond Islam and America, on which efforts are being made to focus the conflict in order to create the delusion of a visible confrontation and a solution based on force. There is, indeed, a fundamental antagonism here, but one which points past the spectre of America (which is, perhaps, the epicenter, but in no sense the sole embodiment of globalization), and the spectre of Islam (which is not the embodiment of terrorism either), to *triumphant globalization battling against itself*. In this sense, we can indeed speak of a world war—not the Third World War, but the Fourth and the only really global one, since what is at stake is globalization itself. The first two world wars corresponded to the classical image of war. The first ended the supremacy of Europe and the colonial era. The second put an end to Nazism. The third, which has indeed taken place, in the form of cold war and deterrence, put an end to Communism. With each succeeding war, we have moved further towards a single world order. Today that order, which has virtually reached its culmination, finds itself grappling with the antagonistic forces scattered throughout the very heartlands of the global, in all the current convulsions. A fractal war of all cells, all singularities, revolting in the form of antibodies. A confrontation so impossible to pin down that the idea of war has to be rescued from time to

time by spectacular set-pieces, such as the [first] Gulf War
or the war in Afghanistan.* But the Fourth World War is
elsewhere. It is what haunts every world order, all hegemonic
domination—if Islam dominated the world, terrorism would
rise against Islam, *for it is the world, the globe itself, which resists
globalization.*

What Baudrillard calls the Fourth World War—the war wherein the
globe itself resists globalization, as he puts it—is actually the first and only
true world war, in the sense that it is only now that for the first time ever
the very issue is raised of whether there will be any genuine *world* at all, and
not just the simulacrum of a world that is manifest in the globe of globalization. In addition, the war at issue is not between nations or nation-states
at all any longer. It is, rather, a war that cuts across all divisions between
nations and states, cutting every nation and state right down the middle.
It is, then, a worldwide *civil* war, in exactly the sense that is at issue for
Giorgio Agamben in *Homo Sacre: Sovereign Power and Bare Life,* which I've
cited before, when he writes (page 180) of the long 'civil war that divides
the peoples and the cities of the earth.' Agamben characterizes that civil
war, which rages everywhere, as one between the People and the people.
That is, the civil war at issue for Agamben is that between those who can
assert their rights as citizens and, therefore, as recognized members of the
state or nation (the People), on the one hand, and those who, although
they are subject to the state and its laws, do not count as citizens with the
standing to assert their rights—what Jacques Rancière (whom Agamben
does not cite, at least in *Homo Sacre*) calls "the part of no part," which is his
definition, much like Agamben's own, of the *demos* ("people") of *democracy*
("rule by the *demos*")—on the other. Agamben gives this lucid summary
(pages 176-177):

Every interpretation of the political meaning of the term
"people" must begin with the singular fact that in modern

---

* Baudrillard wrote these lines after the American invasion of Afghanistan but
before the American invasion of Iraq in the second Gulf War.

European languages, "people" also [that is, in addition to the People] always indicates the poor, the disinherited, and the excluded. One term thus names both the constitutive political subject [which is what he designates by "People," with an upper case 'P'] and the class that is, de facto if not de jure, excluded from politics ["people," with a lower case 'p'].

In common speech as in political parlance, the Italiam *popolo*, the French *peuple*, the Spanish *pueblo* (like the corresponding adjectives *popolare, populaire, popolar* and the late Latin *populus* and *popularis*, from which they derive) designate both the complex of citizens as a unitary political body (as in "the Italian people" or "the people's judge") and the members of the lower classes (as in *homme du peuple, rione popolare, front populaire*). Even the English word "people," which has a less differentiated meaning, still conserves the sense of "ordinary people" in contrast to the rich and the nobility. . . .

. . . . Such a diffuse and constant semantic ambiguity cannot be accidental: it must reflect an amphiboly inherent in the nature and function of the concept "people" in Western politics. It is as if what we call "people" were in reality not a unitary subject but a dialectical oscillation between two opposite poles: on the one hand, the set of the People as a whole political body, and on the other, the subset of the people as a fragmentary multiplicity of needy and excluded bodies' or again, on the one hand, an inclusion that claims to be total, and on the other, an exclusion that is clearly hopeless; at one extreme, the total state of integrated and sovereign citizens, and at the other, the preserve—court of miracles or [concentration/ extermination] camp—of the wretched, the oppressed, and the defeated. . . . If one looks closely, even what Marx called "class conflict," which occupies such a central place in his thought—though it remains substantially undefined—is nothing other than the civil war that divides every people and that will come to an end only when, in the classless society or the messianic kingdom, People and people will coincide and there will no longer be, strictly speaking, any people.

As Baudrillard, Derrida, and Žižek, all three, present it in their analyses of 9/11, and as Agamben presents it in his depiction of the "civil war" raging across the globe in this day when we are all virtual inmates in the camps, contemporary globalization as such, including especially in its inseparability from the very terrorism that supposedly resists it, as well as the "war on terror" that ensues in turn, constitutes what systems-theoretician Gregory Bateson called a "self-escalating system." Such a system is one in which a process, once started, engenders an intensification of the very conditions that the process was originally designed (or at least triggered) to address, which leads in turn to an intensification of the process at issue, aimed at addressing those very conditions. Thus, the system keeps escalating itself, just as the American war in Vietnam kept escalating itself under Johnson and Nixon, or as alcoholism keeps escalating itself, as Bateson argued in 1972 in "The Cybernetics of 'Self.'" According to Bateson, such systems will keep on escalating themselves *until they finally reach a point of overload at which they suffer a complete breakdown*, after which the whole self-escalating system comes crashing down on itself, just as the Twin Towers came crashing down upon themselves on September 11, 2001. For Bateson, such points of *breakdown*, however, are also points of possible *breakthrough*. That is, the points at which the old, unsustainable, dysfunctional, self-escalating system comes apart are precisely the points at which that same system can finally be abandoned, its collapse having cleared the ground for new, sustainable, functional, stable systems and processes to emerge. So, to use Bateson's own example, alcoholism will continue to escalate itself until it finally "hits bottom" or "bottoms-out," as the popular parlance of "recovery" puts it. Only then does a genuine option emerge, for the alcoholic, of abandoning the whole pretense of being able to "handle" alcohol and, instead, admitting "powerlessness" over alcohol and, precisely therein, finding one's way to a new life of "sobriety." In fact, as Bateson presents it, that is the whole "logic" that is ultimately behind self-escalating systems: Such systems are, paradoxically, designed to perform a sort of existential *reductio ad absurdam* on the very theses on which those systems rest, so that those theses can then—and at last—be abandoned.

Just so does the whole process of globalization reduce itself to absurdity on 9/11/01, at least as analyzed by Baurdillard and Žižek (whether Derrida's analysis should also be included is less clear, in my judgment). I have already cited Baurdillard's remark (on page 43 of *The Spirit of Terrorism*) that with the collapse of the two towers "the fragility of global power" was "strikingly proven." If anything, Žižek offers an even clearer statement of the idea, though he couches it the form of a rhetorical question, following a comparison of 9/11 to the end of the Cold War, as well as to the much earlier denunciation of Stalin at the 20ᵗʰ Party Congress of the Soviet Union (*Welcome to the Desert of the Real*, pages 47-48):

Consider the collapse of a political regime—say, the collapse of the Communist regimes in Eastern Europe in 1990: at a certain moment, people became aware all of a sudden that the game was over, that the Communists had lost. The break was purely symbolic; nothing changed 'in reality'—none the less, from that moment on, the final collapse of the regime was merely a matter of days away. . . . [ellipsis in original] What if something of the same order *did* occur on 11 September? Perhaps the ultimate victim of the WTC collapse will be a certain figure of the big Other, the American Sphere. During Nikita Krushchev's secret speech at the Twentieth Congress of the Soviet Party, denouncing Stalin's crimes, a dozen or so delegates suffered nervous breakdowns and had to be carried out and given medical help; one of them, Borislaw Beirut, the hardline General Secretary of the Polish Communist Party, even died of a heart attack a few days later. (And the model Stalinist writer Alexander Fadeyev shot himself a few days later.) The point is not that they were 'honest Communists'— most of them were brutal manipulators without any subjective illusions about the nature of the Soviet regime. What broke down was their 'objective' illusion, the figure of the 'big Other' against the background of which they could exert their ruthless drive to power: the Other on to which they transposed their belief, the Other which, as it were, believed on their behalf, their subject-supposed-to-believe, disintegrated. And did not something analogous happen in the aftermath of September 11? Was not September 11 2001 the Twentieth Congress of the American Dream?

Nietzsche maintained that the "death of God" was such a momentous event that it would take a couple of thousands of years for news of it to reach everyone. Similarly, the news that broke in Manhattan on the morning of September 11, 2001, the news of the collapse of the global world order that was supposed to usher in the end of history, and the news, therefore, of the resumption, as it were, of history—the news that, as Baudrillard put it, events were no longer "on strike"—may take a while, perhaps a very long while, to reach all ears. When I first wrote these lines—in November 2010—a then-current item in what passes for news was the recent scattered outburst of acts of complaint and non-compliance against the recently instituted airport-security use, at some airports, of random full-body scans or, for those who refused to be scanned, invasive "pat-down" procedures. Among the opinions bandied about in various media was one in accordance with which such escalation in the "war on terror" and the concomitant fixation on issues of security is just what the terrorists want, and that to accept such procedures, and the ever increasing costs, monetary and non-monetary, involved in pursuing them, is to "let the terrorists win." Unsurprisingly, what such protest leaves unquestioned is the presupposition that there is indeed a "war" going on, in which either the terrorists or the warriors against terror are in position possibly to win. Nowhere in the currently rising din of such protest—which seemed driven at least as much by what might well be thought of as a right-wing war against the Obama administration, as by any genuine concern with terrorism and securing air-travelers against it—was there any sign of growing awareness of the self-escalating process into which the system binding terrorism and the supposed war against it inseparably together is locked.

By its very nature, there is no "winning" possible for either side in any such self-escalating "war" as that in which "America" and "terrorism" embrace one another as combatants. If and when the "war on terror" is ever over, it will not be because one side or another will have "won"—nor, for that matter, because the two sides have fought one another to a standstill. Rather, it will be because the entire system to which that "war" belongs will finally have come to the point of maximum self-escalation, the point at which the whole system just breaks down. If and when *that* happens, the job before those who survive that breakdown of the whole "world-wide" global order will be to build a human dwelling place amid the ruins, in the space cleared for such a place by the collapse of the global system. The materials, so to speak, out of which such a dwelling place will have to be built will be the remnants left behind after that crash. Since, as Heidegger, for one, insisted, the "political," at the most radical (that is, "root") level, is that which pertains to the building of such a human place, which is Heidegger's definition of the Greek term *polis*, "politics after 9/11" is precisely and only the politics of building such a place, such a *polis*.

However, as Baudrillard and Žižek help us see, the collapse of the world-wide order of globalization, is really no longer something we need still to wait for. That collapse has already happened. That world-wide but world-less global order collapsed with the collapse of the Twin Towers on September 11, 2001. *Now* is already the time *after* the time of globalization. Accordingly, the task at hand now is to continue moving into, and building within, the new space opened up by that collapse, which is to say the space of "ground zero," the space cleared—"symbolic" and "imaginary" as it may be (and, indeed, wholly *effective* for that very reason)—on that date by the collapse of the Twin Towers of the World Trade Center, which, as Baudrillard observed in *The Spirit of Terrorism*, are far more present now in their absence than they ever were when they were physically present.

One way to put the point is to say that the problem with the war on terror, and all that pertains to it, is that the politics of that war only *appear* to be *after* 9/11. In truth, the politics of the war on terror, as well as of the terrorism against which that war is supposedly being waged, is simply an anachronism: It is the same old politics that was being pursued *prior* to 9/11, as though 9/11 never took place, even though by the calendar it is now more than a decade later. However, that pre-9/11 politics proved itself on 9/11—and that is precisely the "meaning" of 9/11—not to be any genuine politics at all, that is, any genuine clearing and care of a livable *polis*, a place of genuinely human dwelling, at all. Genuine politics, in that sense, can only be done "after" 9/11, which rules out all such anachronisms as either terrorism or the war on terror. We might borrow from Marx and, paraphrasing a distinction he made in terms of history, put the point this way: The *pre*-9/11 politics both of terrorism and of the war against it is *pre-politics*, whereas *politics* itself truly only begins *post*-9/11.

Furthermore, not only does such genuine politics, the building of a genuine *polis*, begin only after 9/11. It also takes place nowhere on the entire globe, which is to say the word-*less* "world," of globalization, the one shattered by 9/11. The *polis*, the place where genuine politics takes place, is no more to be found in the space of globalization than is the Kingdom of Oz to be found in Kansas. As Dorothy and Toto in Oz are no longer anywhere in Kansas, so is politics after 9/11 no longer anywhere in the world of globalization, no longer anywhere on that globe. Rather, the place of politics after 9/11 is altogether elsewhere, which will be the topic of the next—and final—section of this chapter on the politics of trauma.

Elsewhere, Politics

What passes for politics everywhere around the globe today—the endless "today" of the globe of globalization, the world-less globe on which history, as Fukuyama proclaimed, has ended—is without relation to politics elsewhere, where there is still world and time for it. The place of politics on our time-less, world-less globe that no longer has any place for it can only be elsewhere—"off-planet," as it were: somewhere else, where politics, the clearing and arranging of a human place, can still take place. Accordingly, too, elsewhere is the only place where human beings can dwell: The globe of globalization may be filled with "human resources," but it is uninhabitable for human beings. Human beings *now*, in that moment of time wherein there is always still time, can dwell only by heeding the call to go elsewhere, as Abraham in Genesis heeded God's call to leave his father's house, and his father's lands, and his father's country and go forth into a new, far place.

The place of genuine politics, as opposed to what passes for politics around the globe in this day of globalization, is not the state. The equation of the *polis* with the *state* enacts, in fact, the subordination—a subordination ever in need of constant, ceaseless reiteration, of performative reassertion—of the former *to* the latter. It is, in effect, the ever more narrowing *enclosure* of the *polis* within the state and, most especially, beginning with the gray dawn of modernity, within the economy. That enclosure process, at its peak, a peak finally attained in the globalization—the going global—of the "market" economy, brings about the *vanishing of the political into the economic*. Contrary to the Marxist hope for the withering away of the state, in the globe of the global market it is *politics* that withers away, as the state grows ever more stately.

As used by historians, "enclosure" refers to the process whereby—largely by literally fencing in: building a fence around—common and/or (supposedly) waste lands were converted to private property—most especially that process as it occurred in Britain in the 18th and early 19th centuries. Thus, the process of enclosure was that of privatizing the land itself, transforming it into what has tellingly come to be called "real estate," since it is the indispensable economic "estate" that constitutes the base capital of the capitalism that emerged through that very process of privatization or "enclosure."

The enclosure of the common lands themselves was as such the enclosing or fencing in—which is also always a matter of simultaneously closing *out* whatever lies beyond the fence and outside the closed-in area—of the *polis* and, therefore, the strict limitation of the political to what went on only *within* the fenced-in area, the "enclosure." As life itself came increasingly to be narrowed down and fenced in, until it became no more than what Agamben calls "bare life," namely, the only life left to the *Muselmänner* in the Nazi death camps, so did politics come increasingly to be confined to what went on within an ever tightening enclosure within economics, until it came to be no more than the sorts of inanities we are currently witnessing as, one after another, all the "advanced" industrialized countries are sacrificing the interests of the people—the *demos*, Rancière's 'part of no part" — to the global economic demand for the elimination of government deficit spending.

Not accidentally, as politics comes more and more to be subordinated to economics, the latter itself becomes ever more "purified" of any of the original elements of the concept, which elements come increasingly to be seen as no more than "adulterations" of the economic. Thus, to cite just one telling example, the Jeffersonian principle that "that government is best, which governs least" eventually degenerates so thoroughly that it becomes, after a little trip from Washington to Chicago to study with Milton Friedman and the "Chicago Boys," the Reaganite shibboleth that "government is not the solution, government is the problem"—where under "government" is lumped everything that could still be called politics, especially everything suggesting anything like the building of a genuinely human place for Ricouer's human pursuit of "the good life, with and for one another, in just institutions."

"Economics" began with the ancient Greeks as a name for the care that saw to opening and arranging the *house-hold* in such a way that it would be a welcoming, life-renewing *home*, into which living human beings could withdraw for such revitalization, and from which they could then reemerge refreshed, to enter again the shared place of the *polis*, and practice the politics that cared for *that* place. Economics ends, however, and in more than one sense of "ends," by being the name, if that's what it still is at all, of the very process whereby, to borrow Nietzsche's phrase, "the wasteland grows," until it finally goes global, leaving no place that still smacks of "home" anywhere at all around that globe. Even if we adhere to Robert Frost's minimalist formulation of the notion of home as "that place where, when you have to go there, they have to let you in," for all the human animals who still crawl about on the globe—all those "virtual *homines sacri*," those virtual Auschwitz inmates, of Agamben's vision—there no longer is, anywhere they might crawl, any such place.

Having delivered all that bad news, however, here's the good news to balance against it: As Bill Murray says in his old summer-camp movie *Meatballs*, "It just doesn't matter!" None of it matters any more than it matters, as Dori Laub saw, that "really" only one smokestack at Auschwitz got blown up by the Jewish inmate-resistance toward the end of World War II, not all four smokestacks, as Dori Laub's Auschwitz-survivor interviewee, remembers it.

The homogeneous, directionless, indifferent "space" in which the whole globe of globalization hangs suspended has no place for places at all, including that globe. That globe is no place at all, any more than any other point in the world-less uniformity of the universal space of the infinity of such points remains a place at all any longer. What is more, just as Laub's survivor's "inaccurate" recollection recollects the *historical truth*, as Laub rightly names it, of the *Sonderkommando* uprising at Auschwitz—the very truth that there was no truth at all in Auschwitz—just so, as Baudrillard saw, was the whole façade of the pretended reality of globalization and its globe shattered into splinters when the Twin Towers collapsed on September 11, 2001. So, too, does the truth of trauma as such — the truth of *all* trauma, which is always fully present as a whole in *any* trauma (whether the trauma be that of a morning in Manhattan in the first year of the 21st century or that of a day in Auschwitz in the middle of the 1940s), in the same way that the whole body of Christ is fully present in each crumb of the bread of a Christian Eucharistic ceremony—consist in putting the lie to the claim of what endlessly puts itself forth as "reality."

In *Living in the End Times*, published in 2010, Žižek cites with approval a book first published in 1972: Menonite scholar-theologian John Howard Yoder's *The Politics of Jesus: Vicit Agnus Noster*. Specifically, what Žižek approves is Yoder's staunch rejection of the linking of Christianity with the power of the state, which linking first and definitively occurred under the Roman emperor Constantine in the fourth century CE. Yoder, writes Žižek (page 129), rejects such "Constantinian-ism," not "on behalf of an ascetic withdrawal from social life," but rather as a full activist engagement in it. Indeed, I would say that Yoder presents such activism as the very keeping open of, and building within, the place of "social life" itself—that very place which *is* the *polis* itself, in any genuine sense of the word. As Žižek himself writes, Yoder, being "aware of the limitations of democracy . . . understood 'being Christian' as involving a non-reconciled *political* standpoint." From that standpoint, "[t]he primary responsibility of Christians is not to take over society and impose their convictions and wishes on people who do not share their faith, but to 'be the church.' By refusing to repay evil with evil, by living in peace and sharing goods, the church bears witness to the fact that there is an alternative to a society based on violence or the threat of violence."

As I read it, Yoder's book makes clear that the sense of the word *is* in saying, with Žižek, that there "is" an alternative to the sham society that has now gone global, is not that another way is *possible*, at least in the normal way of taking the notion of "possibility," in which it is always subordinate to "actuality,' as Aristotle long ago insisted. The "other way" of being political that Yoder indicates is not just waiting around someday to be actualized. Rather, it is *already there*. For a Christian, which Yoder most definitely is, the gospel, the "good news" that it *is* already there, is definitively delivered not only by, but also in, Jesus. And in "the time that remains"—to borrow the title from one of Agamben's recent books, which Agamben, of course, borrows from Paul's witnessing in the Bible—between Jesus's "return to the Father" (his "Ascension," in Christian parlance) and his coming again (this time "in glory," as Christian creedal statements have it), that time opened up by the resurrected Jesus's departure so that the Father might send the Spirit, in that between-time, which is *our* time, that "other way" continues already to be there in and as "the church."

So understood, the Christian church is what I have already referred to as a "remnant community," a term suggested to me by my reading of Agamben's and related works. I can now clarify more fully than heretofore what I have in mind by that term.

One of the key places where Agamben works out his thoughts concerning the essential link between sovereignty and "bare life" is tellingly called *Remnants of Auschwitz*. Not only were the inmates of Auschwitz remnants—cast off by-products, as it were—of the Nazi state. In addition, all we have for testimony from those inmates themselves is no more than the barest remnant of what would constitute full testimony to the horror of the camps. As Primo Levi insisted in giving his own testimony as an Auschwitz survivor, full testimony could only be given by those who did not survive to bear witness.

Basing his discussion on earlier writers such as Agamben and, especially, Rosenzweig, in *The Psychotheology of Everyday Life: Reflections on Freud and Rosenzweig*, a work to which I have made reference before, Eric Santner makes central use of the idea of the "remnant," taken above all in the sense of the "useless," "good for nothing," cast-off remainder of the processes wherein we try to establish our personal and communal "identity." Paradoxically, our *identity*—from the Latin for "the same"—is precisely that which we have in common with others, those others, namely, with whom, as we say, we "identify" ourselves. In the very process of establishing such a common identity we cut off and cast out whatever does not fit, and is therefore rejected as no more than the worthless remnant left over after we have drained all the use out of it, the use for establishing our "identity," establishing just who "we" are.

By reading Freud and Rosenzweig with and against one another, Santner comes to the insight that it is only insofar as we are all such remnants—only at that level where each of us is no more than just such a worthless, good-for-nothing, ready-for-the-junk-heap remnant —that we can be encountered in our pure singularity, our "ipseity" as Santner calls it (following Ricoeur and others), from Latin *se* for 'self' (so that 'ipseity' would be 'it-self-ness,' in effect). Our "identity" is always a matter of social construction and what Santner calls "symbolic investiture." For example, it is only through such symbolic investitures, performed through various ceremonies (such as graduation ceremonies for the awarding of academic degrees, wedding ceremonies, and registering of births) that my own identity as a philosophy professor, father, husband, etc., has been established. In contrast, my ipseity is what is what I am after one subtracts all my identities, all of what can be symbolically invested with any degree of social power and authority.

Santner's use of the idea of the remnant is based perhaps most crucially on Rosenzweig's thought in *The Star of Redemption*, where Rosenzweig traces what he sees as an essential connection between Judaism and that idea. For Rosenzweig, the Jewish diaspora community is just such a "remnant community" as I have in mind: a community alongside and within the dominant—we can say the "sovereign"—society, one which does not set itself up as any alternative to that society, any competitor for sovereign power, but which instead lives out its own rich life as a community *without reference*, we might say, to that environing, dominant, sovereign society. Life in such remnant communities is life lived *outside* the laws that define sovereignty, even if, as with Jewish communities in the diaspora, the individual members of those remnant communities continue to play their various roles in that same sovereign society 'outside' of which the community life is lived out.

Another model of a "remnant" community is provided by Benedictine monasticism, which is an insistently "cenobitic" form of monasticism—that is, the monastic life lived out in communities of monks, which is to say communities of solitaries, who live "alone together," to use a formulation I find helpful. Each Benedictine monastic community lives out its communal life in a certain, definite "withdrawal" from "the world," yet a withdrawal in which the monastery—in the sense of the monastic community as such—always remains connected to, and interactive with, that same "world" in various complex ways. The monastery is a community *"in* the world, but not *of* the world,' as one common formulation puts it. It is a place where the irrelevancy of what in medieval Christian discourse is called "the world" is made known, simply by the fact of communal life being lived at such a place "outside" yet "in" that same "world." (Yet a third example of what I am calling a "remnant community," providing yet a third model of the formation and continuance of such a community, would be a "Twelve Step fellowship" such as Alcoholics Anonymous, but I will not pursue that example any further here.)

Such a community is not only a 'remnant' community in the sense of being in the form of community that is still left behind — in Pauline Christian terms, left behind in that between-time that is itself 'the time that remains' between Christ's first and second coming. It is also a remnant community in the sense of being a community made up of remnants — that is, a community all the members of which are themselves no more than remnants, namely, all those of no account who are left out of the count after everyone who counts has been counted, the no-accounts excluded and rejected as unworthy of being counted in any counting of the members of what counts for society under the state and its sovereignty. A remnant community today is a community of the no-account cast-offs of the global society. It is a community precisely of Rancière's *demos*, "the part of no part." Yoder's "church" is just such a no-account community of no-accounts.

To return to Yoder, as he sees it in *The Politics of Jesus* it is not by trying to make themselves count in the sovereign social accounting, but by taking up and actively *being* the no-accounts that they *are* for any such accounting, that "the church" itself becomes a place where people can still truly live, given that there is no place at all for them in what passes as society among all those who do the counting. He insists that the confrontation between what we might call the politics of the powerful—of all those who count some in, and others out, for the exercise of power in its sovereign form—and the politics of those cast out of power and into powerlessness, is not incidental to who Jesus was, and still is, in and as the church which has become his "mystical body." Rather, that confrontation is essential, and altogether unavoidable.

Already in the second chapter of *The Politics of Jesus*, a chapter entitled "The Kingdom Coming," in a section called "The Epiphany in the Temple"—namely, the epiphany wherein Jesus manifested just who and what he himself was, manifested it in casting the money-lenders out of the Temple once he reached Jerusalem—Yoder argues that, once he had thus "cleansed" the Temple, Jesus is in position to go further. "The coup d'etat" against Rome itself, and all it stood for, is at that point, writes Yoder, "two-thirds won; all that remains is to storm the Roman fortress next door." Then he adds what is decisive, for my purposes here: "But it belongs to the nature of the new order [the one Christ, in coming, has already established] that, though it condemns and displaces the old, it does so not with the arms of the old." Accordingly, he concludes, "Jesus passes up his golden chance and withdraws to Bethany. But," he immediately adds, reinforcing the message that the Kingdom of God is not waiting patiently around some eventual corner of the future, but is already here among us, "the city [that is, Jerusalem—but also that city of cites which is Rome, so far as that goes] will not be the same again."

What is more, for that very reason: " Now it is clear [to the powers that be—"Rome," in all its senses] that he [Jesus] must be killed." Significantly, in the very next lines Yoder goes on to observe that at this point in the story Luke adds, in his Gospel, "a poignant vignette" wherein

> in a kind of prophetic lament Jesus at the gate of the city [Jerusalem] weeps because the city 'did not know its time of visitation.' There is about the coming of the King [namely, the King of the Kingdom of God, but also, as Yoder also insists, a "the King of the Jews"—though an altogether un-kingly King, by all Roman sorts of reckoning] a built-in illustration of that rejection [of that King] which is already sure ["already," that is, as soon as the King enters Jerusalem, and most especially after his cleansing of the Temple]. At the point of the city's most uninhibited welcoming of the Messiah, Luke will not let the reader forget that his rejection was already sealed. Despite the joyous crowds, the man on the donkey is beginning his passion.

Insofar as Jesus, by the Gospel telling, already *knows* all this himself by that point of joyous entry into Jerusalem, and, knowing it, nevertheless insists upon continuing un-deflected along the road he is embarked upon, we could say that Jesus' passion—what he "sets his heart on"—is his passion, in the Christian sense of that term, where it means the very journey to crucifixion and the tomb.

Yoder's point here can profitably be connected (as we will shortly see, Yoder himself will soon note the connection) to the Johannine theme of the "world" not "knowing"—that is, not even recognizing—the very Word that, in and as Jesus, has come to dwell "among us." According to the first letter of John, verses 10-14 (NRSV):

> He was in the world, and the world came into being through him, yet the world did not know him. He came to what was

his own, and his own people did not accept him. But to all who received him, who believed in his name, he gave power to become children of God, who was born, not of blood or of the will of the flesh or of the will of man, but of God. And the Word became flesh and lived among us, and we have seen his glory, the glory of a father's only son, full of grace and truth.

That "worldly" power *must* reject Jesus/the messiah—that the "world" *cannot* know that the Word has come to walk among us—derives from the inescapably *traumatic* nature of "revelation" itself. It is *only* belatedly, in its *re*-turn, a return ever coming (ever futural), that the turn itself can be welcomed and accepted, and thereby "known."

What is more, in such returning turning "that which is Caesar's" gets rendered unto Caesar—and what is God's, to God. That is something that Yoder himself does go on explicitly to connect with the way Jesus, as Yoder puts it, "passes up his golden opportunity" to take power through a coup d'etat when he could have pulled it off, after "the epiphany in the temple." However, Yoder may not see so clearly that it is, in fact, only *in* the refusal *of* power that the power so refused is given what is indeed "due" it. Only in the refusal to assume power, is power rendered its own. The refusal itself *is* the rendering unto power of its due: What we owe power is precisely the *nothing* that the refusal of power reveals power to be "worth." Just so does Jesus' refusal of his "golden opportunity" to assume power render unto power what is its own, precisely as the revelation of the *nothingness of power itself*, its *vacuity*, its own nullity and *im*-potence, its own utter *lack* of all genuine power. And it is precisely because *that* is what is revealed in Jesus, that Jesus must be killed, that whatever lays claim to power must kill him.

Yet it is just as precisely because Jesus' own passion is his passion, as I put it a little while ago, that in so killing him, what lays claim to power gives him even greater life. In killing him, the powers that be render him, the very son of the father, what is his due as that son. What is due the son as son, however, is no less than the full heritage of the father: divine *omni-potence*, the "all" of power itself. In killing Christ power reveals God Godself in full glory and power as the *only* true glory and power, in the glorious shining of which all the illusions of power—above all, the illusion, in effect, that power has any power at all: that the emperor is wearing any clothes—are dispelled, vanishing "like a dream one wakes from," such that "when you wake you dismiss them as phantoms" (Psalm 72 [73]: 20, Grail translation).

John is right in his Gospel: the Resurrection, as the raising up of Christ to life, does not so much come *after* the crucifixion as it comes *in and as* the crucifixion itself. Christ is already raised up in being raised up on the cross. *That* is the wisdom of God: the wisdom of the cross. And it is just that wisdom, just that cross, which, in revealing itself, makes foolish the very wisdom to which the cross itself can be nothing but foolishness.

A bit later in his text, in the very next section of the chapter on "The Kingdom Coming," Yoder points in the same direction. In regard to Luke's later story (later in his Gospel than the story of the crucifixion) of the two travelers whose views are corrected by an apparent stranger on the road to Emmaus, Yoder cites how Jesus asks his two companions if it was not necessary for the Messiah to suffer just as he did, in order to "enter into his glory." That, according to Yoder, was the mistake made by "the unseeing pair"—"they were failing to see that the suffering of the Messiah is the inauguration of the kingdom." Then Yoder adds an important observation: " 'Glory' here cannot mean the ascension [as a rising up into the heavens], which has not been recounted yet. Might it not mean (as with the concept of 'exaltation' in John's Gospel) that the cross itself is seen as fulfilling the kingdom promise? . . . The cross is not a detour on the way to the kingdom; it is the kingdom come."

Yoder then concludes his second chapter by remarking that Christians today can no longer avoid acknowledging that "Jesus was, in his divinely mandated (i.e., promised, anointed, messianic) prophethood, priesthood, and kingship, the bearer of a new possibility of human, social, and therefore political relationships." Nor, according to him, can Christians any longer "avoid his [Jesus'] call to an ethic marked by the cross, a cross identified as the punishment of a man who threatens society by creating a new kind of community leading a radically new kind of life."

Later, in his sixth chapter, "Trial Balance," Yoder returns to the theme of the cross as itself constituting the raising up of Jesus and his followers. "Only at one point," he writes there, addressing all his fellow Christians, "only on one subject—but then consistently, universally—is Jesus our example: in his cross." What is more (with my emphasis added):

> The believer's cross is no longer any and every kind of suffering, sickness, or tension, the bearing of which is demanded. The believer's cross, like that of Jesus, is the price of social nonconformity. . . . Representing as [Jesus] did the divine order now[!] at hand, accessible; *renouncing* as he did the [pretense of] the legitimate use of violence and *the accrediting of the existing authorities*; renouncing as well the ritual purity of noninvolvement, his people will encounter in ways analogous to his own the hostility of the old order.

Carl Schmitt always insisted that any decision establishing a division between what is to count as "political" and what not, is itself a thoroughly political decision. Interestingly, Yoder echoes the same idea a little later in his sixth chapter when he writes: "To say that any position is 'apolitical' is to deny the powerful (sometimes conservative, sometimes revolutionary) impact on society of the creation of an alternative social group. It is to over-rate both the power and the manageability of those particular social structures identified as 'political.' To assume that 'being politically relevant' is itself a universal option so that in saying 'yes' to it one knows where one is going, is to overestimate the capacity of the 'nature of politics' to dictate its own direction." A few lines later Yoder writes that Jesus, on this very point—which Yoder has been saying is the sole point in which Jesus must set the example for all Christians' to follow—"refused to concede that those in power represent an ideal, a logically proper, or even an empirically acceptable definition of what it means to be political. . . . [H]e said, 'your definition of *polis*, of the social, of the wholeness of being human socially is perverted.'"

Still not finished with reiterating his point, Yoder returns to it yet again in his next chapter, the seventh of twelve in the original edition of 1972, on "The Disciple of Christ and the Way of Jesus." "The cross of Jesus was a political punishment," he writes there, "and when Christians are made to suffer by government it is usually because of the practical import of their faith"—and thus *not*, it is worth noting, for their "beliefs,'" as the common view would have it—"and the doubt they cast upon the rulers' claim to be 'Benefactor.'" A bit later, in the penultimate section of the chapter, on "The 'Cross' in Protestant Pastoral Care," he further clarifies his position by arguing that "[t]he cross of Calvary was not a difficult family situation, not a frustration of visions of personal fulfillment, a crushing debt, or a nagging in-law," which is how it is taken most often—as pride, in effect, at the sufferings one is willing to endure in the professed attempt to "follow Jesus," something comfortable and comforting for all self-styled martyrs. Against all such attempts to tame the Christian message by stripping it of its genuinely political core, Yoder insists upon that very core, writing that Jesus' trip to his cross is, rather, "the politically, legally-to-be-expected result of a moral clash with the powers within his society."

Then, in his twelfth chapter, the last in the first edition of the book, Yoder draws his whole, sustained analysis together to argue effectively— or at least faithfully, in a way suggestive of an oft-cited remark of Mother Teressa, in response to a challenge to defend her work with the hopelessly outcast of Calcutta, given the obvious disproportion between the size of her efforts and the size of the problem those efforts addressed—that the Christian call is to *faithful obedience*, not to *effectiveness*. According to Yoder the Christian's job is not to "direct" history but rather to follow Jesus in subordinating oneself to history, only doing so entirely *without compromise*—that is, seeking always to love, never yielding to the temptation to justify resorting to violence/evil in the name of an ultimate or greater good.

At one point in his development of that argument in this culminating chapter, Yoder notes that the book of Revelations is concerned "precisely [with] the question of the meaningfulness of history," though the vision of John in Revelations entails that that very question "cannot be answered by the normal resources of human insight." Yoder goes on from there to observe that "to assume that history is meaningful is itself a Judeo-Christian idea. . . . It is a necessary expression of the conviction that God has worked in past history and has promised to continue thus to be active among us." But John's answer to the question at issue is "not the standard answer." Instead, it is an answer in accordance with which "the cross and not the sword, suffering and not brute power determines the meaning of history." In short, either God is with the powerless against the powerful, or else there is no God. Accordingly, and radically: "The key to the obedience of God's people is not their effectiveness but their 'patience' ([Rev] 13:10)." The triumph of right is not a matter of an eventually effective success at gaining power, but lies in the very relinquishment of all recourse to power, the putting *down* of the sword—but I suggest that "putting down" here be heard simultaneously not only as "laying aside" but also, and crucially (if the pun be permitted), in the colloquial sense of "trashing," "dissing," dismissively belittling. "The triumph of the right [by which he hardly means the triumph of the so-called political right-wing, of course], although it is assured, is sure because of the power of resurrection and not because of any calculation of causes and effects, nor because of inherently greater strength of the good guys."

Yoder then adds a remark that applies no less to Dori Laub's survivor, with her "inaccurate" recollections of the rebellion at Auschwitz demolishing all the crematoria smokestacks, and to Jean Baudrillard's understanding of the collapse of the Twin Towers as being already the full collapse of the global power of "America," than it applies to Jesus' crucifixion as the arrival *already* of the full kingdom of God. "The relationship between the obedience of God's people and the triumph of God's cause is not," writes Yoder, "a relationship of cause and effect but one of cross and resurrection." Jesus' exemplary fidelity or obedience "cost him all his effectiveness; he gave up every handle on history."

Thus, as Yoder reiterates the point a bit later, "Christ renounced the claim to govern history." Yet a bit further on he elaborates, beginning with a reference to the Pauline theme of divine *kenosis* or self-emptying, especially as that is manifest in Jesus not claiming the "equality" with God that his divine son-ship would seem to warrant, but instead "humbling himself, even unto death on the cross." With reference to Jesus letting go of all his bragging rights, as it were, Yoder observes:

> What Jesus [thus] renounced was . . . the untrammeled sovereign exercise of power in the affairs of that humanity amid which he came to dwell. His emptying of himself, his accepting the form of servanthood and obedience unto death, is precisely his renunciation of lordship, his apparent abandonment of any obligation to be effective in making history move down the right track.

Furthermore, it is just this renunciation of lordship that God has ratified in the resurrection and elevated to an entirely new sort of lordship over everything, "thus affirming that the dominion of God over history has made use of the apparent historical failure of Jesus as a mover of human acts"—just as, it is worth noting again, the apparent historical failure of the uprising at Auschwitz, or, nearly six decades later, of the attack against global power on 9/11/01, was far from what Laub, with special regard to the former, convincingly calls the "historical truth" of such incidents.

The cross, writes Yoder, to return to his analysis, points to

> the inevitable suffering of those whose only goal is to be faithful to that love which puts one at the mercy of one's neighbor, which abandons claims to justice for oneself and for one's own in an overriding concern for the reconciling of the adversary and the estranged. 1 Peter 2 thus draws direct social consequences from the fact that Christ "when he suffered did not threaten but trusted him who judges justly.". . . [W]hat Jesus renounced is not first of all violence, but rather the compulsiveness of purpose that leads the strong to violate the dignity of others. The point is not that one can attain all of one's legitimate ends without using violent means. It is rather that our readiness to

renounce our legitimate ends whenever they cannot be obtained by legitimate means itself constitutes our participation in the triumphant suffering of the Lamb.

Thus, "[t]he cross is not a recipe for resurrection. Suffering is not a tool to make people come around, nor a good in itself." Rather, suffering, the cross, is a way of aligning oneself "with the ultimate triumph of the Lamb." Ordinary forms of pacifism or non-violence that make the question one of their being an efficacious non-violent means to achieve assumed ends, continue to rely upon the underlying "axiom . . . that it is a high good to make history move in the right direction." Christ on the cross not only calls that axiom into question, but also cancels it out altogether.

In doing so, he also cancels out the claim of the power he renounces, the power of the lordship of sovereignty rather than that of servanthood, to be counted at all for "reality." Paradoxically, by renouncing all claim to effectiveness—and, therewith, all claim of effectiveness in setting the standards even for effectiveness itself, even for what is to count as *effective agency*—the renunciation and cancellation of all claims to effective power is, we could say, even more effective than effectiveness itself. It effectively *redefines* what it is to have an effect, just as did, by Baudrillard's analysis, the collapse of the Twin Towers as though in a suicidal response of recognition of the attacks upon them. By changing the very coordinates in terms of which effectiveness and the lack of effectiveness are themselves measured, such apparently "merely" symbolic acts out-perform even the most glitteringly successful exercise of everything that passed before for effective, for "practical." Such radically redefining "symbolic" acts do not change anything. Rather, they change everything.

About midway between the date of the original publication of Yoder's *The Politics of Jesus* (1972) and the date of the publication of Žižek's reference to Yoder in *Living in the End Times* (2010), another Christian scholar from a very different denominational background than Yoder's—this time Christian Science, in contrast to Yoder's Mennonism—made the specific point about efficaciousness and "practicality" I am attempting to articulate here perhaps even more effectively and practically than Yoder himself did.

In 1987 in "Theodicy After Auschwitz and the Reality of God," an article published in the *Union Seminary Quarterly Review*, Stephen Gottschalk addressed the issue squarely.*

Classical theodicy attempts to reconcile the doctrine of the conjunction of omnipotence and omni-benevolence in God, on the one hand, with the existence of evil, on the other. However, in the face of such 20th century horrors as Auschwitz, classical theodicy ran up against its limits. Consequently, process theologians, following Whitehead's suggestions, attempted to revise the terms of the problem by abandoning the idea of divine omnipotence. By Gottschalk's analysis, however, both classical theodicy and the critique of it in process theology shared a common assumption that was never subjected to critical assessment. The assumption in question is (page 79) "that God and evil both exist in the same sense in fact and as fact." Both classical theodicy and its critical modifications in process theory "presume that the experience of evil is just what it appears to be: an unchallenged reality against which other realities are to be measured."

It is just this assumption that Gottschalk challenges: "Yet is the same factical quality, as quality of unmistakeable authenticity and concreteness, attributed to humanity's experience of God? Here is the crux of the problem, which turns out to be not so much the problem of evil in the classic formulation as that of the immediacy of this God-experience and the evaluation of its meaning."

Against such an assumption of the unquestioned claim of evil to be reality itself, Gottschalk cites Karl Barth's discussion, in the third volume of *Church Dogmatics*, of the purely nugatory nature of evil. "Barth's treatment of the problem has been subject to strong criticism," writes Gottschalk (page 81), "largely on logical grounds, when appraised alongside other 'solutions' to the dilemma of theodicy. Such criticisms," however, Gottschalk replies,

> while understandable, miss the vital point that Barth is not "doing" theodicy from a purely logical standpoint. He simply will not concede some privileged position without

––

* I thank Shirley Paulson for calling my attention to Gottschalk's essay.

a commitment to (or against) the truth of the Gospel—a commitment that must decisively affect one's conclusions.... He does not move from the problem of theodicy back to the understanding of God; rather, he moves out from the conviction that in the light of the revealed and experienceable reality of a sovereign [in a radically different sense of "sovereignty" than that at play in the ordinary way of understanding that concept, we should add] and good God, evil *must* be described—both with respect to its ontological status and its operative character—in terms of its sheer negation [that is, its sheer negating power: its status as pure "anti-power," we might call it, at least if the cross of Christ is to be given the credence Gottschalk and Yoder both affirm it to deserve, to set the true standard of what constitutes genuine power], as what he calls "das Nichtige" [from the German *Nichts*, "nothing"].

As Gottschalk interprets her work, Mary Baker Eddy, the founder of Christian Science, followed the same path as Barth in her response to evil. "Her aim," writes Gottschalk (page 85),

was not to account for the origin of evil in a logically satisfactory way but to define a new standpoint from which it could be overcome, or reduced, as she once put it, "to its nature of nothingness." . . . For her, the question of evil could only be answered at the existential level of the *demonstration* of the sovereignty [perhaps it would be less potentially misleading to say simply the "reality"] of God through the *act* of reducing evil to its "native nothingness." The only terms in which the problem of evil can be resolved are therefore inseparable from the actual process through which evil is destroyed [or, in accordance with what Gottschalk has been arguing throughout his article, rendered transparent in its nugatory irreality]. . . . The means of redemption must therefore include the recognition of evil as nothing other than the sinful error of life and mind apart from God—an error Christians needed not to account for, but to overcome.

A few pages later (page 91), Gottschalk returns to the issue of Auschwitz, and what response can be adequate to it. In the final line of his article, he sums his whole argument up nicely, by writing that the only way ultimately and adequately to deal with the Holocaust and its effects "would be to *reverse* all that its magnification of evil would accomplish by moving, not back, but forward into a magnified understanding of the reality of God."

I submit that it is precisely the opening up of the possibility of just that forward movement—a going forth actually and concretely to *live* and to *build* in the only true reality—that was accomplished by the rebellion at Auschwitz. At least it was accomplished at the level of the *historical truth*, as Laub revealingly and accurately named it, of that rebellion, the truth captured by his survivor's supposedly "inaccurate" memory. Indeed, that survivor's own coming alive, as Laub recounts, when she recalled the rebellion, with an entirely new vitality, reflected in the sudden change of her entire tone of voice and body posture, bears eloquent witness to the power of that so "failed" rebellion—"failed" as judged by the standards of the evil that, at Auschwitz, lays claim to being reality itself—to seal the failure, instead, of that very evil.

Gottschalk and Yoder would agree, in my judgment, that it was exactly in that same sense that the apparent failure of Jesus' mission in his crucifixion was in truth already of itself the raising up of Jesus to complete victory over the power that hung him on the cross. What is more, what Jesus accomplished in and by his death was an absolutely, definitively *political* act—an act of the clearing and ordering of the *polis*, the place wherein alone a genuinely human life with and for one another in community can be lived. Accordingly, Yoder, to return directly to him, concludes the twelfth chapter of *The Politics of Jesus*, and therewith the whole first edition of the book, with these words—with the ring of which I will also end this chapter of my own, on the politics, not just of Jesus, but of trauma as such:

A social style characterized by the creation of a new community and the rejection of violence of any kind is the theme of the New Testament proclamation from beginning to end, from right to left. The cross of Christ is the model of Christian social efficacy, the power of God for Those who believe.

Vincit agnus noster, eum sequamur.

Our Lamb has conquered; him let us follow.

Of course, one might object that such a line may be heard by Christians as issuing a clarion call to partake of the "freedom of the children of God," as Paul puts it. But what about those who do not consider themselves Christian, who follow other religious or spiritual traditions, or even none at all? My reply is that for non-Christians—which for all I know includes myself—there are, I am grateful to be able to affirm, analogs. I will start with that idea in the next chapter.

Chapter 7

TRAUMA TIME

If being a Christian is the sort of thing John Howard Yoder conceived it to be, then at least for Christians today—a day of the between-time, what Agamben, following Paul, calls "the time that remains," and which we might also call "the time of the cross," both in the sense of the cross of Christ and in that of the crossing-point between two times—the *polis*, the place where truly human habitation in community can occur, has already been definitively opened. What is more, from that same Yoderian perspective, for Christians, at least, humankind has already moved into that place and begun to build there. It did so already in the raising up of Jesus on the cross. That raising up of the cross of Jesus was itself already an act of edification, that is, of building-up. The raising of that cross was, then, the raising of the first building in the newly opened or reopened *polis*. Accordingly, to "follow" Jesus on "the way of the cross" is simply to keep on living, and that means building, there, in that place so opened or reopened up. In turn, so to live and build is the only way truly to keep the cross itself always in mind. Only so can Christians, from the perspective Yoder provides, *remember* the cross, that trauma of traumas, which teaches the irreality of what passes for politics under the sign of Caesar—that is, the state and its sovereignty as such.

Nor is it only in the school of Christ and *his* particular cross that one can learn that particular lesson. Rather, a significant convergence of diverse perspectives across a wide variety of traditions of thought occurs here, at this "crucial point," so to speak. Indeed, insofar as every trauma is *all* trauma, as I have put it before, *every* trauma can be seen ultimately to teach that crucial lesson. To give one example, one important for my present purposes, British international relations scholar Jenny Edkins, whom I cited more than once before, arrives along her own very different way at the same point to which Yoder arrived before her, by way of Christ and his cross.

"Trauma," writes Edkins in one passage already cited before, a passage from "Remembering Relationality: Trauma Time and Politics," her contribution to *Memory, Trauma, and World* (page 107), "is clearly disruptive of settled stories. Centralized, sovereign political authority is particularly threatened by this. After a traumatic event what we call the state moves quickly to close down any openings produced by putting in place as fast as possible a linear narrative of origins."

That remark points to the insight that "sovereign political authority," as Edkins names it, is itself founded in and as the covering over of trauma, covering it over by projecting an illusion of origin and ground, in order to salvage 'sovereign political authority' itself from its own groundless violence and violent groundlessness. Thus, for example, Hobbes traced the emergence of the sovereign back to the trauma of the war of all against all wherein "man is wolf to man," thus *masking* the war of violence the sovereign himself perpetually wages and *must* wage against his own "subjects." All differences aside, however important those differences may otherwise be, the pseudo-justificatory movement at issue is essentially, as I have argued earlier, the same one the wife-abuser makes when he "justifies" the abuse he inflicts on his wife by projecting blame for the abuse back onto the supposed misbehavior of that wife, the very victim of the abuse. What occurs in both cases is, in effect, the *rationalization* of violence, a rationalization that entails, in turn, a denial or at least a gross minimization—and therefore a *compounding*—of the trauma the abuse-victim has suffered.

Edkins follows such French thinkers as Philippe Lacoue-Labarthe and Jean-Luc Nancy in drawing a distinction between *politics*, on the one hand, and *the political*, on the other. She reserves to 'politics' everything usually called by that name within state-dominated society. "Politics,' she thus writes (page 108), 'is the regular operation of state institutions, elections, and such like within the framework of the status quo.' In contrast, by 'the political' she means what, in the preceding chapter, I called 'politics elsewhere" — politics as the building of the genuine *polis*, the place of genuine human life in community—for example, such a place as, for Yoder's Christians, the one opened or reopened up by and at the crucifixion of Christ.

It is "politics," in Edkins' sense of the term, and not "the political," that is "threatened" by trauma; and it is politics that, to counter the threat trauma poses to it, manipulates trauma for the sake of securing sovereign authority against that threat. "The political," in contrast to politics so conceived, ". . . is the moment where established ways of carrying on do not tell us what to do, or where they are challenged and ruptured: in traumatic moments, for example."

Edkins argues that trauma always involves *betrayal*, in a double sense of that term. As she sees it, that doubling of sense goes to the very heart of the matter of how trauma opens the new, multi-dimensional space of "the political" in the midst of the one-dimensional space occupied by the "politics" of sovereignty and the state. On the one hand, to betray is to *break trust*, as when we say that someone we trusted has "betrayed" us by acting contrary to that trust. On the other hand, to betray is to *reveal*, as we might speak of someone's awkward behavior "betraying" a lack of self-confidence. Trauma is the inextricable interweaving of the two, breaking-trust and revelation: The revelation of the breaking of trust is precisely what is traumatic in the fullest sense.

Considered with regard to politics and the political, trauma is just such betrayal of the political, in that double sense of "betrayal": *Political trauma is the revelation that politics has broken trust with the political and as such also the revelation of the radical alterity of the political to all politics.* Thus, Edkins writes (page 109) that

> what traumatic encounter does . . . is reveal the way in which
> the social order is radically incomplete and fragile . . . nothing
> more than a fantasy—it's our invention, and it is one that does
> not 'hold up' under stress. When it comes down to it, for
> example, what we call the state is not a protector, the guardian

of people's security. On the contrary, it is the very organization that can send people to their deaths, by conscripting them in times the state is under threat and sending them to fight its wars. First, there is a betrayal of trust that threatens [ordinary national or family] relationality: relationality expressed as national or family belonging turns out to be unreliable, for example. Second, the radical relationality that is normally forgotten is revealed or made apparent.

Given that trauma thus reveals the betrayal of the *polis* by the state, it is of the utmost importance to the state to do whatever it can to assure itself that trauma—which dispels the illusion on which the state is based and opens a place outside the state, a place where genuine human community is not only still or again possible but also always already actual—will be, and will stay, *forgotten*. "Politics," and the state that defines it, thereby fulfills its own vested interest in keeping the very revelation that comes with trauma from occurring, from *taking place*, as we say in a telling expression. Politics thus attempts to force the *polis*, the place of the political as such, *closed* again, re-securing the *enclosure* of the political within politics. By that enclosure the *polis* is "privatized," in effect. Or at least it is "property-ized," that is, turned into just one more form of "property," so called "public property," which itself is progressively reduced to what is left over after all the "private" property that private interests can lay hands on has been stolen away.

'However,' as Edkins herself goes on to observe (page 108), in contrast to the state and its contentedly safe citizens, 'some people want to try to hold on to the openness that trauma produces.' Such people, already inhabiting the genuinely political place trauma opens up, having migrated there from the state as the place of politics as usual, 'do not want to forget, or to express the trauma in standard narratives that entail a form of forgetting.' Rather, they see clearly that trauma is 'something that unsettles authority,' and something that, furthermore, 'should make settled stories,' such as the Hobbesian sorts of tales sovereignty tells on itself, 'impossible in the future.'

The narrative time that is temporalized by and in such settled, stately stories—the time constituted by such enforced *forgetting* of the traumatic past and thereby rendering impossible of any open future—might well be called *dead time*. It is the time of time's corpse, the time when there is no more time for time.

In such a time, there is also no room for place any longer, no place for it to take place. Instead, all that is left is the placeless space in which no point differs from any other, the indifferent space of global geometry. Most especially, in such a dead time there is no place for the *polis*, the place of human cohabitation. In the dead time of settled, stately narrative, *where nothing ever happens*, the political cannot happen either.

Such dead time, in which nothing happens and nothing is allowed to happen, is precisely the time of politics and the state. In contrast, "it might be useful," as Edkins proposes, "to call th[e] form of time that provides an opening for the *political* 'trauma time', as distinct from the linear, narrative time that suits state or sovereign *politics*." So conceived, trauma time is the time of the place of the political—altogether elsewhere than the place called the state, which is the placeless, un-place-able place of politics.

Trauma time is the time of the political, as opposed to politics. It is the elsewhen of the elsewhere of the polis, *the only place where human habitation, which is always a co-habitation, can truly take place at all.*

Dead Time

One lesson to be learned from Heidegger is that time "is" not—as though it were some sort of container for other things, for example. Time "is" not at all, in that sense. Rather, it "temporalizes": *Time times*, we might say, more closely to mirror Heidegger's German (*"Die Zeit zeitigt"*).

In addition we could say that "what" time times, is events themselves. In short, *time times events.*

Time doesn't time events in the sense that we speak, for example, of "timing" a race, or the boiling of an egg. That latter sense of "timing" means "keeping time," as we also say. It means, often quite literally, "clocking" the duration of some event—that is, measuring that duration in terms of some "time-keeping device" such as a clock or stop-watch. To "time" an event, in that sense, already presupposes that the time being measured is itself already there, already given, and given as just the sort of thing that can be measured by the units at issue in such time-keeping devices—the sort of thing that such devices can keep safely enclosed within the measures of which they count the measure. To time an event in that sense does not mean, then, to open up time or temporality itself for the first time, but rather to count the units of a stretch or segment of an already given time, a counting that counts on that pre-given time's amenability to be measured by such units of chronometry (literally, time-measurement).

Time times, but not in *that* sense—the sense of giving the count for the units of some measurable duration. Instead, time times in the sense that it yields the very e-venting, the very coming forth, of events themselves. Indeed, following Heidegger, we might even say that time yields *the* event itself: the original, originating coming forth of coming forth as such. Times *brings forth* or *lets come forth* coming-forth itself, such that time itself becomes what Heidegger calls *"the eventing of the event"* (*"das Ereignen des Ereignisses"*): Time events the event.

As the eventing of the event, time itself is trauma. What is more, that is reversible: Trauma itself is time. That, at any rate, is the perspective I shall try to articulate in what follows.

Freud taught, in *Moses and Monotheism*, that trauma manifests simultaneously and inescapably both in what he calls its "positive" effects, and in what he calls its "negative" effects. "The former," he writes (page 95), "are endeavors to revive the trauma, to remember the forgotten experience, or, better still, to make it real . . . These endeavors are summed up in the terms 'fixation to the trauma' and 'repetition-compulsion.'" On the other hand, ["t]he negative reactions pursue the opposite aim; here nothing is to be remembered or repeated of the forgotten traumata. They may be grouped together as defensive reactions."

What Freud calls the "negative" effect of, or "defensive" reaction to, trauma, induces, in general, a sort of *numbness* of the traumatized organism toward the traumatic event. The organism as it were numbs itself in the face of trauma and thereby avoids, or at least postpones (a point to which I will return shortly), its impact. The physical reaction to trauma of "going into shock," in which the organism switches itself off, so to speak, in the face of such trauma as sexual abuse or a serious automobile accident, can serve as a model.

By calling such effects "negative," Freud did not mean to indicate that they were somehow harmful for the organism that enacted and/or experienced them in reaction to trauma—far from it. In fact, it is only such numbing, such "going into shock," that allows the organism to *survive* the traumatic "shock" itself, the delivery of the wounding blow that otherwise would kill the organism so struck. In that sense, the "negative" effects of trauma are entirely positive *for the organism as such*. They are what allow the organism to survive the traumatic blow for which it is unprepared and which, as so unprepared, it cannot process. Without its "negative" effect, the trauma would prove deadly. Without such negative effects, the trauma would no longer truly be a trauma at all. It would no longer traumatize. It would simply kill.

Freud's "negative" effects of trauma, accordingly, are actually positive for the traumatized organism: They are life preserving. Those effects are "negative," not in relation to the traumatized organism, but only in relation to the trauma itself, so to speak. They are negative in relation to the trauma, in the sense that they block or impede the impact of the traumatizing blow upon the organism. Alternatively put, they are ways, as Freud himself says, that allow the organism to avoid the trauma, at least in its full impact. As already indicated, such avoidance is absolutely essential, if the organism is to survive the blow at all, rather than completely succumb to it. To put it in paradoxical fashion, going *into* shock— in the sense, for example, of the expression "shell shock," as used during World War I to name what later came to be called "post-traumatic stress disorder"—buffers the organism *against* shock, the very shock of the trauma, the traumatic blow, itself, which would otherwise prove fatal.

Indeed, it is only by *deadening* the organism through such negative effect that trauma achieves the quality of "belatedness" (*Nachträlichkeit*) that, as Freud came to see with great clarity, defines trauma as such. A blow that can be fully experienced at the moment of initial impact is one that the organism, precisely in fully experiencing it, just as fully processes. No sooner has such a fully manageable blow been struck, than it comes to be fully managed. It is already behind the organism just as soon as it has struck at all, rather than still awaiting the organism somewhere in front of it.

But that, once again, would mean that such a blow would not really have been *traumatic* at all. This time, however, that would not be because the blow would have been fatal. The opposite, in effect, would have been the case. Instead of being fatal, the blow would have been no more than just one more routine occurrence in the endlessly ongoing string of routine occurrences that make up the day of the everyday, none of which occurrences ever really rises above the gray, monotonous plain it shares with all the rest—and, in which, then, nothing ever really *happens* at all. Thus, without its *belatedness*, without its having to come reach us across what Freud labeled its period of "latency," trauma would have nothing traumatic about it. It would no longer be any trauma at all.

Equally well, however, trauma would no longer be trauma without what Freud called its "positive" effect, which he defined, above all, in terms of the *compulsion to repeat* the traumatic incident itself. Such *repetition compulsion* is "positive" in relation to the trauma that "effects" it in a sense paired with that in accordance with which numbing or deadening against the blow is "negative" in relation to that same trauma. Just as the negativity of the negative effect of trauma does not as such mean being detrimental to the traumatized organism, so does the positivity of the positive effect not as such lie in somehow benefitting that same organism.

In fact, both the "negative" and the "positive" effects could be said to be positive *in relation to the organism*, allowing it the opportunity not only to survive but also to "fight another day," as we say. At any rate, however that may be, the positivity of Freud's "positive" effect of trauma lies in the relation of that effect not to the organism but to the trauma, just as did the negativity of Freud's "negative" effect.

The negative effect is negative in that it *distances* the organism from the trauma that strikes it. The root negative effect of trauma, the root negative impact of the traumatic shock, is to engender the flattening, damping-down, numbing, or deadening of the impact itself. By its negative impact trauma in effect establishes a distance between the traumatized organism and the traumatic blow or shock, and casts the traumatized organism into that distance, away from the blow. Only such distancing allows the organism to *undergo* the impact, and not simply be destroyed by it. Indeed, to undergo a traumatic impact, as opposed to being eliminated by it, *is* to be cast in such a way into such a distance from it. Only by distancing those it strikes from the impact it delivers does a blow constitute a trauma. As Freud knew, the "latency" period of the unfolding of a trauma was always necessary, not something that could somehow be dispensed with, supposedly to face the trauma directly. At least in that sense, trauma can *never* be met head-on, at the very point of impact. Rather, it can only be approached from the side, indirectly, and only after the fact, "belatedly." In short, what Freud calls the "negative" effect of trauma is inescapable. It is definitive of trauma as such.

In contrast, but in exact parallel, to the way that the negative effect of trauma *distances* the organism from the trauma, the positive effect *keeps the trauma close* to that same organism. The root positive effect of trauma, the root positive impact of the traumatic shock—namely, the compulsion to keep repeating the traumatic encounter—assures that the trauma remains *pending*. As pending, the traumatic event continues to exert pressure, continually demanding to be allowed finally, truly to *happen completely* (or "to complete its happening"), that is, to be allowed fully and truly to *strike* the organism. The trauma remains pending in its demand to "strike" the organism, both in the sense of striking *at* it, and in the deeper, more crucial sense of *striking the very traumatized organism itself*, striking it into that very thing, the traumatized organism, in the same sense that we say of a minting process that it strikes coins.

Without continuing to be impending through that "positive" effect, trauma would no more be trauma than it would if it lost its "negative" effect of deadening the traumatized organism in face of the traumatic blow, distancing the organism from it. Similarly, a blow without Freud's "positive" effect—one that was, then, no longer pending—would simply continue to drop ever further behind whomever it struck, as that one continued on along her way unscathed, untouched in any significant degree by what would have been at most a minor, glancing blow with no lasting impact at all. Trauma, in contrast, is not merely *lasting* in its effects. It is *everlasting*—everlasting precisely as ever-pending and ever-impending. What Freud calls the "positive" effect of trauma is no less definitive of trauma as such than is what he calls its "negative" effect.

What is more, though it may sound paradoxical before a quick reflection, it is only by *postponing* the full impact of the traumatic blow that that blow can be kept *pending*. Thus, the two—the negative and the positive effects of trauma—go together inseparably. That is why Freud himself in *Moses and Monotheism*, right after distinguishing between the "negative" and the "positive" effects of trauma, suggests that the distinction is not to be pushed too far, by writing of what he is calling the "negative" reactions: "Actually they represent fixations on the trauma no less than do the positive reactions, but they follow the opposite tendency."

Only the postponed can truly be pending, and only the pending postponed. The postponed and the pending interpenetrate one another. To postpone is precisely to set (in Latin, *ponere*, to place or put or set, as one sets a brush on a dressing-table) after (*post* in Latin). What is postponed is put off till later, till *after* whatever may come *before* then, whatever comes along to fill the gap created by the postponement.

As Peter Sloterdijk writes in the first line of "Rage as Project: Revenge," a section of "Rage Transactions," the first chapter of his *Rage and Time: A Psychopolitical Investigation*: "The creation of a qualified or existential time, that is, a lived time with a retrospective and anticipatory character, occurs through the deferral of discharge." It may be that, as Sloterdijk's remark suggests when re-contextualized into the general argument of his book, the "rage" of his title may play a special role in the original opening up of "existential" or "lived" time, as he calls it. However, even if what Sloterdijk's calls rage does somehow, for whatever "psychopolitical" reasons, take precedence in that regard over such other fundamental passions or emotions as, say, the anxiety or the boredom to which Heidegger assigns a similar role, it is because Sloterdijk's rage, no less than Heidegger's anxiety or boredom, itself has a *traumatic structure*.

Rage—and the spirit of revenge with which Sloterdijk, following Nietzsche, quite properly connects it—can arise only from the "deferral of discharge" to which Sloterdijk refers in the remark I have just cited. That deferral, in turn, is ultimately *imposed*, at least at the "existential" or "lived" level, to use Sloterdijk's own terms—which is to say, as actually *experienced* by anyone "overcome," as we tellingly put it, by the rage that springs up of itself, from the deferral at issue. Indeed, as Nietzsche well knew, rage might be defined precisely as what wells up of itself in the organism whenever that organism encounters an obstacle to the discharge of any charge (that is, any pulse, impulse, urge, drive, instinct, energy, or the like, anything whatever that would seek to "discharge" itself in the first place), an obstacle imposing a deferral or postponement of such discharge. The organism will experience any such obstacle as a thwarting of the organism's will, as it were. In turn, the thwarted will is the enraged will. Encountering an obstacle to its own will, the will rages—and rage it will, like Achilles on the plains before Troy.

Nor, as Sloterdijk's title for his book shows he also is happy to acknowledge, was Nietzsche ignorant of what it is that the enraged will really rages at. The very spirit of revenge, as he has his Zarathustra say, is (in Walter Kaufmann's well known translation) "the will's ill-will" against *time*—"against time," he says, "and its 'It was!'" From the point of view of rage, what's so objectionable about time, so enraging about it, is expressed precisely by the past tense, the tense of that which is no longer subject to alteration, no longer malleable to the will. The will can work upon the present to change the future, but what has already been, the past itself, is no longer anything that can be changed. In its very being past, the past thus places itself past the reach of the will. The past as such, in its simple past-ness and altogether independent of its actual contents—which may be wholly pleasing to the will, wholly according to its will—*defies* the will, *thwarts* it.

What is more, for a thwarted will, in its enraged frustration, time as a whole, the whole business of "past, present, and future," manifests itself as nothing more than the inexorable mechanism of turning everything into something that "was." Time as such manifests to rage as nothing more than the ever more enraging, ever ongoing, never changing, never changeable transformation of everything into the past, into what "was," but which, precisely as what was, is what still is now and ever will be the one absolutely insuperable limit to the will. So experienced, time is, in effect, a vast engine for devouring everything it touches, all it brings forth—all its children, as Kronos, old Father Time, devours his children in Greek mythology—and turning it all into the pure waste of what is, for the will, deserving only of being discarded, cast away as a useless remnant, what remains after the will has taken all it can from it. For rage, then, there is no need to wait for Auschwitz and Adorno, time itself has always already turned everything into excrement.

Nietzsche can also offer guidance concerning just what rage itself contributes to the very process against which it rages so—the very process of the primordial timing of time as such, the original-originating "temporalization of temporality," in the language of Heidegger's *Being and Time*. "The spirit of revenge," of which Nietzsche's Zarathustra speaks—that spirit of revenge "against time and its 'It was!'"—is also, as he says, "the will's ill-will against itself." As Heidegger, for one, is good at elucidating in his own Nietzsche interpretations, in Nietzsche's thought it is, in effect, the will itself that drives time, that propels and sustains the chronological machine of time, that machine that makes time pass into the past and its "was," turning everything into shit—so far as the will is concerned, at least. The will itself *is* that very machine. It *is* the clock itself, in its very ticking, obscene in the inexorability with which it keeps counting off the moments as they click by from what is not yet, through what is, but, unable to abide, no sooner is than it is gone on by, to become the pure waste of what once was, but as such is no longer.

The will as such is, for Nietzsche, no mere will to preserve itself, as though it were Spinoza's *conatus*, the striving of any being to maintain itself at its present level, which eventually becomes, in Freud, the death-drive whereby the organic defines itself in and as the striving to return to the inorganic. If the will were any such thing, then it would not be pure will. It would be, instead, the will to the very thing, whatever it may be (even if it is nothingness itself, as it may be for a nihilistic will), that *stills* the will— that satisfies it, satiates it, brings it to *cease* its striving, its willing. No, the will as will is no such will to put the will at rest. It is, rather, the will always to keep willing, the will never to be satisfied, the will to will itself. (As Lacan a century after Nietzsche will observe, above all what desire desires, is to desire. *That* is why desire is never satisfied, never has "enough." Or, as Norman Mailer around the same time as Lacan will observe, in regard to both sex and money: Only too much is enough.)

Thus, Nietzsche insists that the will is always the will to increase itself, to subject ever more to its own will, its own power. The will as will is just that, the will to power. Furthermore, as Heidegger especially emphasizes in his interpretations of Nietzsche, as will to power the will as such is always will to *more* power. Otherwise, it would once again become a will that wills to be brought to rest, a will that wills to stop willing. The insatiability of the will to power is just that: insatiability itself.

Accordingly, it is the will itself, as insatiable will to power, the very will to will, that condemns everything that is—condemns it, precisely, *to pass on*. The will to power itself judges every "now" as *deserving* to pass, to get out of the way so the will can keep on going, keep on willing. By announcing that sentence of condemnation, the will *enacts* the very sentence being pronounced: The will is just that "speech-act," the "performative" utterance of the curse of all that is, which utterance as such effects the very *cursing*, the *consigning* of what is to its doom. The will as such passes the very sentence that sentences everything to pass—to turn to shit, against the stench of which the will itself recoils. However, no more than one can recoil from one's own shadow, which continues to shadow one in the very recoil, can the will succeed in escaping the stench of the past from which it recoils. It is, indeed, that very recoil itself that passes the past behind it, as the bowel passes the waste it is designed to pass by spasmodically recoiling itself away from it.

Rage is the form the will itself takes as the recoil that passes the very sentence in the pronouncing of which the very impassable form of passing itself (as Husserl taught time to be in *The Phenomenology of Internal Time-Consciousness*) gets enacted. Yet unless the will pronounces such a sentence, it is no will at all. To will *is* to pronounce that sentence. Thus, the will's rage—the burning rage of the will's spirit of revenge against time and its "It was!"—is rage against *itself*, the "will's ill-will against itself," just as Nietzsche has his Zarathustra also say.

Furthermore, insofar as time or temporality temporalizes itself into the very passing of the sentence of what passes on *to* passing on, *time itself is rage.*

According to one of Heidgger's famous analyses in *Being and Time*, the emotion, mood, or attunement (*Befindlichkeit*) of what he calls anxiety (*Angst*) temporalizes itself into and as the adventing of advent, the coming-to of the to-come (the authentic "future," German *Zukunft*), that retrieves or repeats what has been (*das Gewesene*, the authentic past) in the bare blink of an eye (the authentic moment, now, or present: *Augenblick*, which the old, standard English translation of *Being and Time* by John Macquarrie and Edward Robinson renders as "moment of vision"). So too, according to Heidegger, does every "state-of-mind" (MacQuarrie and Robinson's translation of Heidegger's German term *Befindlichkeit*) temporalize itself in one way or another—*and*, crucially, always as a version either of authentic time, or of inauthentic time, but either way "simultaneously" in all three of time's dimensions.

Just so does the state of mind called rage, too, temporalize itself. Indeed, read as the very spirit of what Nietzsche calls revenge, rage, like what Heidegger calls anxiety, is not just one way among others in which temporality temporalizes itself, but is, instead, a form of *fundamental* temporalization. Rage, conceived along Nietzschean lines, is like Heideggerian anxiety in being what Heidegger will soon enough after *Being and Time* come to call a "fundamental mood" or "fundamental attunement"—a *Grundstimmung*.

However, whereas in the case of the fundamental attunement that is anxiety, time times itself *authentically*, the time of rage—the temporality that temporalizes itself in and as rage, taken as an alternate fundamental attunement—is *inauthentic* time. It is *dead* time—and as such it is also always *deadening* time: that time of the clock that always keeps ticking, time as the never passing, un-transformable, everything-deadening deadness of the very form of passing itself, Nietzsche's rage-inducing time of "It was!"

As deadening dead time, the enraging time of rage, time has no time for itself. It is time as what kills the time that stretches itself so monotonously from now till later, the time that kills the time that must be killed until what's still pending, what has been put off until later—that "later" that never seems to come— finally does come "at last," *after* all the endlessly dead and deadening time of passing on has finally itself passed on.

Life-Time

In the meantime—which is to say, in "the time that remains" until "then," until, that is, time has at last been found for what has so far been postponed and stays pending–in the meantime, however, some way must be found to "kill time," as we say. The time that must be "killed" is precisely the dead and deadening time of rage: All that dead time, that "down-time," we could say, that remains until then must itself be filled in somehow, with some manner of busyness or business. To bide time in the meantime, distractions from how much time remains must be found, then repeated compulsively until all that time no longer remains.

It doesn't really matter just what manner of time-killing activity fills up that time that remains till then, just so long as some manner does. Whatever manner of activity is available will work, provided only it is distracting enough to take up all the interminable dead-time that stretches itself out before us. When the storm rages, any port will do.

The dead time that spreads and stretches forth interminably is the time when nothing really happens, but in which time just keeps ticking on in endless indifference to what may come to fill it. Precisely because it is thus dead, devoid of event or liveliness, that dead time itself is just what must in turn itself be "killed" again, and then again and again on an everyday basis, through all the empty, everyday distractions with the endless repetition of which we do indeed fill every endless day. We must fill in and kill all the dead time when nothing really happens until another time itself returns, until a lively, eventful time of life, a time for living—what we might well call *life*-time—at last strikes again.

However, the empty, dead time that always remains to be killed until such life time finally strikes again does not, as it were, take place at "another" time than that at which the latter time, the time of life, takes place. That is, there is no sort of mediating, third time, besides the two times of dead time and life-time, that would provide some common standard in terms of which those two times could be measured, so that, for example, we might compare their two durations. The two times do not happen at different times as measured in some such third time that is supposed to be common to them both: There *is* no time common to both dead time and life-time. Each of those two times is *all* time.

Indeed, in one sense we could say that, far from happening at two different times, dead time and life time happen *at the same time*. Better: They *are* one and the same time. There is finally only *one* time. However, that is not in any sense that would erase the doubling or bifurcation of time into dead time and life time, turning them into just "one and the same time." Time always does so bifurcate itself "simultaneously" into dead time and life time, but only in the sense that the bifurcation yields two wholly *incommensurable* times "at once," and precisely *not* in the sense of occurring together at one point by some standard that would be common to both— that is, in terms of which *both* could be measured and, thereby, made commensurable with one another.

We might say that dead time and life time are "not-two," in the sense at issue in *Advaita* or "non-dual" Hinduism, whereby to say that x and y are "not-two" does not at all mean to erase the difference between x and y, such that they become simply "one"—"one and the same thing." By the teachings of *Advaita* or "non-duality," mind and matter, for instance, are "not-two." Nevertheless, Bertrand Russell's old quip still holds: "What's mind? Never matter! What's matter? Never mind!"

In fact, it is only because they are not-two that Russell's joke will work at all. It is really only insofar as mind and matter are not-two, that they can be absolutely, radically different—so different as to be strictly "incommensurable." In order for x and y to be two—"two things," such that one could count each in turn to find their total number (namely, 2)—x and y must, of course, have *something in common*, in relation to which they can count as two different instances or particularizations of that third, common thing, that is, two things "of the same kind": "two men," "two birds," "two moons," "two pious acts," or whatever. It is just because mind and matter are *not* two things of the same kind but are, rather, strictly incommensurable, that, for example, Descartes' endeavor to locate the point of their interaction in the pineal gland has so frequently provided grounds for ridicule.

Dead time and life time are not-two. That says both that they are not two things of the same kind, and that they are nevertheless not at all one and the same thing. It says that the two are truly incommensurable.

What could be more different than avoidance and return, distancing from and drawing near, denying and affirming? Yet Freud is right to insist that what he calls the "negative" effects of trauma and what he calls its "positive" effects are not really two different sorts of effect, but always go inseparably together and, as so bound, constitute the traumatic impact as such. They are, in short, "not-two." Trauma itself is just the simultaneous bifurcation of an impact, a shock, into the non-dual duality of such "negative" and "positive" effects. Avoiding a traumatic impact or shock, numbing oneself in the face of it, *is* itself the putting off, the postponing of that impact, which postponement keeps the impact constantly pending. The former does not just accompany the latter; it accomplishes it; it *is* it. The very "registering" of the trauma, its very "impacting" upon the traumatized organism, is exactly the numbing wherein the traumatic impact puts itself off, postpones itself, and, thereby, keeps itself constantly and inescapably impending. But that means that it *opens time itself*—it *times time as such*.

The figure of death is synecdochic for trauma in general. In that regard, it is worth recalling at this point how Heidegger depicts the "certainty" of death for *Dasein*, "that being which each of us is," in the famous analysis of Being-toward-death in the first chapter of the second division of *Being and Time*. It is *certain*, he writes there, that death will come. Yet that very certainty of death is inseparable from the fact that just "when" it will come always remains *indefinite*. My death may come "at any time." It may not come for many years yet, but it may just as easily come in the very next instant, while I am still typing this sentence. It is just that indefiniteness of its coming that makes my death so constant and pervasive a threat to me throughout the whole span of my life, from birth all the way up to death itself. Indefinite and, therefore, equally and fully pending at every moment, the constant threat of my death is one from which I am constantly fleeing, only to find that my death has always run on ahead of me, and is already there waiting for me in any place to which I flee to escape it. Death always keeps its "appointment at Samarra" with me, wherever my own "Samarra" may happen to be.

It is so not only with the trauma of death, but also with all other trauma, for which death serves as the exemplar. Once trauma has struck its first blow, it is certain to strike again, one never knows just when or where. It is the very indefiniteness of its "when" that makes that second blow so certain, and gives it its constantly impending, intensely threatening inexorability. Wherever one may run to try to escape it, trauma will always have run on ahead already, to coil itself there in waiting, biding its time until, in its own good time, it strikes again. Indifferent to all our efforts to avoid it, trauma waits patiently; and by its own indifference toward them it reduces all those efforts themselves, no matter what they may be, to indifference in turn. They all become no more than pointless distractions, one no better or worse than another, to fill all the time that remains until what is constantly threatening to happen at last does happen, and all that dead time itself dies away.

May the time come!

WORKS CITED

Abraham, Karl, and Torok, Maria. *The Shell and the Kernel.* Trans. Nicolas T. Rand. Chicago: The University of Chicago Press, 1994.

Adler, H. G.. *The Journey.* Trans. Peter Filkins. New York: Random House, 2008.

Agamben, Gorgio. *Homo Sacer: Sovereign Power and Bare Life.* Trans. David Heller-Roazen. Stanford, CA: Stanford University Press, 1998.

_____. *Remnants of Auschwitz: The Witness and the Archive.* Trans. David Heller-Roazen. New York: Zone Books, 1999.

_____. *State of Exception.* Trans. Kevin Attell. Chicago and London: University of Chicago Press, 2005.

_____. *The Time That Remains: A Commentary on the Letter to the Romans.* Trans. Patricia Dailey. Stanford, CA: Stanford University Press, 2005.

Améry, Jean. *At the Mind's Limits: Contemplations by a Survivor on Auschwitz and Its Realities.* Trans. Sidney Rosenfeld and Stella P. Rosenfeld. Bloomington and Indianapolis: University of Indiana Press, 1977.

_____. *On Aging: Revolt and Resignation.* Trans. John D. Barlow. Bloomington and Indianapolis: University of Indiana Press, 1994.

_____. *On Suicide: A Discourse on Voluntary Death.* Trans, John D. Barlow. Bloomington and Indianapolis: University of Indiana Press, 1999.

Antelme, Robert. *The Human Race.* Trans. Jeffrey Haight. Evanston, IL: The Marlboro Press/Northwestern University Press, 1992.

Badiou, Allain. *St. Paul: The Foundations of Universalism.* Trans. Ray Brassier. Chicago: University of Chicago Press, 2003.

Bateson, Gregory. "The Cybernetics of 'Self': A Theory of Alcoholism." In *Psychiatry,* vol. 34 (February 1971).

Bell, Duncan, editor. *Memory, Trauma, and World Politics: Reflections on the Relationship between Past and Present.* New York: Pallgrave Macmillan, 2006.

Benjamin, Walter. *On Hashish.* Trans. Howard Eiland et al. Ed. Howard Eiland. Cambridge, MA: The Belknap Press of Harvard University Press, 2006.

_____. "Theses on the Philosophy of History." In *Illuminations.* Trans. Harry Zohn, ed. Hanah Arendt. New York: Schocken Books, 1969.

_____. "The Work of Art in the Age of Mechanical Reproduction." In *Illuminations.* Trans. Harry Zohn, ed. Hanah Arendt. New York: Schocken Books, 1969.

Bergson, Henri. *Le deux sources de la morale et de la religion.* Paris: Presses Universitaires de France, 1932. Ouadrige reimpression of the 9th ed., 2006.

_____. "Le possible et le réel." In *La penseé et le mouvant.* Paris: Presses Universitaires de France, 1938. Ouadrige reimpression of the 9th ed., 2006.

Borradori, Giovanna, ed.. *Philosophy in a Time of Terror: Conversations with Jürgen Habermas and Jacques Derrida.* Chicago: University of Chicago Press, 2003.

Brison, Susan J.. *Aftermath: Violence and the Remaking of a Self.* Princeton University Press, 2002.

Butler, Judith. *Frames of War: When Is Life Grievable?* London and New York: Verso, 2009.

_____. *Precarious Lives: The Powers of Mourning and Violence.* New York: Verso, 2004.

Caruth, Cathy. *Unclaimed Experience: Trauma, Narrative, and History.* Baltimore and London: The Johns Hopkins University Press, 1996.

Cheever, Susan. *Desire: Where Sex Meets Addiction.* New York: Simon and Schuster, 2008.

Chrétien, Jean-Louis. *The Ark of Speech.* Trans. Andrew Brown. New York and London: Routledge, 2004.

_____. *The Unforgettable and the Unhoped For.* New York: Fordham University Press, 2002.

Davis, Colin. *Haunted Subjects: Psychoanalysis and the Return of the Dead.* New York: Pallgrave Macmillan, 2007.

Des Pres, Terrance. *The Survivor: An Analysis of Life in the Death Camps.* Oxford University Press, 1980.

Dupuy, Jean-Pierre. *Pour un catrophisme éclairé.* Paris : Éditions du Seuil, 2002.

Duras, Marguerite. *The War: A Memoir.* Trans. Barbara Bray. New York: Pantheon Books, 1985.

Eisenstein, Paul. *Traumatic Encounters: Holocaust Representation and the Hegelian Subject.* Albany, NY: State University of New York Press, 2003.

Ellman, Richard. *James Joyce: A Literary Biography.* New York: Oxford University Press, 1959

Faulkner, William. *Light in August.* New York: Random House, 1950.

Freud, Sigmund. *Beyond the Pleasure Principle.* Trans. James Strachey. New York and Longon: Norton, 1961.

_____. *The Interpretation of Dreams.* Trans. James Strachey. New York: Basic Books, 2010.

_____. *Moses and Monotheism.* Trans. Katherine Jones. New York: Random House, 1939.

Fukyama, Francis. *The End of History and the Last Man.* New York: Penguin Books, 1992.

Gass, William H.. *The World Within the Word.* Boston: Nonpareil Books, 1979.

Gottschalk, Stephen. "Theodicy After Auschwitz and the Reality of God." *Union Seminary Quarterly Review.* Vol. XLI, Nos. 3 & 4, 1987.

Hardt, Michael, and Negri, Paulo. *Commonwealth.* Cambridge, MA: The Belknap Press of Harvard University Press, 2009).

Hawkes, John. *Adventures in the Alaskan Skin Trade.* New York: Simon and Schuster, 1985.

Heidegger, Martin. *Being and Time.* Trans. John Macquarrie and Edward Robinson. New York: Harper & Row, 1962.

_____. *Contributions to Philosophy: From Enowning.* Trans. Parvis Emad Emad & Kenneth Maly. Bloomington, IN: Indiana Univeristy Press, 2000.

_____. *Nietzsche.* 4 vols. Trans. David Farrell Krell. New York: Harper, 1991.

Heilbrunn, Jacob. "Telling the Holocaust Like It Wasn't." In *The New York Times*, Sunday, January 9, 2009.

Henry, Michel. *Du communism au capitalism: Théorie d'une catastrophe.* Lausanne, Switz.: L'Age d'Homme, 2008.

_____. *L'essence de la manifestation.* Paris: Presses Universitaire de France, 1963.

_____. *Marx.* 2 vol.—*I: Une Philosophie de la reality; II: Une Philosophie de l'économie.* Paris: Editions Gallimard, 1976.

Husserl, Edmund. *The Phenomenology of Internal Time-Consciousness.* Indianapolis and Bloomington: Indiana University Press, 1971.

Jones, Serene. *Trauma and Grace: Theology in a Ruptured World.* Louisville, KY: Westminster John Knox Press, 2009.

Kakar, Sudhir. *The Colors of Violence: Cultural Identities, Religion, and Conflict.* Chicago: University of Chicago Press, 1996.

Klein, Naomi. *The Shock Doctrine: The Rise of Disaster Capitalism.* New York: Picador, 2007.

LaCapra, Dominick. *History and Memory after Auschwitz.* Ithaca and London: Cornell University Press, 1998.

_____. *Writing History, Writing Trauma.* Baltimore: Johns Hopkins University Press, 2001.

Laclau, Ernesto. *Emancipation(s).* London and New York: Verso, 1996.

_____. *On Populist Reason.* London and New York: Verso, 2005; paperback edition 2007.

_____ and Mouffe, Chantal. *Hegemony and Socialist Strategy: Towards a Radical Democratic Politics.* 2nd edition. London and New York: Verso, 2001. Original edition, 1985

Lacoue-Labarthe, Philippe. *Typologies.* Palo Alto, CA: Stanford University press, 1989.

Laub, Dori, and Felman, Shoshana. *Testimony: Crises of Witnessing in Literature, Psychoanalysis, and History.* New York and London: Routledge, 1992.

Levi, Primo. *The Drowned and the Saved.*

Lifton, Robert Jay. *Broken Connections: Death and Life Continuity.* New York: Simon and Schuster, 1979.

_____. *Super Power Syndrome: America's Apocalyptic Confrontation with the World*. New York: Thunder's Mouth Press/Nation Books, 2003.

Lubin, Orly. "Masked Power: An Encounter with the Social Body in the Flesh." In *Trauma at Home*. Ed. Judith Greenberg. Lincoln and London: University of Nebraska Press, 2003.

Lyotard, Jean-François. *Heidegger and "the jews"*. Trans. Andreas Michel and Mark S. Roberts. Indianapolis: University of Minnesota Press, 1990.

Marion, Jean-Luc. *Being Given: Toward a Phenomenology of Givenness*. Trans. Jeffrey L. Kosky. Stanford, CA: Stanford University Press, 2002.

Marcos, Subcomandante Insurgente. *The Speed of Dreams:: Selected Writings 2001-2007*. San Francisco: City Lights, 2007.

McCarthy, Cormack. *No Country for Old Men*. New York: Alfred A. Knopf, 2005.

Nancy, Jean-Luc. *The Creation of the World, or Globalization*. Trans. François Raffoul and David Pettigrew. Albany, NY: State Univesity of New York Press, 2007.

_____. *Dis-Enclosure: The Deconstruction of Christianity*. Trans. Bettina Bergo, Gabriel Malenfant, and Michael B. Smith. New York: Fordham University Press, 2008.

Nietzsche, Friedrich. *Thus Spoke Zarathustra*. Trans. Walter Kaufmann. In *The Portable Nietzsche*. Ed. Walter Kaufman. New York: The Vintage Press, Inc., 1954.

Novitch, Miriam. *Les Passages des Barbares*. Nice: Presses du Temps présent, no date.

Peck, M. Scott, with Patricia Kay and Marilyn Von Waldner. *What Return Can I Make? The Dimensions of the Christian Experience*. New York: Simon and Schuster, 1985.

Pollack, Michael. *L'experience concentritionaire*. Paris: Éditions Métailié, 2000.

Ricoeur, Paul. *Oneself as Another*. Trans. Kathleen Blamey, Chicago: University of Chicago Press, 1995.

_____. *The Symbolism of Evil*. Trans. Emerson Buchanan. Boston: Beacon Press, 1969.

Rosenzweig, Franz. *The Star of Redemption*. Trans. William W. Hallo. Notre Dame, IN: University of Notre Dame Press, 1985.

Santner, Erik. *The Psychotheology of Everyday Life: A Reading of Freud and Rosenzweig*. Chicago: University of Chicago Press, 2001.

Sauter, Gerhardt. *Questions of Meaning: A Theological and Philosophical Orientation*. Trans. Geoffrey W. Bromiley. Grand Rapids, MI: Eerdmans, 1996.

Sebald, W. G. *On the Natural History of Destruction*. Trans. Anthea Bell. New York: Random House, 2003.

Sloterdijk, Peter. *Rage and Time: A Psychopolitical Investigation*. Trans. Mario Wenning. New York: Columbia University Press, 2010.

Schmitt, Carl. *The Concept of the Political*. Trans. George Schwab. Chicago: University of Chicago Press, 1996.

_____. *Political Theology: Four Chapters on the Concept of Sovereignty*. Trans. George Schwab. Chicago: University of Chicago Press, 1985.

Sebald, W. G.. *On the Natural History of Destruction*. Trans. Anthea Bell. New York: Random House, 2003. (Orig. Ger. Ed. *Luftkrieg und Literatur*. Germany: Hansen, 1999.)

Seeburger, Francis F.. "9/11 Never Happened, President Bush Wouldn't Let It: Bob Dylan Replies to Henri Bergson." *Electronic Book Review* 2006-12-12. http://www.electronicbookreview.com/thread/musicsoundnoise/eventual.

_____. *The Stream of Thought*. New York: The Philosophical Library, 1984.

Solnit, Rebecca. *A Paradise Built in Hell: The Extraordinary Communities That Arise in Disaster*. New York: Viking, 2009.

Sontag, Susan. *Regarding the Pain of Others*. New York: Farrar, Straus, and Giroux, 2003.

_____. *On Photography*. New York: Farrar, Straus, and Giroux, 1977.

Spiegelman, Art. *Maus*. Two volumes.

_____. *In the Shadow of No Towers*. New York: Pantheon Books, 2004.

_____. *MetaMaus*. New York: Pantheon Books, 2011.

Taylor, Mark. *After God*. Chicago: University of Chicago Press, 2007.

Updike, John. *Memories of the Ford Administration*. New York: Alfred A. Knopf, 1992.

Vattimo, Gianni. *After Christianity*. Trans. Luca D'Isanto. New York: Columbia University Press, 2002.

_____. *Belief.* Trans. David Webb and Luca D'Isanto. Stanford, CA: Stanford University Press, 1999.

Walker, Alice. *Possessing the Secret of Joy.* New York: Houghton Mifflin, Harcourt, 1992.

Winter, Jay. "Notes on the Memory Boom: War, Remembrance and the Uses of the Past." In *Memory, Trauma, and World Politics.* Ed. Duncan Bell. New York: Pallgrave Macmillan, 2006.

Wolfe, Thomas. *You Can't Go Home Again.* New York: Harper & Row, 1932.

Yoder, John Howard. *The Politics of Jesus: Vicit Agnus Noster.* 2nd ed.. Grand Rapids, Michigan: William B. Erdmans, 2nd edition, 1994.

Žižek,Slavoj. *In Defense of Lost Causes.* London and New York: Verso 2008.

_____. *Organs Without Bodies: Deleuze and Consequences.* New York and London: Routledge, 2004.

_____. *The Puppet and the Dwarf: The Perverse Core of Christianity.* Cambridge, MA: The MIT Press, 2003.

_____. *The Ticklish Subject: The Absent Centre of Political Ontology.* London and New York: Verso, 1999.

_____. *Welcome to the Desert of the Real: Five Essays on September 11 and Related Dates.* London and New York: Verso, 2002.

Index

Lightning Source UK Ltd.
Milton Keynes UK
UKHW020017100522
402711UK00009B/2016